Boricuas in Gotham

Puerto Ricans in the Making of Modern New York City

Boricuas in Gotham

Puerto Ricans in the Making of Modern New York City

Essays in Memory of Antonia Pantoja

EDITED BY
Gabriel Haslip-Viera
Angelo Falcón
and
Félix V. Matos Rodríguez

Markus Wiener Publishers
Princeton

Copyright © 2005 Gabriel Haslip-Viera, Angelo Falcón, and Félix V. Matos Rodríguez

All rights reserved. No part of this book may be reproduced or transmitted in any form or by any means, electronic or mechanical, including photocopying, recording, or by any information storage or retrieval system, without permission of the copyright owners.

Book Design: 'Damola Ifaturoti

For information write to: Markus Wiener Publishers
231 Nassau Street, Princeton, NJ 08542
www.markuswiener.com

Library of Congress Cataloging-in-Publication Data

Boricuas in Gotham : Puerto Ricans in the making of New York City /
edited by Gabriel Haslip-Viera, Angelo Falcón, and Félix V. Matos Rodríguez.
  p. cm.
  Essays in memory of Antonia Pantoja.
  Based primarily on a series of presentations and commentaries from a symposium held at the Graduate Center of the City University of New York on Sept. 22, 2000.
  Includes bibliographical references and index.
  ISBN 978-1-55876-356-2 (paperback)
  ISBN 978-1-55876-355-4 (hardcover)
  1. Puerto Ricans—New York (State)—New York—Social conditions—Congresses. 2. Community life—New York (State)—New York—Congresses. 3. Puerto Ricans—New York (State)—New York—Congresses. 4. Puerto Ricans—New York (State)—New York—Economic conditions—Congresses. 5. New York (N.Y.)—Ethnic relations—Congresses. 6. New York (N.Y.)—Social conditions—Congresses. I. Haslip-Viera, Gabriel. II. Falcón, Angelo. III. Matos Rodríguez, Félix V., 1962-   IV. Pantoja, Antonia.
  Fl28.9.P85B67   2004
  9747'.1004687295—dc22
                    2004016684

CONTENTS

Introduction ix
*Angelo Falcón, Gabriel Haslip-Viera,
and Félix Matos Rodríguez*

1. Building the New York Puerto Rican Community,
   1945–1965: A Historical Interpretation 1
   Virginia Sánchez Korrol

   Commentary. A Nuyorican's View of our History
   and Language(s) in New York, 1945–1965 21
   Ana Celia Zentella

2. The Changing Socioeconomic and Political Fortunes
   of Puerto Ricans in New York City, 1960–1990 37
   José E. Cruz

   Commentary. From Civil Rights to the "Decade of
   the "Hispanic": Boricuas in Gotham, 1960–1990 85
   Angelo Falcón

3. Puerto Rican New Yorkers in the 1990s: A
   Demographic and Socioeconomic Profile 107
   Francisco L. Rivera-Batíz

   Commentary. Boricuas in 1990s New York: A
   Decade of Accomplishments and Disappointments 131
   Gabriel Haslip-Viera

4. De'tras Pa'lante: Explorations on the Future
   History of Puerto Ricans in New York City 147
   Angelo Falcón

Commentary. Forging a New, New York: The
Puerto Rican Community, Post-1945 195
Clara E. Rodríguez

Commentary. A Stronger Puerto Rican New York 221
Hon. Fernando Ferrer

Appendix: Puerto Ricans in New York: A Historical
and Community Development Perspective (1989) 227
Antonia Pantoja

List of Contributors 239

INTRODUCTION

Passengers bound for New York City at the preflight inspection area of San Juan's Isla Grande Airport, circa 1948. (Historical Archives of the Puerto Rican Migration. *Courtesy: Center for Puerto Rican Studies, Hunter College, (CUNY)*

Introduction

Angelo Falcón, Gabriel Haslip-Viera, and Félix Matos Rodríguez

> If you consider that the largest wave of Puerto Ricans came to New York starting in 1945, our group has been in the city for only fifty-five years. During these fifty-five years, we who came without the knowledge of English, with few skills and no economic resources, have been able to accomplish many important projects and build many institutions ... I believe that other New Yorkers evaluate our situation using standards that only find failure and poverty. Considering that we came to this country with many odds against us, I believe we have done well in a short period of time, given the realities that we faced as an immigrant group of nonwhite people coming from a country that had been colonized by the United States.
> —Antonia Pantoja, 2000

This book, *Boricuas in Gotham: Puerto Ricans in the Making of Modern New York City,*, is based primarily on a series of presentations and commentaries that were made at a symposium titled, *Contra Viento y Marea: Puerto Ricans in New York City—Past, Present, and Future,* which was held at the Graduate Center of the City University of New York on September 22, 2000. Dr. Antonia Pantoja, the tireless educator, social worker, and activist who, at the age of seventy-eight, had recently returned from Puerto Rico to continue her work with New York's Puerto Rican community, inspired the gathering. The planning for this event began when Dr. Pantoja met with the three of us at the Center for Puerto Rican Studies (the "Centro") at Hunter College to discuss the status of research on this community.

Originally, her idea was to hold a small closed session of scholars and graduate students, but given Dr. Pantoja's legendary preference for big events, this quickly evolved into a major all-day citywide symposium on the historical development of the Puerto Rican community in New York City. The event was cosponsored by the Centro in cooperation with the PRLDEF Institute for Puerto Rican Policy, the Gotham Center of the City University of New York, and the Center for Continuing Education at the City University Graduate Center.

The symposium was motivated in part by Dr. Pantoja's wish to reenergize Puerto Ricans to explore new directions in community organizing and development and in part by a recognition that the status of the community needed updating and reassessment. The symposium was also part of Dr. Pantoja's plan to use the conference papers to inform the writing of her memoirs, which were eventually published just weeks before her passing in 2002 with the title, *Memoir of a Visionary: Antonia Pantoja* (Arte Público Press).

Perhaps Dr. Pantoja's most extended and sharply drawn written assessment of the history and status of the Puerto Rican community in New York City was a short article titled "Puerto Ricans in New York: A Historical and Community Development Perspective," which appeared in the spring 1989 issue of the *Centro Journal*. In this article, Dr. Pantoja is very critical of the city's Puerto Rican leadership and institutions. She notes that in the 1980s, the Puerto Rican community's political base was "fragmented and deteriorates in a void of an effective leadership." She also notes that "a leadership crisis develops" and talks about the problem of "an unethical leadership (that) threatens to destroy the institutions we have and to create a climate of distrust in our own people" (see appendix, p. 227). When Dr. Pantoja returned to New York in 1998, after being in Puerto Rico for a number of years, she was struck by the leadership vacuum that existed in the Puerto Rican community and the poor state of many of the institutions she had helped to establish.[1] She then set out to implement, at the start of a new century, the plan of action that she had proposed in her 1989 article, which she described as "a strategy for community development and community restoration" (p. 235), a process cut short by her death on May 24, 2002.

In our planning of the symposium, in which Dr. Pantoja's longtime colleagues, Dr. Wilhemina Perry and Louis Nuñez, joined us, we decided to focus on reconstructing the history of Puerto Ricans in New York City since 1945 and promoting a discussion of this community's future. We identified the major presenters from among our leading scholars. The symposium, which filled the auditorium and attracted some 400 people, became a major event in the Puerto Rican community in 2000. Dr. Pantoja's original notion of a relatively small roundtable discussion of researchers and graduate students had become, as she had been for some time, larger than life.

The editors all benefited greatly from their association with Dr. Pantoja. Angelo Falcón first met Dr. Pantoja as an Aspirante (a student involved with

Aspira of New York) when he was in high school and, in 1968, participated in Aspira's annual summer leadership trip to Puerto Rico; the trip included fellow Aspirantes Fernando Ferrer and Ninfa Segarra, among others. He later had occasion to work with Dr. Pantoja in his development of the Institute for Puerto Rican Policy, on whose advisory board she served for a number of years. In November 1999, he introduced Dr. Pantoja to Dr. Gabriel Haslip-Viera, who was then acting director of the Center for Puerto Rican Studies; this was at the time when Dr. Pantoja had returned to New York City to stay and was beginning work on her memoirs. It was, curiously, the first time, according to Dr. Pantoja, that she had ever visited the Centro, but it became the beginning of her serious collaboration with that more than thirty-year-old research institution.

When Félix Matos-Rodríguez took over as director of the Centro, he met with Dr. Pantoja and deepened her new relationship with this research center. Dr. Matos-Rodriguez is, for example, finishing a book on the history of Aspira that he began jointly with Dr. Pantoja before her passing, and Dr. Pantoja donated her personal papers to the Centro Library. When she died at the age of eighty, her life stood as a testament of her vision for the Puerto Rican community and a legacy that all three editors now feel a part of in the development of this book.

The Literature on the Puerto Rican Experience

One of the purposes of this symposium was to document the history of Puerto Ricans in New York City. In the process of doing so and compiling and editing this volume, we conducted an extensive review of the existing literature on the subject as a way to assess scholarship in this area and explore ways to promote it. From this assessment, we found that quite a number of books and edited volumes published from the early 1970s to the late 1980s and generally accessible to the public had focused primarily, or at least in part, on Puerto Ricans in New York.

These publications include, in chronological order, Joseph P. Fitzpatrick, *Puerto Rican Americans: The Meaning of Migration to the Mainland* (1971; Englewood Cliffs, NJ: Prentice-Hall, 1987); Alfredo López, *The Puerto Rican Papers: Notes on the Re-Emergence of a Nation* (New York: Bobbs-Merrill, 1973); Stan Steiner, *The Islands: The Worlds of the Puerto Ricans* (New York: Harper and Row, 1974); Clara E. Rodríguez, *The Ethnic Queue in the United States: The Case of Puerto Ricans* (San Francisco: R&E Research Associates, 1974); Ruby Rohrlich Leavitt, *The Puerto Ricans: Culture Change and Language Deviance* (Tucson: University of Arizona Press, 1974); Kal Wagenheim, *A Survey of Puerto Ricans on the U.S. Mainland in the 1970s* (New York: Praeger, 1975); Luis Nieves Falcón, *El emigrante puertorriqueño* (Rio Piedras, P.R.: Editorial Edil, 1975); Manuel

Maldonado-Denis, *The Emigration Dialectic: Puerto Rico and the United States* (1976; New York: International Publishers, 1980); *Puerto Ricans in the Continental United States: An Uncertain Future* (Washington, DC: U.S. Commission on Civil Rights, 1976); Ramón Colón, *Carlos Tapia: A Puerto Rican Hero in New York* (New York: Vantage Press, 1976); James Jennings, *Puerto Rican Politics in New York City* (Washington, DC: University Press of America, 1977); Alan Harwood, *Rx: Spiritist as Needed: A Study of a Puerto Rican Community Mental Health Resource* (1977; Ithaca, N.Y.: Cornell University Press, 1987); Rosa Estades, *Patterns of Political Participation of Puerto Ricans in New York City* (Rio Piedras: Universidad de Puerto Rico, 1978); José Oscar Alers, *Puerto Ricans and Health: Findings from New York City* (New York: Hispanic Research Center, Fordham University, 1978); Joseph Fitzpatrick and Douglas T. Gurak, *Hispanic Intermarriage in New York City: 1975* (New York: Hispanic Research Center, Fordham University, 1979): Barry B. Levine, *Benjy Lopez: A Picaresque Tale of Emigration and Return* (New York: Basic Books, 1980); Ian A. Canino, Brian F. Early, and Lloyd H. Rogler, *The Puerto Rican Child in New York City: Stress and Mental Health* (New York: Hispanic Research Center, Fordham University, 1980); Virginia Sánchez-Korrol, *From Colonia to Community: The History of Puerto Ricans in New York City* (1983; Berkeley: University of California Press, 1994); José Hernández, *Puerto Rican Youth Employment* (Maplewood, NJ: Waterfront Press, 1983); Lloyd H. Rogler and Rosemary Santana Cooney, *Puerto Families in New York City: Intergenerational Processes* (Maplewood, NJ: Waterfront Press, 1984); Manuel Alers-Montalvo, *The Puerto Rican Migrants of New York City: A Study of Anomie* (New York: AMS Press, 1985); Frank Bonilla and Ricardo Campos, *Industry and Idleness* (New York: Centro de Estudios Puertorriqueños, 1986); Julio Morales, *Puerto Rican Poverty and Migration* (New York: Praeger, 1986); Clara E. Rodríguez, *Puerto Ricans: Born in the U.S.A.* (1989; Boulder, CO: Westview Press, 1991); and José E. Figueroa, *Survival on the Margin: A Documentary Study of the Underground Economy in a Puerto Rican Ghetto* (New York: Vantage Press, 1989).

Several anthologies or edited volumes were also published during this period, including Francesco Cordasco and Eugene Bucchioni, eds., *The Puerto Rican Community and Its Children: A Source Book for Teachers, Social Workers and Other Professionals* (1968, 1972; Metuchen, NJ: Scarecrow Press, 1982); Young Lords Party and Michael Abramson, eds., *Palante: The Young Lords Party* (New York: McGraw-Hill, 1971); Francesco Cordasco and Eugene Bucchioni, eds., *The Puerto Rican Experience: A Sociological Sourcebook* (Totowa, NJ: Littlefield, Adams, 1973); Adalberto López and James Petras, eds., *Puerto Rico and Puerto Ricans: Studies in History and Society* (Cambridge, MA: Schenkman, 1974); Edward Mapp, ed., *Puerto Rican Perspectives* (Metuchen, NJ: Scarecrow Press, 1974); Catarino Garza, ed., *Puerto Ricans in the U.S.: The Struggle for Freedom* (New

York: Pathfinder Press, 1977); Centro de Estudios Puertorriqueños, History Task Force, ed., *Labor Migration under Capitalism: The Puerto Rican Experience* (New York: Monthly Review Press, 1979); Edna Acosta-Belen, ed., *The Puerto Rican Woman* (1979; New York: Praeger, 1986); Clara E. Rodríguez and Virginia Sánchez Korrol, eds., *Historical Perspectives on Puerto Rican Survival in the U.S.* (1980; Princeton, NJ: Markus Wiener, 1996);[2] Adalberto López, ed., *The Puerto Ricans: Their History, Culture and Society* (Cambridge, MA: Schenkman, 1980); James Jennings and Monte Rivera, eds., *Puerto Rican Politics in Urban America* (New York: Praeger, 1984); María E. Sánchez and Antonio Stevens-Arroyo, eds., *Towards a Renaissance of Puerto Rican Studies: Ethnic and Area Studies in University Education* (Boulder, CO: Social Science Monographs, 1987); Cynthia García Coll and María De Lourdes Mattei, eds., *The Psychosocial Development of Puerto Rican Women* (New York: Praeger, 1989).

Quite a number of these books and edited volumes were written in response or reaction to earlier publications by social scientists, journalists, and other writers, especially Anglo Americans. Lawrence Chenault's *The Puerto Rican Migrant in New York City* (New York: Columbia University Press, 1938) was the first book by a social scientist to attempt a comprehensive study of the city's Puerto Rican population and its development during the first four decades of the twentieth century. Other books by social scientists followed in fairly quick succession during the years of the great migration from 1945 to 1970, including C. Wright Mills, Clarence Senior, and Rose Goldsen, *The Puerto Rican Journey* (New York: Columbia University Press, 1950); John H. Burma, *Spanish Speaking Groups in the United States* (Durham, NC: Duke University Press, 1954);[3] Fernando Sierra Berdecia, *La emigración puertorriqueña: realidad y política pública* (San Juan, PR: Editorial de la Universidad de Puerto Rico, 1956); Martin B. Dworkis, *The Impact of Puerto Rican Migration on Government Services in New York City* (New York: New York University Press, 1957); Elena Padilla, *Up From Puerto Rico* (New York: Columbia University Press, 1958);[4] Beatrice Berle, *Eighty Puerto Rican Families in New York City* (New York: Columbia University Press, 1958); Oscar Handlin *The Newcomers: Negroes and Puerto Ricans in a Changing Metropolis* (Cambridge: Harvard University Press, 1959); Clarence Senior, *The Puerto Ricans: Strangers—Then Neighbors* (1961; Chicago: Quadrangle Books 1965); Nathan Glazer and Daniel Moynihan, *Beyond the Melting Pot: The Negroes, Puerto Ricans, Jews, Italians, and Irish of New York City* (1963; Cambridge: The M.I.T. Press, 1970); Oscar Lewis, *La Vida: A Puerto Rican Family in the Culture of Poverty—San Juan and New York* (New York: Random House, 1965); Patricia Cayo Sexton, *Spanish Harlem: Anatomy of Poverty* (New York: Harper and Row, 1965); Federico Ribes Tovar, *El libro puertorriqueño de Nueva York*, 2 vols. (New York: Plus Ultra, 1968); and Jesús de Galíndez, *Puerto Rico en Nueva York: sociología de una inmigración* (Buenos Aires: Editorial

Tiempo Contemporáneo, 1969).

Publications from this earlier period also include books by journalists and other nonacademic writers, such as the *Handbook on Puerto Rican Work* (New York: Puerto Rican Affairs Committee, Communist Party USA, 1954); Christopher Rand's unsympathetic *The Puerto Ricans* (New York: Oxford University Press, 1958); Dan Wakefield's supportive *Island in the City: Puerto Ricans in New York* (New York: Corinth, 1959); Piri Thomas's autobiographical *Down These Mean Streets* (New York: Alfred A. Knopf, 1967); *Savior Savior, Hold My Hand* (Garden City, NY.: Doubleday, 1972) also by Piri Thomas; and Nicky Cruz's memoir, *Run Baby Run* (Plainfield, NJ: Logos International: 1968).

Previously unpublished documents and memoirs on New York's Puerto Ricans from the pre-1945 period also played a role in the creation of books and edited volumes in the 1970s and 1980s. These included Cesar Andreu Iglesias, ed., *Memoirs of Bernardo Vega: A Contribution to the History of the Puerto Rican Community in New York* (1977; New York: Monthly Review Press, 1984); Jesús Colón, *A Puerto Rican in New York and Other Sketches* (New York: International Publishers, 1961); and other important compilations, such as *Sources for the Study of the Puerto Rican Migration, 1879–1930* (New York: Centro de Estudios Puertorriqueños, 1982); Juan Flores, ed., *Divided Arrival: Narratives of the Puerto Rican Migration* (New York: Centro de Estudios Puertorriqeños, 1984); and *Extended Roots: From Hawaii to New York* (New York: Centro de Estudios Puertorriqueños, 1986). Other books like these have been published more recently, including Jesús Colón, *The Way It Was and Other Writings* (Houston: Arte Publico Press, 1993); Felix V. Matos-Rodríguez and Pedro Juan Hernandez, eds., *Pioneros: Puerto Ricans in New York City 1896–1948* (Charleston, S.C.: Arcadia Publishing, 2001); Jesús Colón, *Lo que el pueblo me dice...* (Houston: Arte Publico Press, 2001); and Joaquin Colón López, *Pioneros Puertorriqueños en Nueva York, 1917–1947* (Houston: Arte Publico Press, 2002);

A number of unpublished but important doctoral dissertations were also completed during the 1970s and 1980s. These include among others, "Rituals and Politics of the Puerto Rican Community in New York City," by Judith Herbstein (City University of New York, 1978); "Sterilization among Puerto Rican Women: A Case Study in New York City," by Iris López (Columbia University, 1985), "Housing Puerto Ricans in New York City, 1945 to 1984: A Study in Class Powerlessness," by José Ramon Sánchez (New York University, 1990), and the much cited "Managing Migration: The Migration Division of Puerto Rico and Puerto Ricans in New York City, 1948–1968," by Michael Lapp (John Hopkins University, 1990). Edgardo Melendez's recently published *Puerto Rican Government and Politics: A Comprehensive Bibliography* (Boulder, CO: Lynne Rienner, 2000) is a good resource for all unpublished and published works connected to government and politics.

Introduction

The number of books and edited volumes that were published on New York's Puerto Rican community declined after the 1970s and early 1980s as the focus seemed to shift to the immigrant experience of other Latinos and to Puerto Ricans in other parts of the country.[5] In many instances, the books that were published after 1985 placed New York's Puerto Ricans within a larger Latino or North American context, with an increasing emphasis on issues of ethnic identity and popular culture. Books of this type included Felix Padilla's *Latino Ethnic Consciousness: The Case of Mexican Americans and Puerto Ricans in Chicago* (Notre Dame, IN: University of Notre Dame Press, 1985) and his *Puerto Rican Chicago* (Notre Dame, IN: University of Notre Dame Press, 1987). They also included Asela Rodríguez De Laguna, ed., *Images and Identities: The Puerto Rican in Two World Contexts* (New Brunswick, NJ: Transaction Publishers, 1987); Edna Acosta-Belén and Barbara R. Sjostrom, eds., *The Hispanic Experience in the United States: Contemporary Issues and Perspectives* (New York: Praeger, 1988); Edwin Meléndez, Clara E. Rodríguez, and Janis Barry-Figueroa, eds., *Hispanics in the Northeast and the Changing Economy* (Cambridge, MA: Plenum, 1990); Rodolfo O. de la Garza, Louis DeSipio, F. Chris García, John García, and Angelo Falcón, eds., *Latino Voices: Mexican, Puerto Rican and Cuban Perspectives on American Politics* (Boulder, CO: Westview Press, 1992); the collected essays of Juan Flores in *Divided Borders* (Houston: Arte Publico Press, 1993) and *From Bomba to Hip Hop* (New York: Columbia University Press, 2000); James Jennings, ed., *Blacks, Latinos and Asians in Urban America: Status and Prospects for Politics and Activism* (Westport, CT: Praeger, 1994): Jay P. Dolan and Jaime R. Vidal, eds., *Puerto Rican and Cuban Catholics in the U.S., 1900–1965* (Notre Dame, IN: University of Notre Dame Press, 1994); Andrés Torres, *Between Melting Pot and Mosaic: African Americans and Puerto Ricans in the New York Political Economy* (Philadelphia: Temple University Press, 1995); Ruth Glasser, *My Music Is My Flag: Puerto Rican Musicians and Their New York Communities, 1917–1940* (Berkeley: University of California Press, 1995); Gabriel Haslip-Viera and Sherrie L. Baver, eds., *Latinos in New York: Communities in Transition* (Notre Dame, IN: University of Notre Dame Press, 1996); Clara E. Rodríguez, ed., *Latin Looks: Images of Latinas and Latinos in the U.S. Media* (Boulder, CO: Westview Press, 1997); Frances Aparicio, *Listening to Salsa: Latin Popular Music and Puerto Rican Cultures* (Middletown, CT: Wesleyan University Press, 1997); Frances Negrón-Muntaner and Ramón Grosfoguel, eds., *Puerto Rican Jam: Essays on Culture and Politics* (Minneapolis: University of Minnesota Press, 1997); Lourdes Torres, *Puerto Rican Discourse: A Sociolinguistic Study of a New York Suburb* (Mahwah, NJ: Lawrence Erlbaum Associates, 1997); José E. Cruz, *Identity and Power: Puerto Ricans and the Challenge of Ethnicity* (Philadelphia: Temple University Press, 1998); Ellen Bigler, *American Conversations: Puerto Ricans, White Ethnics and Multicultural Education* (Philadelphia: Temple University Press, 1999);

Clara E. Rodríguez, *Changing Race: Latinos, the Census, and the History of Ethnicity in the United States* (New York: New York University Press, 2000); Juan González, *Harvest of Empire: A History of Latinos in America* (New York: Viking, 2001); Carmen Teresa Whalen, *From Puerto Rico to Philadelphia: Puerto Rican Workers and Postwar Economies* (Philadelphia: Temple University Press, 2001); Lisa Sánchez González, *Boricua Literature: A Literary History of the Puerto Rican Diaspora* (New York: New York University Press, 2001); Arlene Dávila, *Latinos Inc.: The Marketing and Making of a People* (Berkeley: University of California Press, 2001); Gabriel Haslip-Viera, ed., *Taíno Revival: Critical Perspectives on Puerto Rican Identity and Cultural Politics* (Princeton, NJ: Markus Wiener, 2001); Agustín Lao-Montes and Arlene Dávila, eds., *Mambo Montage: The Latinization of New York* (New York: Columbia University Press, 2001); Jorge Duany, *The Puerto Rican Nation on the Move: Identities on the Island and in the United States* (Chapel Hill: University of North Carolina Press, 2002); Ed Morales, *Living in Spanglish: The Search for Latino Identity* (New York: St Martin's Press, 2002); Raquel Z. Rivera, *New York Ricans from the Hip Hop Zone* (New York: Palgrave Macmillan, 2003); Ramón Grosfoguel, *Colonial Subjects: Puerto Ricans in a Global Perspective* (Berkeley: University of California Press, 2003); Ana Y. Ramos-Zayas, *National Performances: The Politics of Class, Race and Space in Puerto Rican Chicago* (Chicago: University of Chicago Press, 2003); and Nicholas De Genova and Ana Y. Ramos-Zayas, *Latino Crossings: Mexicans, Puerto Ricans and the Politics of Race and Citizenship* (New York: Routledge, 2003).[6]

Of course, books and edited volumes that focus on Puerto Ricans in New York and utilize a more standard social science and humanities approach also continued to be published during the 1990s and into the current century. These included Andrés Pérez y Mena, *Speaking of the Dead: Development of Afro-Latin Religion Among Puerto Ricans in the U.S.* (New York: AMS Press, 1991): Ana Maria Díaz-Stevens, *Oxcart Catholicism on Fifth Avenue: The Impact of the Puerto Rican Migration upon the Archdiocese of New York* (Notre Dame, IN: University of Notre Dame Press, 1993); Joseph A. Fernández, *Tales Out of School: Joseph Fernandez's Crusade to Rescue American Education* (Boston: Little, Brown, 1993); Carlos Antonio Torre, Hugo Rodríguez Vecchini, and William Burgos, eds., *The Commuter Nation: Perspectives on Puerto Rican Migration* (Rio Piedras: Universidad de Puerto Rico, 1994); Cynthia García Coll and Lamberty Gontran, *Puerto Rican Women and Children: Issues of Health, Growth and Development* (New York: Plenum, 1994); Camille Rodríguez and Ramón Bosque Pérez, eds. *Puerto Ricans and Higher Education Policies: Issues of Scholarship, Fiscal Policies and Admissions* (New York: Centro de Estudios Puertorriqueños, 1995); Roberto Santiago, ed., *Boricuas: Influential Puerto Rican Writings—An Anthology* (New York: Ballantine Books, 1995); Altagracia Ortíz, ed. *Puerto Rican Women and Work: Bridges in Transnational Labor* (Philadelphia: Temple University Press, 1996);

Introduction

Francisco L. Rivera-Batíz and Carlos E. Santiago, *Island Paradox: Puerto Rico in the 1990s* (New York: Russell Sage Foundation, 1996); Malve von Hassell, *Homesteading in New York City, 1978–1993: The Divided Heart of Loisaida* (Westport, CT: Bergin and Garvey, 1996); Joseph P. Fitzpatrick, *The Stranger Is Our Own: Reflections on the Journey of Puerto Rican Migrants* (Kansas City, MO: Sheed and Ward, 1996); Bonnie Urciuoli, *Exposing Prejudice: Puerto Rican Experiences of Language, Race, and Class* (Boulder, CO: Westview Press, 1996); Ana Celia Zentella, *Growing Up Bilingual: Puerto Rican Children in New York* (Malden, MA: Blackwell, 1997); Vicky Muñiz, *Resisting Gentrification and Displacement: Voices of Puerto Rican Women of the Barrio* (New York: Garland Publishing, 1998); Andrés Torres and José Velázquez, eds., *The Puerto Rican Movement: Voices from the Diaspora* (Philadelphia: Temple University Press, 1998); Edna Acosta-Belén et al., eds. *"Adiós, Borinquen querida": The Puerto Rican Diaspora, Its History, and Contributions* (Albany: CELAC, State University of New York at Albany, 2000); Sonia Nieto, ed., *Puerto Rican Students in U.S. Schools* (Mahwah, NJ: Lawrence Erlbaum, 2000); and Miguel Meléndez, *We Took the Streets: Fighting for Latino Rights with the Young Lords* (New York: St. Martin's Press, 2003).

The attempt in this book to reconstruct the history of Puerto Ricans in New York City since 1945 made it evident that general histories of this period do not exist for this community. The existing literature, dominated largely by sociology and, more recently, by cultural studies, is for the most part ahistorical or highly specialized. Broad-gauged analyses that attempt to characterize medium- and long-term trajectories of the Puerto Rican experience in this city are not being produced, and it seems that there are few incentives to do so. This book, as a result, makes some original (and possibly reckless) efforts to begin this process of historical reconstruction and analysis for this recent and current period. Rather than being definitive in this endeavor, our hope is to generate some useful questions and map out some broad historical coordinates that would help shape future research on the subject.

How This Book Is Organized

As previously noted, the current volume is an attempt to update and reassess the evolution and status of New York's Puerto Rican community from the perspective of what is currently known about the subject as we move deeper into the twenty-first century. Following the format established during the September 2000 symposium, the chapters and subsequent comments are organized chronologically.

In the first chapter, "Building the New York Puerto Rican Community, 1945–1965," historian Virginia Sánchez Korrol, focuses on the years of the "great migration," but with references to the earlier Puerto Rican community that served as the basis for this community's expansion after 1945. Sociolinguist

Ana Celia Zentella provides a fascinating and humorous commentary based on her personal experiences growing up Puerto Rican (and bilingual) in New York City.

This chapter is followed by "The Changing Socioeconomic and Political Fortunes of Puerto Ricans in New York City, 1960–1990" by political scientist José A. Cruz, who analyzes the political activities and economic status of Puerto Ricans during a tumultuous period characterized by great hopes and quite a number of disappointments. His chapter sparks what we hope will become a lively debate about how to interpret the Puerto Rican experience during this period in a commentary by his fellow political scientist, Angelo Falcón.

In the third chapter titled, "Puerto Rican New Yorkers in the 1990s: A Demographic and Socioeconomic Profile," economist Francisco Rivera Batíz discusses the status of New York's Puerto Ricans during a decade when this community came under increased attack by the right-wing, neoconservative forces that took control of the city after Rudolph Giuliani's election as mayor in 1993. Historian Gabriel Haslip-Viera extends Rivera Batíz's analysis beyond the chapter's empirically based socioeconomic analysis to look at other aspects of the Puerto Rican experience during this decade.

This chapter is followed by "*De'tras Pa'lante:* Explorations on the Future History of Puerto Ricans in New York City" by Angelo Falcón, who discusses the current status of Puerto Ricans in New York and speculates about their future prospects. Sociologist Clara E. Rodríguez offers an extended commentary that expands on Falcón's analysis and raises fundamental issues for future analyses and research on the Puerto Rican experience in New York.

The book concludes with comments that were made at the September 2000 symposium by former Bronx Borough President Fernando Ferrer, who was at the time about to launch his inspiring but ultimately unsuccessful campaign to become New York's first Puerto Rican mayor. As a former Aspirante, his achievements stand as a living testament to Dr. Pantoja's legacy as well as a barometer for those Puerto Rican New Yorkers who have had similar or different experiences.

Boricuas in Gotham, although about Puerto Ricans in New York City, takes on a broader significance because of the special place that this community's experience has played historically for Puerto Ricans wherever they reside. For so many decades, the stateside Puerto Rican experience was, by definition, a New York City experience because Puerto Ricans were consistently concentrated in this city in such large numbers. But even as this community dispersed more and more after the 1960s to Chicago, California, and Florida, among other places, the "Nuyorican" presence and experience was always present in some form wherever Puerto Rican communities emerged.

Introduction

The impact of this presence extended more and more to Puerto Rico itself with the beginnings of a significant return migration in the 1970s and the growth of the stateside Puerto Rican population, which by the early 2000s approached the size of the island population. With the dramatic growth of the Latino immigrant population in New York and elsewhere in the United States, there is much for these newer communities to learn from the history of Puerto Ricans in this city. "Boricua" and "Gotham" are both alternative terms by which to call communities that are pregnant with history specific to each, in the process metaphorically joining Agüeybana with Washington Irving and simultaneously evoking specificities and universalities, with all the tensions and insights this brings. As a result, we hope that this book resonates as widely as the New York Puerto Rican experience has.

The editors would like to thank Markus Wiener, Willa Speiser, and the staff of Markus Wiener, Publishers, for their support and assistance in the completion of this project. We would also like to show our appreciation to Louis Nuñez, Eddie González, and Dr. Wilhelmina Perry for their important contributions to the symposium upon which this book is based. Finally, this volume is dedicated to the memory of a life well lived by Dr. Antonia Pantoja, or simply Toni as we knew her, who brought us all together to work and guided us on this project. It was a very productive collaboration for the three of us, which we hope has translated into a stimulating and useful collection for our readers.

Angelo Falcón
PRLDEF Institute for Puerto Rican Policy
New York

Gabriel Haslip-Viera, Ph.D.
The City College of the City University of New York

Félix Matos-Rodríguez, Ph.D.
Center for Puerto Rican Studies at Hunter College (CUNY)

New York
October 2003

Notes

1. These included ASPIRA, the Puerto Rican Forum, Boricua College, the Puerto Rican Association for Community Affairs (PRACA), the Graduate School of Community Development in San Diego, and Producir and its subsidiaries on the island of Puerto Rico.
2. Originally published as *The Puerto Rican Struggle: Essays on Survival in the U.S.* (New York: Puerto Rican Migration Research Consortium, 1980), with José Oscar Alers also as coeditor.
3. Reprinted (Detroit: Blaine Ethridge Books, 1974).
4. Anthropologist Elena Padilla was the first Puerto Rican to publish a study of the diaspora with a specific focus on New York's East Harlem community. However credit should also be given to Patria Aran Gosnell, a Puerto Rican sociologist, who completed an unpublished doctoral dissertation on the New York community in 1945.
5. It should be noted that Lloyd H. Rogler's *Migrant in the City: The Life of a Puerto Rican Action Group* (New York: Basic Books, 1972) was probably the first book to focus specifically on a Puerto Rican community outside New York City. Reference also should be made to the pre-1985 publication of Daniel Flores Duran's, *Latino Communication Patterns: An Investigation of Media Use and Organizational Activity Among Mexican, Cuban and Puerto Rican Residents of Chicago* (New York: Arno Press, 1980).
6. The Puerto Rican experience in New York and in other parts of the country has also been discussed in a more diminished or generalized manner in the plethora of books that have focused on Latinos in general since 1985. These include, among others, Ilan Stavans, *The Hispanic Condition: Reflections on Culture and Identity in America* (New York: Harper Collins, 1995); Geoffrey Fox, *Hispanic Nation: Culture, Politics, and the Construction of Identity* (Secaucus, NJ: Carol Publishing, 1996); Ray Suárez, *The Old Neighborhood: What We Lost in the Great Suburban Migration* (New York: The Free Press, 1999); Héctor Cordero Guzmán, Robert C. Smith, and Ramón Grosfoguel, eds., *Migration, Transnationalism and Race in a Changing New York* (Philadelphia: Temple University Press, 2001); Marcelo M. Suárez-Orozco and Mariela M Páez, eds., *Latinos: Remaking America* (Berkeley: University of California Press, 2002); and Rodney E. Hero, *Latinos and the U.S. Political System: Two-Tiered Pluralism* (Philadelphia: Temple University Press, 1992). To a significant degree, the Puerto Rican experience has also been trivialized or distorted in a number of these books. See, for example, Lewis H. Gann and Peter J. Duignan, *Hispanics in the United States: A History* (Boulder, CO: Westview Press, 1986); Linda Chavez, *Out of the Barrio* (New York: Basic Books, 1991); Earl Shorris, *Latinos: A Biography of the People* (New York: W. W. Norton, 1992); Philippe Bourgois, *In Search of Respect: Selling Crack in the Barrio* (New York: Cambridge University Press, 1995); Michael Jones-Correa, *Between Two Nations: The Political Predicament of Latinos in New York City* (Ithaca, NY.: Cornell University Press, 1998); and Roberto Suro, *Strangers Among Us: Latino Lives in a Changing America* (New York: Alfred A Knopf, 1998).

CHAPTER ONE

Typical Puerto Rican family owned neighbourhood grocery store or *bodega*, late 1950s. (Justo A. Marti Photographic Collection. *Courtesy: Center for Puerto Rican Studies, Hunter College, CUNY*).

Chapter 1

Building the New York-Puerto Rican Community, 1945-1965:
A Historical Interpretation

Virginia Sánchez Korrol

I remember when we had just one Puerto Rican grocery store, one Puerto Rican restaurant and one such barbershop in all of New York City. No matter where you lived you had to take the old nickel IRT to 145th Street and Madison Ave. if you wanted a haircut in a Puerto Rican barbershop so you would not be discriminated against because of race, color, nationality or accent. That was more than forty years ago. Today over a half a million Puerto Ricans live in greater New York alone. Statistics say that we will be one solid million in this city by 1960.[1]
—Jesús Colón

Writing in 1958, Jesús Colón's observations were not far wrong. Following World War II, the numbers of his compatriots in the United States escalated from roughly 301,375 in the 1950s to 1,391,163 some twenty years later. More than 42,000 *puertorriqueños* were estimated to have arrived in the United States every year between 1946 and 1956, and the majority of them stayed in New York City.[2] Emerging communities were already visible in key industrial and agricultural states including California, Connecticut, Florida, Illinois, Massachusetts, Michigan, New Jersey, Ohio, and Pennsylvania, and Puerto Ricans appeared in the census records of all the states of the union.

However, the site that would rapidly become identified with the Puerto Rican migration, the first airborne movement of American citizens, would be the city of New York. This narrative recounts the challenges confronted by Puerto Ricans during the period of 1945 to 1965, the strategies used to overcome those challenges, and the contributions made in the process of building community.

There were many reasons why New York City would indeed attract the bulk of the migrant flow. As the nation's financial and industrial hub, the port city had traditionally been the site of immigrant disembarkation. Since before the turn of the twentieth century, the city served as the focal point for early migrants. Puerto Ricans and Cubans who engaged in liberation struggles in the last decades of the nineteenth century found New York City to be an excellent haven for expatriation. The exile community of political émigrés included banished Latin Americans as well as individuals from the Hispanic Caribbean (Haslip-Viera 1996: 3–29). The culmination of the Spanish-Cuban-American War in 1898 set the stage for a predominantly working-class emigration, but students and some professionals also made up part of that migrant flow.

In New York, the *colonias* established during the 1918–1939 interwar period by Puerto Rican pioneers soon spread beyond the boundaries of Brooklyn and Manhattan, into the South Bronx, Queens, and other locations. These were, for the most part, vibrant, intact neighborhoods where language, customs, traditions, and other cultural manifestations welded connectivity in ways that solidified diasporic communities. These, in turn, were interwoven not only with island concerns, but also with the affairs of the broader Spanish-American and Caribbean world. It was to these communities that the post–World War II migrants would gravitate (Sánchez Korrol 1994).

Post–World War II New York Puerto Rican Community

At the end of World War II, the sheer numbers of Puerto Rican migrants in New York City would no longer be ignored. Migrants came by plane, and as American citizens they faced no immigration barriers. If the size of the postwar migration was impressive, the city of the late 1940s and 1950s was also strikingly different from the New York of the interwar, pioneer generation. Gone was the heyday of the earlier cigar industry and other sectors with unique traditions and labor organizations. The decline of cigar making, along with skilled employment in munitions and other World War I–related industries trapped Depression-era Puerto Ricans into a realm of fierce competition with others, including American ethnics, for low-paying blue-collar work, and this competition would remain difficult to overcome. Throughout the

1940s, employment in essential industries, civil service, and garment-related sectors alleviated conditions in the barrios to some extent, but this was to be temporary.

To be sure, like their counterparts during the early decades of the twentieth century, post–World War II migrants also came full of hope and ambition. The number of women equaled the number of men among the migrants leaving the island; wives followed military husbands, recently discharged from the armed forces; children came in family groups or with relatives to join parents who had come before them. Forced by political and economic factors to leave their island home in search of better opportunities, they soon found themselves confronting urban decay in a concrete jungle, fierce discrimination, low status employment, poor health conditions, substandard housing, and inadequate education.

Throughout the late forties and fifties, displaced island workers were initially lured to New York and other cities by a booming postwar economy and the opportunities it afforded. In many respects, the economy did indicate new growth in areas such as retail and wholesale; in building and construction. Recruited as well by continental industry and agriculture as contract workers, some 20,000 to 30,000 Puerto Ricans arrived annually to work on the farms of Long Island, the Connecticut River valley, and the southwestern agricultural regions of New Jersey. Echoing the contractual labor conditions of the early decades of the century when Puerto Rican workers became a surplus labor pool and were sent to Hawaii, Arizona, Mexico, New York, and other locations, seasonal employment often resulted in the founding of new settlements, establishing enclaves for future migrations. A number of postwar communities outside of New York emerged precisely because seasonal migrants remained in the region of their initial contractual employment; these included the earliest barrios in Chicago, Illinois; Milwaukee, Wisconsin; Gary, Indiana; Lorain, Ohio; Dover, New Jersey; and Hartford and Bridgeport, Connecticut (Sánchez Korrol 1999).

In New York City, Puerto Rican laborers were marginal to the economic boom and concentrated in blue-collar occupations: restaurants, hotels, manufacturing, garment factories, light industry, manual labor, and laundries. Stymied by restrictive trade union practices, low-wage work in the service and manufacturing sectors, including kitchen help, waiters, porters, and hospital workers, offered Puerto Ricans little chance for upward mobility. Some trickled into civil service, teaching, and the health professions and women found employment in the garment industry, where they were deemed an essential labor force. By mid-century however, women's integration into the workforce also faced impending decline. As a case in point, Puerto Rican women, ages fourteen and over, accounted for 38.9 percent of women working in the garment-related industries in 1950, but by 1970, that figure had been reduced to 29.8 percent (Santana Cooney and Colón 1996: 71-72).

Frequently stereotyped as lazy, opportunistic, and eager to fill the city's welfare rolls, the increasing migrant population was unaware that it had entered a city undergoing enormous changes (Rodríguez 1989: 9–21). The industrial base that had in the past provided the first jobs and glimmers of financial security for newcomers had ceased to expand. As the city moved from manufacturing to finance and professional services, Puerto Rican labor rested on tenuous foundations, positioned in marginal or declining sectors. Employment prospects were meager as the jobs where migrant workers were concentrated suffered severe contraction. Technological changes in production and automation promoted profound changes, and companies began to relocate offshore or to other regions of the country such as the southeastern states, where labor was cheap and plentiful. Between 1958 and 1965, for example, 87,000 factory jobs and 227 manufacturing companies were lost to the city (Berrol 2000: 126). Gender-segregated employment sectors also experienced change, and although Puerto Rican women continued to find jobs as sewing machine operators and in related occupations, this sector, on the verge of severe reduction, now incorporated such practices as section or piecework, which often carried lower wages. Historian Altagracia Ortíz points to women workers in the New York metropolitan region as the "first in the area to experience on a large scale the negative consequences of the production and labor market changes that resulted from the globalization of the industry after the 1960s" (Ortíz 1996: 73).

Nevertheless, it is important to point out that were it not for the labor of Puerto Ricans in the city, cheap and exploited as it may have been, many more companies would have fled New York. In the words of Raymond Vernon, "The rate of Puerto Rican migration to New York is one of the factors that determine how long and how successfully the New York metropolitan region will retain industries which are under competitive process from other areas. To the extent that some of these industries have hung on in the area, they have depended upon recently arrived Puerto Rican workers, who have entered the job market of the New York area at the rate of about 13,000 each year."[3]

As the city context to which the migrants came is acknowledged, so too must we understand the factors and conditions in the "sending" society. In Puerto Rico, conditions were no better throughout the late forties and fifties. In fact, the move from the land to the factory as the key unit of economic production had paved the way for the extensive emigration that found its way to New York City. Following World War II, Puerto Rican planners and politicians pushed for a redefinition of the island's legal status. The result was the creation of the Commonwealth in 1952 with Luis Muñoz Marín, the island's first elected governor, at the helm. Commonwealth leadership with U.S. support and encouragement developed Operation Bootstrap, the plan for the island's industrialization, modernization, and overall economic growth. However, industrialization by invitation, along with its built-in lucrative tax exemptions, rested on a projected emigration of more than a third of the island's population. The relocation of workers was aggressively promoted, often recruited by stateside businessmen and politicians, and envisioned by island planners as the "safety valve" that would insure the success of industrialization.[4]

Female sterilization as a means of controlling excess or surplus population was yet another strategy promoted by island planners. During this period, Puerto Rico became the testing ground for contraceptives. Many of the first companies that came to the island under Operation Bootstrap were in the garment production business. Women were skilled in this craft, learned needlework in the schools, and conditioned for decades to work for lower wages. They were thus increasingly needed and courted for such employment in the factories. Persuasive campaigns were launched in health-care clinics, government offices, and schools to tout the benefits of two children per family, leaving women the opportunity to work outside the home. Along with an enhanced image of middle-class status, the concept of sterilization as a means of controlling family size swayed thousands of women, who then entered the workforce in large numbers.[5]

For the most part, industrialization was not the panacea it was expected to be. It rapidly replaced agricultural production and drew the unemployed and underemployed to industrial centers where factory jobs paid more than agriculture. As the initial manufacturing and tourism phases gave way to heavy industry and pharmaceuticals, a highly skilled work force was required. For many who did not have the education or the skills to fill these jobs, migration presented a viable alternative.

New York City's Dubious Progress

For both, the newly arrived migrants of the postwar era and the pioneer migrant generation, physical changes in New York City's landscape would have a profound effect on their communities. Intent on redesigning and revitalizing crumbling neighborhoods and building highways, roads, and bridges, Title 1 funding enabled Robert Moses, then Mayor William O'Dwyer's city construction coordinator, and other planners to move ahead on an expansive vision for a new Gotham. By 1949, Title 1 of the Housing Act—the Federal Urban Redevelopment Program—empowered local governments to purchase or condemn land for government-sponsored projects. Funding was made available for private projects, as well.[6] These funds, however, would be allocated to state or city agencies only if every structure in a designated zone was slated for demolition. New bridges and super highways served as a two-way street. Improved transportation allowed people and goods to enter the city, but also to leave it. As Puerto Ricans and blacks spread into other neighborhoods in Brooklyn and the South Bronx, middle-class white families seized the opportunity to leave the city for greener suburbs. Encouraged by the wide use of the automobile, highways attracted many individuals and families who could afford to move and commute, but not necessarily the blacks and Puerto Ricans. By 1952 these groups, generally lingering on the brink of or below the poverty line, and subject to patterns of residential segregation, already made up 10 percent of the city's population (Berrol 2000: 125–148).

The rebuilding of New York included impressive landmark institutions like Lincoln Center, the Guggenheim Museum and the recently demolished New York Coliseum at Columbus Circle. Countless families were dislocated when private and public housing projects were constructed between 1946 and 1956, under the supervision of the New York City Housing Authority in partnership with private concerns. Displaced families waited to be called back into the public housing that replaced original neighborhoods, but affordable lodging stood at a premium. Many families were turned away from primary neighborhoods or new ones because of patronage or racial preferences (Sánchez 1996: 259–301). Others continued to live in deteriorated "old law" tenement apartments that bore the scars of time and neglect.

While neighborhoods like El Barrio and the Brooklyn Navy Yard remained intact, old, mostly working-class, or poor and powerless neighborhoods were demolished. Previously untouched communities disintegrated as highways such as the Gowanus Expressway in Brooklyn, the Brooklyn-Queens Expressway, and the Cross Bronx Expressway suddenly sprouted in their stead. Slum clearance and public housing in Harlem, Morrisania, and Brownsville displaced thousands of blacks and Puerto Ricans, as did renovations in Washington Square South, Manhattantown, and Corlear's Hook on the Lower East Side.[7] Neighborhoods fragmented and their inhabitants scattered to different sectors of the city. Small businesses, including *farmácias, bodegas,* and *botánicas,* were forced to relocate or shut down entirely, taking with them experienced leadership developed over decades and exercised by their owners. Extended families divided, moving back to Puerto Rico, or into unfamiliar boroughs, other neighborhoods, or to the suburbs, where they encountered old patterns of discrimination based on color, class, language, or culture. Ironically labeled "urban renewal," the destruction of Puerto Rican pioneer settlements in the South Bronx, South Brooklyn, and Lower Manhattan, with their internal institutions, leadership, and structures necessary for cushioning the massive postwar migration, compounded the plight of a population already in crisis.

So it was that at a time when the *barrio hispano* was inundated with a peak migration, invigorating and reinforcing the city with human potential, the economic, communal, institutional, and organizational structures of the Puerto Rican community were in a state of transition. Many pioneer associations, mutual aid societies, trade union, professional, and sociocultural organizations simply did not have sufficient resources or political power to broker for an increased, broadly dispersed population. Some, like Casita María in the Bronx, a religious multiservice association in the tradition of immigrant settlement houses, continued to provide essential social services to the Puerto Rican community opening offices in areas of high Spanish-speaking concentrations; but others did not (Sánchez Korrol 1999). The growing numbers of Pentecostal churches reinforced identity and offered support and pastoral services to their congregants, but these sects were often insular by design, limiting outreach and resources to church members and isolating themselves from broader community social action. Catholic Charities and the Mission Society succored the poor. However, the Catholic Church also entered a period of reorganization in the fifties and sixties that included abolishing the traditional national parishes with their focus on maintaining bilingual-bicultural ministries. Effective with past immigrant populations, these ministries softened the impact of Americanization by encouraging cultural bonds with the European countries of origin (Stevens Arroyo 1996: 153–165). New models of social action and pastoral care were devised for the Puerto Ricans, more often than not replicating American concepts of assimilation. Throughout the fifties and sixties, the New York archdiocese initiated several such programs including the Fiesta de San Juan; the Intercultural Institute, a program to train new clergy; and, ultimately, the Cursillo movement based on preparing lay persons for apostolic participation.

Indeed, many nonreligious groups throughout the city were also forced to formulate programs to assuage what was called the "Puerto Rican problem" and the migration adjustment process. Basically intent on rapid assimilation into mainstream culture, public and private organizations offered instruction in the English language and formed committees to deal with issues of employment, health, and housing. The Mayor's Committee on Puerto Rican Affairs, formed in 1949, conducted several studies on the city's Puerto Ricans. This committee included representatives from the major community organizations and city and state agencies. Associations including chapters of unions within the AFL, CIO, UFT, Amalgamated Clothing Workers, International Ladies' Garment Workers Union, Hotel and Restaurant Workers, National Maritime Union, Building Service Employees, and Toy and Novelty Workers also established programs to work with the population. Although a few of these efforts incorporated Spanish as the language of communication, almost none understood the plight of the Puerto Rican worker or the cultural dimensions of the Puerto Rican community.[8]

Agencies such as the Welfare Council, the health and welfare departments, and the state employment services conducted yet more studies on the Puerto Ricans in efforts to understand this ethno-racial, Spanish-speaking group of American citizens whose numbers had so overwhelmed city services. Along with Catholic Charities and the Mission Society, settlement houses including the Henry Street Settlement, Hudson Guild, Community Service Society, and the Good Neighbor forum provided additional programs to mediate in the process of assimilation and acculturation. However well intentioned these groups may have been, they lacked the human resources necessary to bring about meaningful change. Bilingual-bicultural personnel were rarely represented in city or state agencies, or in the schools or community-based organizations. The Puerto Rican community was remarkably young, and an experienced, educated leadership corps that could occupy decision-making positions in labor, education, and/or politics was still in the process of gestation.

In 1949, the city's board of education had succeeded in hiring ten bilingual professionals to assist in public instruction, and it subsequently employed more individuals in the same capacity throughout the eighteen years leading up to bilingual education licensure. By 1950 the Department of Welfare had hired one hundred and thirty-eight bilingual-bicultural social workers. Individuals in these professions went on in their careers to develop important institutions and organizations, structure the sociopolitical, communitarian, and cultural aspects of the community, but in terms of numbers, at mid-century they were but drops in the proverbial bucket.

Perpetuating Stereotypes

In spite of yeoman efforts, city agencies, unions, churches, and other institutions were hard pressed to eradicate stereotypical notions and discrimination, often found within their own ranks and as prevalent in the broader society. The notion that Puerto Ricans posed social problems and predominantly engaged in drug usage and street crime persisted in spite of any evidence to the contrary. If, as early as the 1930s, scholarly studies like Lawrence Chenault's *The Puerto Rican Migrant in New York City* (1938) portrayed Puerto Rican in negative tones as unreliable, lacking ambition, and having pathologically sensitive dispositons, the popular literature of the forties and fifties was far more scathing. In 1947, the government of Puerto Rico attempted to gauge the perception of the group from an American perspective and discovered the findings to be so destructively negative that they were never published (Puerto Rican Forum 1964: 61). Their findings would certainly have included columnists like the *Daily Mirror's* Jack Lait and Lee Mortimer who described the group as "mostly crude farmers... [Who] turn to guile and wile and the steel blade, the traditional weapon of the sugar cane cutter, mark of their blood and heritage."[9] Another journalist painted Puerto Ricans as the perpetrators of lower educational standards, "because of the language problem, and when Puerto Rican children are in a majority on a street they can, like any such majority, make life almost unbearable for other children" (Rand 1958: 5).

The literary critic Sandoval Sánchez and the sociologist Clara E. Rodríguez cite two examples that contributed overwhelmingly to stereotyped perspectives because of their broad impact on American culture and international circulation. One was the 1957 production of the Broadway hit *West Side Story*, an ethno-racial retelling of Shakespeare's classic *Romeo and Juliet* with white ethnics and Puerto Ricans transformed into the feuding Montagues and Capulets. The other was Oscar Lewis's *La Vida*, a generalization of Puerto Ricans based on a poor family in a San Juan slum. Highly regarded in academe and in the American theatre, both works have contributed toward perpetuating a conformist image of the Puerto Rican in America devoid of positive values, historical legacy or culture. The musical highlights the urban, segregated territoriality of New York City, and in the patriotic song "America" presents the island as "an underdeveloped country with all kinds of natural disaster, socio-economic and demographic problems, and crime" (Sandoval Sánchez 1997: 174).

Lewis's anthropological approach overgeneralizes both the island and the realities surrounding the migration experience. Through the lens of one poor, extended family group engaged in prostitution as a way of life, the writer offers a San Juan barrio, the city's unofficial red light district, as the prototype of the Puerto Rican experience (see Rodríguez 1995: 230–236). Throughout the fifties and sixties, both the book and the play became synonymous with New York Puerto Ricans.

Without a doubt, the city failed the Puerto Rican community. What was needed was (1) a clear understanding of the roots of the problems and an agenda for their solutions; (2) strategies for raising the community utilizing existing internal leadership and organizations; (3) the creation of a new leadership cadre that could broker with the city and state in the name of the community; (4) integration of such a cadre into key institutions and agencies where they could be effective as agents for change. In addition, to reenergize community solidarity, promote identity, encourage political action and empowerment, and provide guidance to overcome the challenges and disadvantages plaguing New York's Puerto Ricans, leadership needed to come from within the community itself. That required awareness that the Puerto Rican community in New York in the forties, fifties, and sixties was not monolithic but already a diverse entity. This community incorporated recent arrivals, settled pioneers, U.S.-born "Americanized Hispanics," individuals who clung steadfastly to a traditional island culture, and those who had forged a stateside blended brand of *lo puertorriqueño*. Race, class, gender, and generational perspectives had also influenced the development of New York Puerto Ricans in ways that would require a revaluation of who and what actually comprised the Puerto Rican community.

Organizing for Advancement

Although many of the pre-1945 associations continued to exert some degree of leadership, other groups, new or refocused units, such as the hometown clubs, emerged and worked with the remaining older groups to promote a common agenda. Many were committed to the understanding that the integration of Puerto Ricans into New York City could be achieved only if and when Puerto Ricans themselves were engaged in defining and devising the means of integration (Puerto Rican Forum 1964: 66). The fifties, but in particular the sixties and early seventies, energized by the civil rights movement and militant demands on behalf of students and community leaders for equality and justice, witnessed the emergence of Puerto Rican political radicalism along with organizations that functioned on behalf of the community at the city, state and eventually the national level. Leaders like Gilberto Gerena Valentín, Evelina Antonetty, and Antonia Pantoja championed political representation and engaged in progressive organizing.[10] Among the groups that surfaced were the Migration Division of the Office of Puerto Rico, the Puerto Rican Forum, the Puerto Rican Family Institute, Aspira, the Puerto Rican Association for Community Affairs (PRACA), and the Institute for Puerto Rican Culture (Sánchez Korrol 1994: 224-231).

Established by the government of Puerto Rico, the Migration Division, a New York branch of the island's Department of Labor, opened its doors in 1948. Its mission was to ameliorate the adjustment process of newly arrived migrants and to mediate between Puerto Rico and the diasporic communities.[11] An agency tied to the government of Puerto Rico was not considered unusual. For the most part, migrants viewed their stay in the U.S. as a temporary hiatus, fully expecting to return to Puerto Rico once they had secured financial stability. The migration itself was cyclical in nature, characterized by a circular movement of individuals entering and leaving depending on the economic trends of the nation. Indeed, by the late sixties, a noticeable return migration of retirees from the pioneering generation, in tandem with the return of workers, upheld that premise (Hernández Alvarez 1976).[12]

In addition, the office was expected to help public and private institutions in their interactions with the Puerto Rican community, including facilitating language and other cultural differences. In 1951, the national office was directed by the sociologist Clarence Senior and extended services to employers throughout the industrial and agricultural regions of the country. Affiliated with the U.S. Employment Service, the national office fulfilled labor demands throughout the country (Senior 1952). By 1955, the Migration Division opened a branch in Chicago, followed by branch offices in Pennsylvania, Massachusetts, New Jersey, Ohio, and other areas to which the migrant flow was diverted. Before long, the agency was encouraging nonseasonal workers to take up residence in many states such as Connecticut or New Jersey, or even in far-flung destinations like California, Illinois, Michigan, and Wisconsin. Within five years, 45 percent of the Puerto Ricans leaving the island were destined for New Jersey; another 20 percent responded to the need for cheap labor in Connecticut's tobacco regions (Senior 1952: 44).

Under the leadership of Joseph Monserrat, the New York office monitored seasonal contract workers and served as a clearinghouse on jobs, housing, welfare, education, and health services. The Migration Division gained currency as the arbitrator for Puerto Rican affairs, a situation that more often than not served to inhibit and undermine grass-roots leadership emanating from diaspora communities. In fact, the virtual exclusion of stateside Puerto Ricans from the political scene during the fifties and sixties can be traced in great measure to the intermediary role assumed by the Migration Division, subsequently known as the Office of the Commonwealth.[13]

Some New York Puerto Ricans questioned the agency's political ties to the island as counterproductive to city and stateside interests. Pledged to develop community leadership, the Office of the Commonwealth tended to bypass internal authority figures on issues affecting the New York community, instead consulting island superiors on matters where they were not experienced. Nonetheless, the Migration Division also served to counterbalance the actions and attitudes of an inhospitable, bigoted American society. Within the migrant community, other Puerto Ricans, including many who were U.S. born, accepted the representation of their communities by a quasi-political, highly visible entity, precisely because of its promise to develop the community and its leadership. Overall, the Migration Division's mandate to work with existing community groups and foster the creation of new associations as needed was supported.

Among the earliest grass-roots associations connected with the Migration Division was the Hispanic Young Adult Association (HYAA). This group initially focused on the interests of young professionals and college students and advanced the adoption of mainstream U.S. mores and middle-class values. Among HYAA's membership were Luis and Cecilia Núñez, Antonia Pantoja, Joe and Josie Morales, Josephine Nieves, Eddie González, Alice Cardona, Yolanda Sánchez, and others, including college-educated social workers who believed that social intervention would eventually solve the community's problems. By 1956, however, commitment to issues of identity motivated many in the HYAA's leadership to reject assimilation and question the use of the term Hispanic. Although the group's primary objective—to create an effective Puerto Rican leadership responsive to community—remained in place, the Hispanic Young Adult Association redefined itself as the Puerto Rican Association for Community Affairs (PRACA) (Pantoja 2002: 77–78).

El Congreso de Pueblos, or the Council of Hometown Clubs, exemplifies an older organization that worked closely with the Migration Division. The council incorporated eighty clubs, many of which had been in existence since the era of the pioneer generation. Traditionally the first to take root on U.S. soil wherever Puerto Rican concentrations built a community, the importance of the hometown clubs cannot be underestimated. The clubs had provided a home away from home predominantly oriented toward sociocultural and political affairs, and they continued to do so in the fifties and sixties, sponsoring baseball teams, sports leagues, and beauty pageants. Alone, the clubs served an important function in coalescing community, but incorporated under the council and led by the astute activist, Gilberto Gerena Valentín, the clubs became substantial political agents utilized by both island and mainland politicians. Hometown clubs formed the backbone of the Puerto Rican Day Parade and took political positions when necessary against injustice, police brutality, racism, and discrimination; raised funds for the indigent, provided shelter, and job opportunities. The most visible display of Puerto Rican solidarity was (and continues to be) the Puerto Rican Day Parade where the hometown clubs in concert with other organizations transcended their island roots and unfurled the full potential and vitality of the increasingly transnational community.

Another example of grass-roots organizing was the Puerto Rican Forum. This nonprofit civic coalition of multiple associations surfaced in 1957 to challenge the domination of the Migration Division. Initially known as the Puerto Rican Hispanic Leadership Forum, the group patterned itself after the NAACP and the American Jewish Committee, and sought to become the citywide representative of the Puerto Rican community. Supported by a cadre of community volunteers, the forum was privately funded and promoted community enterprises. Fueled by the organizational strengths of the community, the forum produced a plan for a comprehensive community development project. Some sixty organizations participated in the initial planning and argued for constructing strategies to promote community advancement in family income, education, health, and housing. Above all, they espoused building strong family units through the creation of cultural, economic and educational programs (Puerto Rican Forum 1964).

Although some of the ideas envisioned in their publication, *A Study of Poverty in the Puerto Rican Community*, were initiated, many were not. Disagreement surfaced over priorities, disbursement of funds, mode of operation, and directorship. However, at least two alternative strategies for community development that resulted did in fact help the Puerto Rican community to move forward. The first prioritized immediate action and intervention to confront the daily socioeconomic problems facing the community. The second placed the youth of the community at center stage and promoted a premise of advancement through leadership based on long-range educational and professional programs. These programs were necessary in order to hone management skills, raise the level of consciousness regarding identity and self-image, and nurture the desire and opportunity to attain higher educational credentials.

Aspira (1961), the Puerto Rican Educators' Association, and other groups like the Society of Puerto Rican Auxiliary Teachers well understood and supported long-range planning strategies focused on education. Other organizations, exemplified by the Puerto Rican Family Institute (1960), chose to confront immediate needs. Directed by Augustín González, the Family Institute became a citywide agency that recreated a traditional support system using the concept of the extended family as a model. From the early days of its humble beginnings in volunteers' apartments to the present, these programs provided social services. These included prevention and intervention in mental health, child placement, residential services, education, and research. A multiservice agency with a strong new arrivals program, the institute identified a cadre of experienced families who were then invited to serve as *padrinos* or godparents to a newly arrived family. The godparents would serve as role models and advise on issues affecting the newcomers. The mental health component stressed family therapy as the family unit continued to be the focal point of all the Institute's programs. In all, the Family Institute prioritized short-range strategies and immediate intervention that dealt head-on with a multitude of problems affecting the migrant family.

By contrast, under the auspices of the Puerto Rican Forum and led by the dynamic community activist Antonia Pantoja, Aspira (1961) focused on correcting the miseducation of Puerto Rican youth in the New York City school system. The key to social change was education, and Aspira directed its energies to reversing dismal graduation and drop out rates. The organization aimed to develop the talents of barrio youth to their fullest potential, and that, in turn, would ultimately lead to political and economic community empowerment. Toward this end, Aspira created chapters in secondary schools designed to guide the youth toward professional, business, academic, and artistic goals. Such chapters provided an empowering, nurturing atmosphere where members were tutored and taught to master the school curriculum. Students were enriched by knowledge of their history and culture, and along with their families received counseling about college opportunities requirements, financial aid, campus visits, and general orientation about higher education. From its humble beginnings as a small, nonprofit counseling agency, Aspira grew into a national association with branches in five states, Puerto Rico, and Washington, D.C. Today, many *aspirantes* in important decision-making positions bear witness to Aspria's success.[14]

The Schools and Puerto Rican New Yorkers

If the community agencies of the fifties and sixties arose through coalition and collective action to combat the ills plaguing Puerto Ricans, the schools provided yet another arena of fierce contestation. Since the late forties, when the great migration brought thousands of Puerto Rican children to city schools, the community had encountered a rigid, bureaucratic system no longer experienced in teaching language-minority children. The first attempts to amend the situation centered on the hiring of bilingual teachers, mostly from the island, who were employed as substitute auxiliary teachers (SATs). Their role was not only to teach the children the English language but also to serve as liaisons with their community. The SATs received waivers to bypass the board's stringent speech requirements and proved to be enlightened professionals, champions of community causes, and leaders in raising a political consciousness among the community's parents, many of whom became leaders in their own right.[15]

The second attempt resulted from suggestions made in the *Puerto Rican Study*, a comprehensive review of Puerto Rican children in the city's public schools carried out with the purpose of creating new methods for their instruction (Morrison 1958). Recommendations based on the study included the hiring of bilingual-bicultural teachers, coordinators, school-community personnel, counselors, and administrators.

By the late sixties, the struggles over bilingual- bicultural education, community control, desegregation, and decentralization of the New York City schools set the stage for ideological confrontations that could potentially serve to unite the community in a common front. The failure to educate American students who happened to speak another language became the rallying cry for institutionalization of bilingual education. Alarming statistics and the virtual exclusion of Puerto Ricans and other Spanish-speaking students from a university education set the tenor for the 1968 Aspira conference, *Hemos Trabajado Bien*. Participants included Puerto Ricans, Mexican-Americans, and Euro-American educators who pledged their support for bilingual education, access to the university, and a renewed campaign for the right of self-definition and determination. In the wake of political fervor and the civil rights movement, Aspira, in partnership with the Puerto Rican Legal Defense and Education Fund, launched a class-action suit against the large and powerful New York City Board of Education on behalf of the non-English-speaking children in the public schools. The result was the Aspira Consent Decree of 1974, which guaranteed equal educational opportunities for all language minority children in the city.

By this point in time, the Puerto Rican community demonstrated a high degree of solidarity. Radical student movements brought together barrio youth with college students, particularly from the campuses of the City University of New York, parents' organizations, and community groups. All joined in the struggles for social justice, fair housing standards, jobs, health care, and meaningful education. Barrio parents argued for improving the neighborhood schools and against the busing of their children into hostile areas of the city. They mobilized to elect Puerto Ricans and other Spanish-speaking individuals to community school boards. And students, mostly U.S.-born second generation, supported by the community, argued for accountability and representation in university curricula. So it was that after two decades of disarray and dislocation, the Puerto Ricans of New York stood prepared to bring about significant transformations to their city. And this was merely the beginning.

Final Thoughts
Clearly, the period from 1945 to 1965 was a challenging one for the New York Puerto Ricans in terms of employment, housing and other critical indicators, but it was also a period of fundamental strides that essentially engaged New York Puerto Ricans in a process of unification and self-definition. The emergence of major organizations that brokered for the community on city, state, and national levels became the vehicles for serving a national constituency that continues to provide political representation and multi-services for Puerto Ricans and other Latinos throughout the nation. Furthermore, the struggles of this community during this time period created the environment and support system for the unprecedented immigrations from the Hispanic Caribbean, Central America, and South America that originated in the sixties. Ultimately, these organizations pressed for the creation of a Puerto Rican

leadership emphasizing a bilingual-bicultural construct. Along with the community they represented, such leaders took center stage as agents for social, political and educational change.

REFERENCES

Berrol, Selma. 2000. *The Empire City: New York and Its People, 1624–1996*. Westport, CT: Praeger.

Caro, Robert. 1974. *The Power Broker: Robert Moses and the Fall of New York*. New York: Alfred A. Knopf.

Centro de Estudios Puertorriqueños, History Task Force, ed. 1979. *Labor Migration Under Capitalism: The Puerto Rican Experience*. New York: Monthly Review Press.

Chenault, Lawrence. 1938. *The Puerto Rican Migrant in New York City*. New York: Columbia University Press.

Colón, Jesús. 1993. *The Way It Was and Other Writings*. Houston: Arte Publico Press.

Haslip-Viera, Gabriel. 1996. "The Evolution of the Latino Community in New York City: Early Nineteenth Century to the Present," in *Latinos in New York: Communities in Transition*, Gabriel Haslip-Viera and Sherrie L. Baver, eds. Pp. 3–29. Notre Dame, IN: University of Notre Dame Press.

Hernández Alvarez, José. 1976 [1967]. *Return Migration to Puerto Rico*. Westport, CT: Greenwood Press.

Lapp, Michael. 1990. "Managing Migration: The Government of Puerto Rico and Puerto Ricans in New York City, 1948–1968." Ph.D. dissertation, Johns Hopkins University.

Meyer, Gerald. 1992. "Marcantonio and El Barrio," *Centro de Estudios Puertorriqueños: Bulletin* 4: 2 (spring): 66–87.

Morales Carrion, Arturo, ed. 1983. *Puerto Rico: A Political and Cultural History*. New York: W.W. Norton.

Morrison, J. Cayce. 1958. *The Puerto Rican Study, 1953–1957: A Report on the Education and Adjustment of Puerto Rican Pupils in the Public Schools of the City of New York*. New York: New York City Board of Education.

Ortiz, Altagracia. 1996. "'En la aguja y el pedal eché la hiel:' Puerto Rican Women in the Garment Industry of New York City, 1920–1980," in *Puerto Rican Women and Work: Bridges in Transnational Labor*, Altagracia Ortíz, ed. Pp. 55-81. Philadelphia: Temple University Press.

Pantoja, Antonia. 2002. *Memoir of a Visionary*. Houston: Arte Público Press.

Puerto Rican Forum. 1964. *A Study of Poverty Conditions in the New York Puerto Rican Community*. New York: Puerto Rican Forum, Inc.

Puerto Ricans in the Continental United States: An Uncertain Future. 1976. Washington, DC: U.S. Commission on Civil Rights.

Ramírez de Arellano, Annette and Conrad Seipp. 1983. *Colonialism, Catholicism and Birth Control in Puerto Rico: The History of Sterilization in Puerto Rico*. Chapel Hill: University of North Carolina Press.

Rand, Christopher. 1958. *The Puerto Ricans*. New York: Oxford University Press.

Rodríguez, Clara E. 1989. *Puerto Ricans: Born in the U.S.A*. Boston: Unwin and Hyman.

———. 1995. "Puerto Ricans in Historical and Social Science Research," in *Handbook of Research on Multicultural Education*, James A. Banks and Cherry A. McGee Banks, eds. Pp. 223–244. New York: Macmillan.

———. 1996. "Economic Survival in New York City," in *Historical Perspective on Puerto Rican Survival in the U.S.*, Clara E. Rodríguez and Virginia Sánchez Korrol, eds. Pp. 37–53. Princeton, NJ: Marcus Wiener Publications.

Rodríguez, Clara E., and Virginia Sánchez Korrol, eds. 1996. *Historical Perspective on Puerto Rican Survival in the U.S.* Princeton, NJ: Marcus Wiener Publications.

Rodríguez Fraticelli, Carlos, and Amilcar Tirado. 1989. "Notes Toward a History of Puerto Rican Community Organizations in New York City," *Centro de Estudios Puertorriqueños: Bulletín* 2: 6 (summer): 34–47.

Sánchez, José. 1996. "Puerto Rican Politics in New York City: Beyond Second Hand Theory," in *Latinos in New York: Communities in Transition*, Gabriel Haslip-Viera and Sherrie Baver, eds. Pp. 259–301. Notre Dame, IN: University of Notre Dame Press.

Sánchez Korrol, Virginia. 1994. *From Colonia to Community: The History of Puerto Ricans in New York City.* Berkeley, CA: University of California Press.

———. 1999. *Teaching U.S. Puerto Rican History.* Washington, D.C.: American Historical Association, Teaching Diversity Series.

Sandoval Sánchez, Alberto. 1997. "West Side Story: A Puerto Rican Reading of 'America,'" in *Latin Looks: Images of Latinas and Latinos in the U.S. Media*, Clara E. Rodríguez, ed. Pp. 164–179. Boulder, CO: Westview Press.

Santana Cooney, Rosemary, and Alice Colón Warren. 1996. "Work and Family: The Recent Struggles of Puerto Rican Women," in *Historical Perspectives on Puerto Rican Survival in the United States*, Clara E. Rodríguez and Virginia Sánchez Korrol, eds. Pp. 69–85. Princeton, NJ: Markus Wiener Publishers.

Senior, Clarence. 1952. *Strangers- Then Neighbors: The Story of Our Puerto Rican Citizens.* New York: Anti-Defamation League of B'nai B'rith.

Stevens Arroyo, Anthony M. 1996. "Struggles in the Catholic Church," in *Historical Perspectives on Puerto Rican Survival in the United States*, Clara E. Rodríguez and Virginia Sánchez Korrol, eds. Pp. 153–165. Princeton, NJ: Markus Wiener Publishers.

Tattenbaum, Ian S. 1997. "Renewal for the 1990s: An Analysis of New York City Redevelopment Programs in Light of Title I of the Housing Act of 1949." *New York University Environmental Law Journal* 6, 1 (spring): 221-226.

Torres, Andrés, and José E. Velásquez, eds. 1998. *The Puerto Rican Movement: Voices From the Diaspora.* Philadelphia: Temple University Press.

NOTES

1. From the article "A Growing Minority," originally published in *The Worker*, March 30, 1958. Cited in Colón (1993: 84).
2. Figures are based on "Population Trends of Puerto Ricans on the U.S. Mainland by Region, State, and City, 1950, 1960, 1970," in *Puerto Ricans in the United States: An Uncertain Future* (1976: 23).
3. Raymond Vernon, *Metropolis, 1985* (Cambridge: Harvard University Press, 1960).

Cited in Rodríguez (1996: 48).
4. Many historians and economists have written about industrialization and migration. Centro de Estudios Puertorriqueños, History Task Force (1979) and Morales Carrión (1983) are still excellent sources for their detailed analysis of this issue. Clara E. Rodríguez also cites a *New York Times* article about former Mayor Robert F. Wagner's visit to San Juan in which he told Puerto Ricans that mainland communities needed migrants to fill jobs. See Rodríguez (1996: 46-47).
5. For detailed information on sterilization in Puerto Rico see Ramírez de Arellano and Seipp (1983).
6. The Housing Act of 1949 contained six titles. Title I was "Slum Clearance and Community Development and Redevelopment. The Act sanctioned several actions. It gave control of urban redevelopment projects to local governments and required any area designated for redevelopment to be defined as blighted. See Tattenbaum (1997).
7. See Robert Caro's detailed portrayal of Robert Moses and his transformation of New York in *The Power Broker: Robert Moses and the Fall of New York* (1974).
8. See Altagracia Ortíz (1996: 55–81). In this essay, Professor Ortíz cites the work and testimony on these issues by Herbert Hill, who appeared before the Labor Sub-Committee of the U.S. House of Representatives Committee on Education and Labor on August 17, 1962. The focus of Hill's work was on discriminatory practices in the ILGWU against African Americans, but also includes Puerto Ricans.
9. Cited in Meyer (1992: 76–77). This quote appeared on the dust cover flap of John Lait and Lee Mortimer's book, *New York Confidential!* (Chicago: Ziff-Davis, 1948).
10. For an excellent overview of radical student and community organizing in the sixties, see Torres and Velázquez, eds. (1998).
11. An excellent study of the role of the Migration Division in community formation is Michael Lapp, "Managing Migration: The Government of Puerto Rico and Puerto Ricans in New York City, 1948–1968" (1990). On this issue, also see Rodríguez Fraticelli and Tirado (1989: 37–38).
12. See also *Puerto Ricans in the Continental United States: An Uncertain Future* (1976: 29).
13. Antonia Pantoja was among those who believed that the work of the Office of the Commonwealth was not in the best interests of developing community leadership. See Pantoja (2002: 78).
14. For a more detailed discussion of Aspira and the Puerto Rican Family Institute, see Sánchez Korrol (1994: 224-231).
15. The New York City Board of Education required prospective teachers to take an oral speech test. Persons with accents were denied licenses to teach in the schools. Thus, many professional Puerto Rican teachers were kept out of teaching positions. Among these, many accepted positions as case workers with the city.

CHAPTER ONE
Commentary

Author's childhood residence (1945-1965) at 881 Intervale Avenue in South Bronx. (*Photo: courtesy of the author*)

COMMENTARY

A NUYORICAN'S VIEW OF OUR HISTORY AND LANGUAGE(S) IN NEW YORK, 1945–1965

Ana Celia Zentella

The story of the dramatic expansion of the New York Puerto Rican community between 1945 and 1965 deserves to be written in a multitude of compelling styles. Virginia Sánchez Korrol's solid histories, first about the pioneers who shaped a *colonia* into a community (Sánchez Korrol 1994) and now of the development of its major organizations and institutions in the face of New York's ignorance and hostility, provide the essential grounding in a keen analysis of historical records. To complete the story and bring it fully alive, we would need to tell it via the sounds and music and voices that surrounded Puerto Ricans: at home and on their *bloques* every day, on the way to work and school from Monday to Friday, at the *londris* and *La Marqueta* on Saturday mornings, in the house parties and dance halls on Saturday night, and in church on Sundays.

What a great CD that would make! Begin with the *paso doble* theme song of *La Hora Hispana—tan tan taaaaan tantantántararan—España Cañí*, which invoked *la madre patria* for a community whose *abuelitos* remembered Spanish rule and the *Yanqui* takeover in 1898. Include Rafael Hernández's lament

---

I dedicate this paper to the loving memory of the wonderful Puerto Ricans/Nuyoricans who guided and enriched my life while they were alive, especially mami, my brother-in-law Salvador Vivó, mi madrina Josefa Mercado, Delia Torres, Zoila and Santos Tomei, Rosa Reguero, William Acevedo, Emérita Cruz, Antonia Pantoja, and Tito Puente.

(*Lamento Borincano*) of the disastrous poverty of the late 1920s that forced my mother's family and other precursors of the massive post–World War II migration to flee the island. Daniel Santos's sad song to Puerto Rican mothers about their sons away at war in the early 1940s and Noel Estrada's frustrated dreams of returning for good to *Mi Viejo San Juan* ("*pues lo quiso el destino*" because fate wanted it) in the fifties remain unforgettable. Also unforgettable is the rumble of the packed *sobueyes* that took us to school or work, mainly the Lexington Avenue local, *el número seis*, from the bowels of Loisaida through El Barrio in Manhattan and beyond Hunts Point in the Bronx, or the 7th Avenue Express that took us above the rooftops of Simpson, Intervale, and Prospect Avenues, and connected us at the Grand Concourse to the Woodlawn train for the trip to Yankee Stadium ($.25 CENTS on Ladies Day!). Ok, there were some unlucky folks living in Brooklyn who rooted for the Dodgers, but the sound of Bronx cheers was deafening during the glorious string of World Series championships. More universally appreciated were the *rumbas, mambos,* and *guagancos* that we danced to all Saturday night in crowded apartments (*esos "paris" chéveres*), or at the big clubs. To mention just a few: the Tropicana on Westchester Avenue and the *Club Cubano Interamericano* on Prospect, the Hunts Point Palace on Southern Boulevard, *El Club Caborrojeno*, and the Broadway Casino on the West Side, and the world-famous Palladium (where one envied girlfriend said she danced with Marlon Brando). Three giant TITOs stood out among the musicians who thrilled us: Tito Curet Alonso, Tito Rodríguez, Tito Puente. And what about those *corta vena boleros* ("vein-cutting ballads") that made it very hard to hold on to St Athanasius's definition of a good girl? (*Ay, Vicentico Valdés, "la gloria eres tú."*)

I leave the musical history of those years to the ethnomusicologists, but I want to make clear that just as our music was our flag (Glasser 1995), so was our language. In keeping with my training as a linguist, which began in the South Bronx, this chapter focuses on the many contributions that Puerto Ricans in New York made to the city's linguistic history. Those contributions were not well received, in part because we arrived during the period (1920s–1950s) identified as the most restrictive in language policies in the history of New York City (García 1997). The xenophobia of the post–World War I era had given rise to many restrictive policies against immigrants and their languages. Negative attitudes persisted through the World War II era, perpetuated by the children of the immigrants of the first part of the century. Sadly, they had internalized the pessimistic views of languages other than English and of bilingualism that their parents had been subjected to.

The languages and language behaviors of Puerto Ricans were attacked for reasons linked to linguistic as well as racial and class prejudices. Puerto Rican Spanish was deemed unacceptable because it differed from that of

Spain, although those very same critics would never expect the United States to speak the English of Great Britain. Puerto Rican English was ridiculed for its Spanish accent and second-language errors, although their immigrant parents had mangled English too. Most misunderstood was our bilingualism, particularly the ways in which we used both languages to speak about our new experiences. The bilingual style was rarely used in writing, but *Trópico en Manhattan, una novela* about *puertorriqueños en Nueva York* in the late 1940s, ends with a two-page glossary of "Neoyorquismos."[1] *El autor,* Guillermo Cotto-Thorner (1951), provides *la versión en español* of 80 items that a *monolingüe* readership might not understand, alongside the English words or expressions from which they were derived. It is among the earliest lists, to my knowledge, of the *anglicismos* that pepper what is widely known today as "Spanglish," of the New York Puerto Rican (NYPR) variety.[2] Some of the loans are no longer *de moda* because the reality they captured has disappeared. For example, those were the days when it was common for single men to *rentar un "cuarto furnido"* (furnished room) in a boardinghouse, or become *"bordantes"* (boarders) in the apartments of families who could not *soportarse* (support themselves) *con el "rilif"* (the city's Home Relief supplement), and who lived in fear of *un "desposes"* (eviction). But the majority of the novel's *"neoyorquismos"* are still in everyday use, for example, *"lonchar"* (to lunch), *"londri"* (laundry), *"piquels"* (pickles), *"beibito"* (little baby), *"chequear"* (to check), *"liquear"* (to leak), *"chipe"* (a cheap person). And we have new terms for some of the same old problems, including *guelfer* or *wilfrido* for welfare and *cupones* for food stamps. Like most of the words that Puerto Ricans borrowed from English in order to communicate their new experiences in New York, they reflect the historical realities that Virginia Sánchez Korrol documents in her chapter.[3] The community that grew from 60,000 in 1945 to 610,000 in 1960 shook up and reshaped Puerto Rico and New York and Spanish and English, creating strong but often disparaged blends of languages and identities.

The Spanish and English labels—some imposed and some of our own choice—that have identified us as a group reflect the linguistic and cultural transformations we have participated in. At different periods and sometimes at one and the same time, we have been *puertorriqueños, antillanos, caribeños, marín taiguers, grinjornes, jíbaros, hispanos, latinos, boricuas, pororicans,* Spanish, Hispanics, Spiks, Puerto Ricans, Nuyoricans.[4] Those of us who answer to the "Nuyorican" label with pride, now spanning at least three generations, remain bonded to each other and to Puerto Rico, New York, Spanish, and English by the linguistic inventions that took hold in the post–World War II decades and defined the "Nuyorican." Our inventions sometimes took the form of new meanings for old words (for example, *"yarda"* became the schoolyard and back alley in addition to the standard measurement), but English words with Spanish pronunciations were more generative. Some of our adaptations of borrowed items were characteristic of the transformations made by all Spanish speakers learning English. These include changing the soft <th> sounds to <t>, as in *trifti* (thrifty), the <sh> to <ch> as in *chopin* (shopping bag), the hard <j> to <y> as in *los proyectos* (the project), or adding an /e/ to words that begin with /sp/, /st/, or /sk/ as in "I no espeak espanis in eskul." In addition, by substituting English <h> or Spanish <j> sounds of aspiration in place of <s> at the end of syllables, as in *ejtoj* < *estos* and changing final /r/ to /l/, as in *paltil* < *partir*, we Puertoricanized the words we borrowed, so that "to scratch" becomes *ejcrachal* . Mixed together with our island's *puertorriqueñismos*, which include antiquated Spanish terms (*prieto* "dark/black"), Taíno words (*mimes* "no see'ums"), Canary Island Spanish (*guagua* "bus"), African loans (*ñangotarse* "to squat"), and homegrown creations (*cur cur/cul cul* "to drink down quickly," *tostao* "crazy," *picao* "tipsy," *enfogonao* "angry"), to name just a few, we created a truly Nuyorican *asopao*.[5] Because these creative combinations helped make me and the people I love most who and what we are, they remain identity markers that distinguish potential friend from stranger. When I hear them, I assume that speaker will laugh appreciatively at my jokes, sympathize with my problems, and agree with me as to who is *buena gente*, "good people" or *un comemierda* (literally, a shit-eater). In these pages, I reflect on the loans and labels that stir deep emotions in me because they are so tightly linked to my growing up during the decades of the most significant growth of the New York Puerto Rican community, and because they continue to bond me to my fellow Nuyoricans.

For almost all of the period from 1945 to 1965, I lived at 881 Intervale Avenue, between Beck and Fox Streets in the South Bronx. In the accompanying picture of my *"bildin"* (building), which was taken in 1940 (Facing p. 20), the window of my room is on the third floor to the right.[6] On the left is the *faia ejquei* (fire escape) where we sometimes sat on steamy nights, and where we hung handmade streamers for *papi*'s joyous return from World War II (the first memory I can recall). You can see the stoop where we played stoopball, y *donde jangueábamos* (where we used to hang out). We weren't allowed to *janguear en el jol o en el "rufo"* (to hang out in the hall or on the roof); only *títeres, putas y bones* (hooligans, whores, and bums) did that. To the left of the stoop was *"el beijman"* (the basement), where *el supel* (the super/superintendent), also known as *el janitol* (the janitor) lived. That's where we went to complain *que no hay "ejtin" y nos estamos "frizando" aún con el "cou" puesto, dígale al "lanlol" que arregle la "boila"* (that there's no steam and we are freezing even with our coats on; tell the landlord to fix the boiler) From the sidewalk, my sister and I yelled ¡*MAMI, tírame cinco chavos!* (Ma, throw down five cents) for the strolling vendors who sold sweet potatoes, jelly apples, and *coco* (coconut) slices. If we heard the bell of the Bungalow Bar ice cream truck we asked for *un daim* (a dime) or *una cuora/ "cuara"* (a quarter), to buy *aijcrim* (ice cream). But our favorite hawker was the Italian who sold watermelons in the summer, causing every Puerto Rican to roar with laughter when he bellowed his version of "watermelon," "*Huélemelo, huélemelo*" (literally, smell my thing).

Language jokes and language itself were frequent topics of conversation in apartment 3C, where my Puerto Rican *mami* and Mexican *papi*—who had met in Spanish Harlem—discussed the difference between *frijoles* and *habichuelas* and taught us to love their *tostones* and *tortillas*, *pasteles* and *tamales*, Rafael Hernández and Agustín Lara, *la Virgen de la Providencia* and *la Virgen de Guadalupe*. *Papi*, who became "Daddy" because he communicated with us in native-like New York City English, was a perfect example of Weinreich's "ideal bilingual" (Weinreich 1953), capable of switching flawlessly from one language to the other, in formal and informal registers. He also switched between two Spanish lexicons with ease. He never sounded like a Puerto Rican even after 44 years of marriage to *mami*, and despite being surrounded by Puerto Ricans at home and at work, but he made sure to order a *bizcocho*, not a *pastel*, from Valencia Bakery and he referred to *aretes*, not *pantallas*, at the Centro Mexicano.[7] Under his tutelage, my introduction to the basic tenets of sociolinguistics began quite early.

As for *mami*, in addition to learning Mexican Spanish at home, she learned Yiddish and English from her Jewish neighbors and coworkers in the garment district. Yiddish was very handy on Intervale in those days because of the yentas who sat downstairs in their shmattas, kvetching about the meshugunas who passed by, and lamenting, "Oy gevalt," "Oy veis mihr, over the tsurris in their lives. "Gesundheit" competed with "Salud" in our everyday vocabulary. Years later, I learned that the deep blue numbers on some arms identified Holocaust survivors, and in their honor "Sie gesunt" remains one of my special blessings.

The most important English lessons *mami* had learned were taught in her grade school in Aguadilla less than 20 years after the U.S. takeover in 1898, when she was forced to study in a language she did not understand. The first sentence in English she memorized was, "I cannot tell a lie, I chop [sic] down the cherry tree"—indisputable proof of George Washington's honesty and by extension, proof of the decency and good will of his nation and the deserved supremacy of its government and language. Those benevolent views were put to the test in New York's garment district *factorías* where she worked hard days for 34 years—*"partaim," "ful taim," "haciendo piswor"* (doing piecework), with little pay and frequent *"ley-of,"* despite the efforts of *la unión* (the ILGWU).[8] Workers usually were laid off around Chanukah/Christmas when *el boj o la bosa* ('the boss'), whom Italian coworkers often called "*sadamanbiches*" ('sons of bitches'), went to Florida. El *rosheo, trobol, taxes, la renta, y los biles* were everyday worries. In the garment district *mami* learned that the way you spoke English could stigmatize you forever, and she knew her accent made her a marked woman. Yet she could not speak her own language because it was considered impolite to speak Spanish in front of English speakers, even if you were not talking to them. Conflicted, she advised us not to yell "mami" from the street, but to say "Moder." So my sister and I immediately ran downstairs and screamed MO——DER, a loving name that stuck for as long as she lived.

From Intervale it was a short walk up Fox to Tiffany Street every Sunday and holy day of obligation for mass at St. Athanasius where, *bendito*, my sister had been refused admission by the school's nuns in the early 1940s. By the 1960s so many parishioners and students were Puerto Rican that the parish had become a solid political base for Father Louis Gigante, whose bulk lent credibility to our Spanish pronunciation of his Italian last name: *higante* (giant). Gigante's power and links to local poverty programs, and the impact of the Catholic archdiocese's decision to limit the number of masses a parish could offer in Spanish, is another piece of our history that remains to be written.[9] Not everyone went to St. Athanasius. The attraction of small Spanish-speaking storefront Pentecostal churches, led by local Puerto Rican ministers, resulted in many defections from Roman Catholicism. We called them *"Aleluyas"* with some disdain, and we were amazed by the females' strict adherence to clothing and makeup codes, but we loved their joyous Spanish hymns, the hand clapping and tambourine playing. The pulsating beat of *"Yo quiero más y más a Cristo"* sounded as if it had a lot more healing power than the ballad-like "Holy God, we praise thy name." To this day, the prayers I said with *mami* in Spanish mean more to me than the English versions we learned during Tuesday afternoon's religious instruction classes, when we Catholic kids trouped, en masse, to St. Athanasius from P.S. 39.

Catholics, *Pentecostales*, Jews, and many *"Negroes,"* including Colin Powell, the present secretary of state, studied together in P.S. 39 on Longwood Avenue and Beck Street. The massive influx of Puerto Rican students in the post–World War II period transformed that school and challenged the entire system. We brought a new language and a racially mixed group into schools controlled by teachers and administrators of European backgrounds who were unprepared for such diversity. Most of them no longer spoke the language of their immigrant parents or considered it a language worth speaking, particularly Yiddish, and they expected us to follow their example. Instead, our Spanish, English, and Spanglish grew to reflect all of our influences, including the New York City standard spoken by teachers and *la principal* (the principal), and the popular varieties of English spoken by our Jewish, Irish, and African American playmates in *la yarda* (the yard).

My lifelong connection and identification with African Americans began in P.S. 39. The Puerto Rican migration was happening on the heels of a major Black move from southern fields to northern factories between the wars, and neither group knew much about the other. Nor did we understand why we felt so battered or neglected in our classes that most of us did not graduate from high school. Remember that "Negroes" or "colored people," as they were called then, were still living under Jim Crow laws and being hunted and lynched like wild animals in the South. In the North, they were depicted as violent, lazy, and dirty, like their Puerto Rican neighbors. Newspapers that carried those stories also included reports on "crazy Puerto Rican Nationalists/terrorists" because of an armed revolt against U.S. domination on the island and the assassination of one of the president's guards in Washington, D.C., in 1950, and a shooting in Congress in 1954. I often wonder how those events shaped teachers' and other gatekeepers' views of Puerto Ricans and "Negroes," and what impact their views had on our efforts to succeed. The liaisons forged between the children and parents who bore the brunt of racist prejudices deserve to be documented in full, including local collaborations like that of Mrs. Zentella and Mrs. Tyson in P.S. 39's PTA.[10] They helped lay the foundation for the mutual Puerto Rican and African American support in the face of discrimination that continues to this day, notwithstanding the rough spots along the way. Puerto Ricans learned the hard way that the phenotypic complexities captured in their distinctions between *blanco, negro, grifo, jabao, indio, trigueño,* and *mulato* were lost on Americans of all races. Americans recognized only two color boxes, white and black, and respected only one. "Negro" did not have any positive connotations, as *negro* did/does in Puerto Rican Spanish, albeit alongside the negative. In the United States it easily became "nigger," an epithet even worse than the Spik label that Puerto Ricans endured. Soon "dirty Spiks and niggers" became a common refrain in the mouths of those who despised us.

During this period in our history, "Puerto Rican" became synonymous with Spik, with *gangas* (gangs) like the Sharks depicted in *West Side Story*, who "rumbled" and ran from *la jara* (the police), with teenage killers like the demonized "Capeman," and with *joloperos* (muggers/literally, hold-uppers), *drogadictos* (drug addicts), alcoholics, whores, and welfare cheats who (supposedly) came to New York to sponge off the city. When they couldn't cut the mustard here, they returned to Puerto Rico and perpetuated a vicious cycle of social deviance and return migration, according to chronicles like Oscar Lewis's *La Vida* (1965). Dismay about the public perception of Puerto Ricans and the city's inability to deal with the community's problems prompted Antonia Pantoja and others to organize HYAA, the Hispanic Young Adult

Association. As Toni poignantly recalls in her memoir, they agonized, trying to find a way out:

> During this period [1950–1953], the daily newspapers were carrying many articles about the problems that Puerto Ricans were bringing to the city. All the reports were negative.... Our discussions covered many issues: Why did our parents emigrate? Why do Americans hate us? Why do Americans accuse our women of being prostitutes and our men of being lazy? Why are we accused of coming to New York to get on welfare? Why? Why? Why?" (Pantoja 2002: 73–74).

Even in scientific research, the primary reference to our presence denoted deviance: the "Puerto Rican Syndrome" became the clinical label for hyperkinetic seizures, of the type suffered by women who shook uncontrollably in response to a family tragedy. We got another label instead of a solution.

Puerto Rico's elites did not treat us much better. Nuyoricans were viewed as adding fuel to the fifty-year-old fire that raged around the political status of Puerto Rico and the U.S. impact on Puerto Rican culture. More than half a million Puerto Ricans who lived on the U.S. mainland instead of the island and spoke English or a despised Spanglish instead of a "pure" Spanish, challenged the essentialist notions of the Puerto Rican nation championed by traditional *hispanófilos* and worried *independentistas* (Duany 2002). One solution was to exclude us from *la gran familia puertorriqueña*, as Seda (1972) suggested.[11] A parallel move was to direct the Office of the Commonwealth of Puerto Rico in New York City to pursue an assimilation agenda without the advice or consent of the community, as Sánchez Korrol and Pantoja document. Fortunately, the members of HYAA sought their own solutions via direct community activism. Beginning in the 1950s and extending into the 1970s, Antonia Pantoja and other members of HYAA helped create ASPIRA, the most important Puerto Rican self-help institutions in the United States.[12]

After a few years, the Hispanic Young Adult Association renamed itself the Puerto Rican Association for Community Affairs (PRACA), not because "Hispanic" was discredited as it is today in some circles, but because Pantoja believed it necessary to identify as Puerto Ricans first. She won a close vote on the name change by challenging her fellow members: "Are we ashamed of calling ourselves Puerto Ricans? I think we should change our name to identify our Puerto Rican origin" (Pantoja 2002: 76).

When New York City became home to a larger and increasingly diverse number of Latin American immigrants, each group continued to prefer to identify with its nation of origin, but a debate about the appropriate umbrella term, "Hispanic" or *"Latino,"* heated up. Many of today's activists reject the

English rubric vehemently, believing it was imposed by government officials. For them, *"Latino"* sends a message, in Spanish, of identification with Latin America instead of Spain. But the term "Hispanic" was popular with Puerto Ricans and other Latin American immigrants in New York way before Nixon's census officials appropriated it in the early 1970s (occasioned by "his-panic," some claim facetiously), primarily because it grouped them together on the basis of their language, and colonization by Spain. Toni points out that at the time HYAA was organized, "most of the major groups serving Spanish-speaking populations were all called Hispanic" (Pantoja 2002: 76). This was understandable, because *hispano* had a long and illustrious history in the city as the unifying term for the early immigrants, primarily from Spain, Puerto Rico, and Cuba. The Spanish newspaper *El Diario*, established in 1915, called itself *La Voz de los Hispanos* (The Voice of the Hispanics). *La Liga Puertorriqueña e Hispana* (The Puerto Rican and Hispanic League) was established in 1926. In the 1940s, *La Hora Hispana* was a prominent Spanish radio program. And Cotto-Thorner refers to *"la colonia hispana"* frequently in his 1951 *novela*, including this reminder of a reality that persists today: *"No se puede pensar en la colonia hispana de Nueva York, ni en Harlem, sin pensar en la bolita, el negocio de los números.* (It's impossible to talk about the Hispanic community of New York, or Harlem, without thinking about 'la bolita,' the numbers racket.)" (Cotto-Thorner 1951: 57).

Logically, "Hispanic" was the popular choice when organizations adopted English names. On our *bloques* (blocks), however, "Spanish" was the common identity label, shorthand for "Spanish-speaker," as in "I'm Spanish." Since it might also refer to someone who came from Spain, sometimes "I'm Spanish" was a cop-out, a way to avoid identifying as Puerto Rican. When Lolita Lebrón went to apply for a job in a factory in the early 1940s, the African American elevator operator warned her to say she was "Spanish," not Puerto Rican. The patriot, who later spent 25 years in jail for leading the 1954 Nationalist attack on Congress, took his advice.

Given the hostility and pervasive images of immorality and inferiority that plagued Puerto Ricans in New York, how did we manage to get to the point where we eagerly lined Fifth Avenue by the thousands every first Sunday in June (beginning in 1959), making *La Parada* (the parade, *El Desfile Puertorriqueño*) New York's largest parade? And what source of inner strength produced all those Puerto Rican flags on cars and in windows, and the buttons and T-shirts that said "I'm Puerto Rican and proud," or "Kiss me, I'm Puerto Rican?" Visionaries including Antonia Pantoja helped lead the way by highlighting our Puerto Rican ancestry in the names and programs of the organizations they established: the Puerto Rican Forum, Universidad Boricua, Aspira's Madrinas (godmothers) and its *Areyto* Initiation Ceremony. Since then we have demanded the right to identify as Puerto Ricans, in defiance of those Americans who want us to adopt a hyphenated -American label and those islanders who would prefer we drop any reference to "their" homeland. Why, then, do we also lay proud claim to "Nuyorican?" My answer: because "Nuyorican" makes a graphic statement—in a term that is emblematic of our mixing of Spanish and English—about our roots, our hybrid identities, and our complementary allegiances. "What part of Puerto Rico do you come from?" a caller was recently asked by a radio announcer on *La Mega*. "The Bronx," she answered. "Nuyorican" joins me to that caller, to the children of El Barrio whose bilingualism I documented (Zentella 1997), and to all those who worked so hard for so long and so little, in defiance of demeaning labels and racist stereotypes. But not only those of us who were born in New York can be Nuyoricans; anyone who embraces our cause and us is welcome. Antonia Pantoja did not move to New York until she was in her twenties, but "I am a Nuyorican" is the triumphant last line of her memoir.

CONCLUSION

> *"Si no hubiera nacido en la tierra en que nací, Estuviera arrepentido de no haber nacido aquí"* (If I had not been born in the land where I was born, I would have felt sorry about not having been born here).

For many years, these key lines in Rafael Hernández' song, "El buen borincano," sung with great feeling at patriotic activities, left me feeling as if I had missed out on an essential part of being Puerto Rican. But now I, and thousands of others, reinterpret those lines to mean that we celebrate having been born Puerto Rican in New York.[13] Personally, I consider it a privilege to have been born into the New York Puerto Rican community during the defining period of its history. And I consider it my obligation to set the record straight for those who dismiss us as an immigrant group that went wrong because of a lack of significant social and structural assimilation by the third generation. Critics ignore the extent of our linguistic, cultural, educational, organizational, and economic achievements. Our *bodegueros* (bodega/grocery store owners), poets, musicians, teachers, garment workers, community activists, and others are missing from the history books. In spite of a colonized homeland that used our migration and sterilization as "escape valves," and inhospitable social and economic policies in the new land that constructed us as semilingual pathological misfits, we left an indelible imprint on New York.

The voice of that imprint is "Spanglish," a misnomer if it gives the impression that a third language has been created. Instead, as Miguel Algarín noted in his Introduction to the now-classic anthology *Nuyorican Poetry*, "the average Nuyorican has a working command of both [English and Spanish] and normally uses both languages simultaneously" (Algarín and Piñero 1975: 18). In fact, the great majority of the poems in the anthology are primarily in English, with a few words and phrases in Spanish. Basically, Spanglish is a colorful way of switching between varieties of English and Spanish, adopted because "a new day needs a new language or else the day becomes a repetition of yesterday" (Algarín and Piñero 1975: 18). Principally it consists of borrowed words and meanings, constituting a New York Spanish lexicon. Every Spanish-speaking country has its unique lexical items and features, and we have ours. Just as Costa Ricans cannot be accused of inventing a new and corrupted language when they say "Se te deschocho´el colocho" (Your curl has come undone), New Yorkers who say "Tengo que vacunear la carpeta" (I have to vacuum the carpet) are not destroying Spanish, or hobbling their communication.[14] Instead, "the interchange between both [languages] creates new possibilities" (Algarín 1975: 15). The real problem isn't the number of English words that we have borrowed into Spanish, or switching from one language to the other, but the fact that our young people are losing Spanish altogether.

My generation asked to be recognized as Puerto Ricans with a Nuyorican style that blended two languages. Because we were rejected in both of our homelands and little was done to help us develop and pass on oral and literate skills in Spanish, the newest generations are claiming that it is not necessary to speak Spanish to be Puerto Rican. Not surprisingly, given the fact that they want to leave room for all members of their family *en la gran familia puertorriqueña*, even those who were born on the island support this view (Zentella 2002).

All Nuyoricans understand this claim to be a demand for respect for those who no longer can express themselves in Spanish but who still feel and act Puerto Rican, thereby challenging a narrow territorial and language based definition of who or what is a Puerto Rican. Have we learned enough from the high price we paid for dismissing the creative contributions of the Nuyoricans of the mid-twentieth century to help today's English dominant youth affirm and strengthen the Spanish-speaking part of their identity? *Ojalá, bendito.*

REFERENCES

Algarín, Miguel. 1975. "Introduction," in *Nuyorican Poetry: An Anthology of Puerto Rican Words and Poetry*, Miguel Algarín and Miguel Piñero, eds. Pp. 9–20. New York: William Morrow.

Algarín, Miguel, and Miguel Piñero, eds. 1975. *Nuyorican Poetry: An Anthology of Puerto Rican Words and Poetry*. New York: William Morrow.

Alvarez-Nazario, Manuel. 1961. *El elemento afro-negroide en el español de Puerto Rico.* San Juan, PR: Instituto de Cultura Puertorriqueña.

_____. 1977. *El influjo indígena en el espaõl de Puerto Rico.* Río Piedras, PR: Editorial Universitaria.

_____. 1990. *El habla campesina del país.* Río Piedras: Editorial Universitaria.

Cotto-Thorner, Guillermo. 1951. *Trópico en Manhattan: Novela.* San Juan, PR: Editorial Occidente.

Duany, Jorge. 2002. *The Puerto Rican Nation on The Move: Identities on the Island and in the United States.* Chapel Hill: University of North Carolina Press.

García, Ofelia. 1997. "New York's Multilingualism: World Languages and Their Role in a U.S. City," in *The Multilingual Apple: Languages in New York City*, Ofelia García and Joshua A. Fishman, eds. Pp. 3–50. Berlin: Mouton de Gruyter.

Glasser, Ruth. 1995. *My Music is My Flag: Puerto Rican Musicians and Their New York Communities, 1917–1940.* Berkeley: University of California Press.

Lewis, Oscar. 1965. *La Vida: A Puerto Rican Family in the Culture of Poverty—San Juan and New York.* New York: Random House.

Malaret, Augusto. 1955. *Vocabulario de Puerto Rico.* 2nd ed. New York: Las Américas Publishing.

McWilliams, Carey. 1990 [1948]. *North from Mexico: The Spanish-Speaking People of the United States.* New York: Greenwood Press.

Núñez de Ortega, Rosario and Isabel Delgado de Laborde. 1999. *Los que dicen ¡ay bendito!: Dichos, modismos y expresiones del habla coloquial puertorriqueña.* San Juan, PR: Editorial Plaza Mayor.

Pantoja, Antonia. 2002. *Memoir of a Visionary.* Houston: Arte Público Press.

Rosario, Rubén del. 1965. *Vocabulario puertorriqueño.* Sharon, CT: Troutman Press.

Sánchez Korrol, Virginia. 1994. *From Colonia to Community: The History of Puerto Ricans in New York City.* Berkeley: University of California Press.

Seda Bonilla, Eduardo. 1972. "El problema de identidad de los niuyoricans," *Revista de Ciencias Sociales* 16 (4): 453–462.

Tió, Salvador. 1992. *Desde el tuétano.* San Juan, PR: Editorial Cultural.

Weinreich, Uriel. 1953. *Languages in Contact: Findings and Problems.* New York: Linguistic Circle of New York.

Zentella, Ana Celia. 1997. *Growing up Bilingual: Puerto Rican Children in New York.* Malden, MA: Blackwell.

_____. 2002. "Latin@ Languages and Identities," in *Latinos: Remaking America*, edited by Marcelo M. Suárez-Orozco and Mariela M. Páez, eds. Pp. 321–338. Berkeley: University of California Press.

NOTES

1. I am grateful to Pedro López Adorno for bringing the *glosario* to my attention.
2. Puerto Rican essayist Salvador Tió claimed to have coined the term "Spanglish," which he lampooned mercilessly, in 1948 (Tió 1992: 5). It was his claim to fame, and decades later, he lamented not having patented the term: "*el invento no fue patentado y todo el mundo lo ha seguido usando sin ningún respeto por los derechos del*

autor...." (Tió 1992: 6). But the borrowing and mixing of Spanish and English had been occurring in Mexican communities in the southwest for decades before Tió supposedly "named" it. Aurelión Espinosa published a list of 300 words in 1917, and by 1930, words that would become part of New York Spanish were common in the southwest, including those based on "taxes," "truck," "boarder," "ice cream," "lunch," "laundry", "boss" (McWilliams 1990).

3. Other items in the *glosario* were never widespread, or are apocryphal, e.g., *"toquear"* < to talk, *"craca"* < cracker, *"flaua"* < flower, *"caque"* < cake (Cotto-Thorner 1951: 243–44). Loans in quotation marks in this text denote those that appear in Cotto-Thorner's *glosario*. Other loans, the majority, appear in italics without quotation marks, as do all standard Spanish segments, because they have become an integral part of New York Puerto Rican Spanish. English glosses are in single quotations, in parentheses.

4.. *Antillanos* (Antilleans) refers to the island chain of the Antilles, and *caribeños* recalls the surrounding Caribbean Sea. The *Marine Tiger* was one of the ships that brought émigrés from the island before direct air flights. Newcomers were often dubbed *marín taiguers* or *grinjornes* (greenhorns), disparagingly. *Jíbaros* are the peasants from the countryside, but to be called a *jíbaro* meant you were a hick, not street smart. "Spiks" was the ethnic slur directed at all Spanish speakers, perhaps because they tended to say "espeek" for "speak." And "pororican" was based on the early U.S. name for the island, Porto Rico.

5. For lists of Puerto Rico's *criollismos, africanismos,* and *tainismos,* consult the work of Malaret (1955), Rubén del Rosario (1965), and Manuel Alvarez-Nazario (1961, 1977, 1990). Typical expressions have been collected by Núñez de Ortega and Delgado de Laborde (1999).

6. Every building in New York City was photographed in 1939–1940, and you can buy a picture of any one of them. Contact or visit the Municipal Archives at the New York City Department of Records at 31 Chambers Street in New York City (10007). Photographs of each building cost $25.00.

7. My father was one of the founders of the Centro Mexicano, a social-cultural club, in the late 1920s. He continued to be active for more than 50 years, until his death in 1987, serving as director of its Ballet Folklórico and often as president.

8. The International Ladies Garment Workers Union.

9. In the 1990s, "Fr. G." was questioned about his knowledge of his brother's role in organized crime. That brother, Vincent "The Chin" Gigante, was connected to the Lower East Side Mafia, but Father Gigante denied having any knowledge of his brother's affiliations.

10. Mrs. Tyson's son Cyril became a prominent member of the Democrat Party in New York City government in the 1980s, while Colin Powell became the country's leading African American Republican.

11. Seda's experiences in the tumultuous early days of Puerto Rican Studies at Hunter College with students and colleagues, including *su servidora*, who challenged his academic style and views, cemented his negative opinion of New York Puerto Ricans.

12. Aspira had offices in several cities, including one in Puerto Rico. Details about the founding of Aspira and the other organizations are in the chapter by Sánchez Korrol and Pantoja's memoir.
13. U.S. Puerto Ricans are due to surpass the number of island Puerto Ricans in 2010.
14. For a description of the grammatical forms and discourse functions of Spanglish, see chapters 5 and 6 in Zentella (1997).

CHAPTER TWO

Deputy Mayor and former congressman Herman Badillo (2nd left) with Assemblyman and current congressman José Serrano at 1978 south Bronx ribbon cutting ceremony with Evalina Antonetty, the head of United Bronx Parents, a community based advocacy group. (Records of the United Bronx Parents. *Courtesy: Center for Puerto Rican Studies, Hunter College, CUNY*)

CHAPTER 2

THE CHANGING SOCIOECONOMIC AND POLITICAL FORTUNES OF PUERTO RICANS IN NEW YORK CITY, 1960–1990

José E. Cruz

This chapter examines the socioeconomic status and political activities of Puerto Ricans in New York City during a crucial period in their history in the United States. During the 1960s, the experience of Puerto Ricans in New York was regarded as an anomaly relative to the experience of previous immigrants. In contrast to the pattern of political incorporation and upward mobility of the Irish and Italians of New York, Puerto Ricans were seen as mired in political apathy and socioeconomic disadvantage. This prognosis did not change much during the 1970s and continued to be held throughout the 1980s. What the chapter does is reexamine notions about Puerto Ricans as lacking in organizational drive, leadership resources, and political activity by taking a closer look at their economic performance and record of political

---

This chapter would not have been possible without the assistance and cooperation of Carlos E. Santiago. I am also grateful to Anthony Affigne, John Bretting, Lisa García-Bedolla, Gabriel Haslip-Viera, and Edgardo Meléndez for their comments and suggestions.

activities during those crucial three decades. The analysis then considers the role of community and political leaders in bringing about significant change in the status and well-being of the community.

New York City has long been the city of largest settlement of Puerto Ricans outside the island. In many respects, the fortunes of the inhabitants of Puerto Rico and Puerto Ricans in general have been inextricably linked to the flow of people, goods, and intellectual, artistic, and political developments that have, in one way or another, ties to the great metropolis that is New York City. While New York City was a magnet for Puerto Ricans prior to the Great Migration of the 1950s, it is in the post–World War II period that the size of the Puerto Rican population becomes an increasing and significant fraction of the city's total population. The initial migration flow of Puerto Ricans outside the island in the 1950s was truly monumental, particularly in light of the island's population at the time (Santiago 1992). During the 1950s nearly a quarter of the island's labor force migrated to the United States, predominantly to New York City. While birth and mortality rates declined dramatically on the island, the demographic transition experienced by Puerto Rico during that time was due primarily to migration. It was primarily an agricultural labor force that was being dislocated from the island and gradually moved into the low-skill–low-wage echelons of the New York City labor market and occupational hierarchy.

During the 1960s, net migration from Puerto Rico to the United States declined relative to the preceding decade. While the net immigration flow was still in the direction of New York City, return migration patterns were already being felt, thus reducing the rate of growth of the Puerto Rican population in New York City compared to the 1950s (Hernández Álvarez 1976). By 1970, the Puerto Rican population made up approximately 11 percent (844,303 people) of the population of New York City, a fraction that had declined a bit to 10.5 percent (887,573 people) by 1990 (see table 1). The growth in the number of Puerto Ricans living in New York City between 1980 and 1990 was extremely low compared to previous decades, with an increase of only 73,000 people. Despite the relative constancy of the fraction of New York City residents who were Puerto Rican, an upsurge in Puerto Rican migration during the 1980s did not translate into a significantly larger Puerto Rican-born New York City population. As Rivera-Batiz and Santiago point out:

> The migration of Puerto Ricans to the United States slowed considerably in the 1970s but picked up again in the 1980s, when close to 120,000 people left the island on a net basis. This resurgence of out-migration differed from previous migration flows in that the emi-

grants dispersed more widely than in the past. As a result, substantial Puerto Rican communities now exist throughout the United States, from southern California to Texas, to upstate New York and western Massachusetts (Rivera Batíz and Santiago 1996: 43).

Table 1
PUERTO RICANS IN THE NEW YORK CITY SMSA, 1970-1990

Year	Total Population and Average Annual Growth Rate			
	New York City		Puerto Ricans	
1970	7,881,284	---	844,303	---
1980	8,215,920	0.42%	887,500	0.50%
1990	8,408,590	0.23%	887,573	0.001%

Source and Notes for Tables 1-12:
1. The data for 1980 and 1990 are extracted from the Public Use Microdata Sample, 5% New York State files, for the New York City MSA or PMSA.
2. The data for 1970 are extracted from the Integrated Public Use Microdata Sample 5% for SMSAs.
3. The 1990 and 1970s data analysis are weighted by the housing unit's and person's weights.
4. Employment status is recorded for persons 14 years of age and older for 1970, and for persons 16 years of age and older for both 1980 and 1990.
5. The 1970s occupational and industry codes are somewhat different from those of 1980 and 1990.
6. The 1970 PUMS does not include the household income variable.

By 1980, 43 percent of the Puerto Rican population residing outside the island lived in New York City, again making up almost 11 percent of that city's population. Ten years later, the fraction of Puerto Ricans residing in New York City fell to a third of the total number of Puerto Ricans living outside the island. These changes represent a growing dispersion of Puerto Ricans throughout the fifty states and the emergence of new urban concentrations, particularly in cities like Hartford and Bridgeport, Connecticut; Camden, Passaic, and Paterson, New Jersey; and Lawrence, Massachusetts. There is also clear evidence of Puerto Ricans moving southward and westward. These demographic changes in no way diminish the importance of Puerto Ricans within the life of New York City, but they do represent the emergence of new locales of rising influence outside the New York City hub.

The initial growth of the Puerto Rican population in New York City was driven exclusively by migration from the island. Over the last thirty years, however, it is the natural increase in the population—that is, increasing birth rates and declining death rates—that is more fundamentally determining population growth. While Puerto Ricans remain a relatively younger population than the rest of the city's population, the gap in age structure is closing fast. A relatively young population is apt to have higher current and potential population growth rates compared to an older population. Table 2 shows that by 1970, approximately 75 percent of Puerto Ricans residing in New York City were younger than 35 years of age compared to 53 percent for the city as a whole. Twenty years later that 22 percentage point gap fell by half to 11 percentage points.

Behind these changes in the age structure of the Puerto Rican population in New York City lie a number of demographic factors. For one, they reflect the decline in Puerto Rican migration to the city.[1] Secondly, they correspond to an upsurge in new younger immigrants from the Dominican Republic, Central America, Mexico, and Asia. Immigrants tend to be younger than the native population. While the fraction of the city's population over 35 years of age hovered around 35 percent of the total population between 1970 and 1990, the age structure of the Puerto Rican population, for that age group, increased from 22 to 32 percent of the Puerto Rican population over that same time period. As new, younger immigrants continuously arrive in the city, the demographic profile of Puerto Ricans more closely approximates that of the city at large. A third factor influencing these demographic patterns is that the exodus of Puerto Ricans from New York City has been disproportionately of the younger population, particularly women of childbearing age. This has the effect of immediately shifting the age distribution upward and reducing birth rates in the years to come. It is important to keep these demographic trends in mind when considering the changing socioeconomic and political conditions of the Puerto Rican population in the city.

From the Culture of Poverty to the Poverty of Politics

The 1960s was a buoyant period as far as economic growth in the United States was concerned. The decade represented the longest economic expansion on record at the time and the inflationary pressures brought on by military expenditures during the Vietnam conflict had not been fully realized. The economic high water mark was 1965. Paul W. McCraken, chairman of President Nixon's Council of Economic Advisors from 1969 to 1972, described the U.S. economy during the mid 1960s in the following terms: "From 1960 to 1966 real output grew at the average annual rate of 4.8 percent per year quite impressive for an economy whose long-run growth rate has been about 3.5 percent. Moreover, there has been no recession since 1961 (though the expansion suffered a prolonged interruption in late 1962 and early 1963, and a recedence in the first half of 1967" (McCraken 1972: 175).

Table 2
AGE STRUCTURE OF THE POPULATION IN NEW YORK CITY, 1970-1990
(in percent of total population)

Group	New York City			Puerto Ricans		
	1970	1980	1990	1970	1980	1990
0-34 Years Old	53.24	53.57	51.54	75.57	69.95	62.20
0-15	25.93	22.34	20.40	43.38	35.20	29.20
16-24	13.89	14.70	12.65	15.93	17.97	15.55
25-34	13.45	16.53	18.49	16.26	16.78	17.45
Over 34 Years Old	34.42	33.21	35.38	21.85	26.24	31.93
35-44	11.46	11.93	15.25	11.24	12.07	14.08
45-54	11.81	10.78	11.12	6.61	8.75	10.62
55-64	11.15	10.50	9.01	4.00	5.42	7.23
Over 65 Years Old	12.34	13.22	13.08	2.58	3.81	5.87

Source: See Table 1 above.

In New York City a similar pattern was coupled with evidence of problems to come. There was clear advance warning of the difficulties down the road.[2] According to Fred Ferretti, Robert F. Wagner, mayor of New York City from 1954 to 1965, set the tone by conducting the City's business in the following manner: "During the last ten years [1965-1975], as the city's expenses have been outstripping revenues by about 15 percent to 6 percent, mayors, beginning with Robert Wagner, the father of the practice, have fulfilled the legal requirements to produce a balanced budget by overstating income and underestimating expenses. Deficits and excesses have been hidden in bewildering columns of figures" (Ferretti 1976: 28).

Both John V. Lindsay, who succeeded Wagner as mayor and served in that capacity from 1966 to 1973, and Abraham D. Beame, who succeeded Lindsay as mayor in 1974 and soundly criticized both Wagner and Lindsay for these practices while city comptroller, fell into similar patterns of "fiscal gimmickry." Ten years after Wagner's last year in office (1965), the city of New York was on the brink of financial default. This was to have serious repercussions on the socioeconomic status of Puerto Ricans, both those living in New York City and those on the island.

In the early 1960s the preeminent Puerto Rican institution in New York City was the Migration Division of the Department of Labor of the Commonwealth of Puerto Rico. This was the case, in part, due to a "lack of vigorous competition from other groups." The agency was *for* Puerto Ricans but not *of* them (Lapp 1990: 295, 296). Therefore, it was eventually overshadowed by the myriad new organizations that emerged during the decade.

The starting point of this process is 1956, when Mayor Robert Wagner established the Commission on Intergroup Relations. It was from the Commission's director, Frank Horne, that Antonia Pantoja, then a staff member, received the first encouragement to form what later became the Puerto Rican Forum and Aspira. But before these two organizations came to be, there was the Hispanic Young Adult Association, which was nurtured by the Migration Division. The Forum was subsequently founded in 1957 and Aspira in 1961 (Lapp 1990: 298-299).

The Forum's emphasis was on self-help, focusing on the Puerto Rican family, Puerto Rican youth, and the educational needs of the community. In 1964, the Forum sought antipoverty funds to promote bilingual education and Puerto Rican studies. Political organization to achieve representation was not part of the agenda at this point, even though the agency believed that ethnic identity and solidarity—which were part of the political arsenal of earlier immigrant groups—were essential to the task of educating Puerto Rican youth (Lapp 1990: 300-303).

According to Michael Lapp (1990: 303–304), the Migration Division was different from emerging groups such as the Forum by its top-down as opposed to grass-roots approach to community development. The record suggests another difference: an emphasis on centralization by the Division compared to an emphasis on decentralization by the Forum. Both organizations wanted Puerto Ricans to solve their problems mostly on their own. However, while in 1964 the Forum argued that "a strong central organization, if it provided direct services, would weaken existing organizations and destroy local initiatives" (Lapp 1990: 304), the Division, for its part, touted as accomplishments the creation of a Council of Organizations in East Harlem and the revitalization of a similar federation in Brooklyn. In that year, the East Harlem organization, in particular, recommended several Puerto Ricans as candidates for local school boards and community planning boards.[3]

Lapp also argues that the political success of the civil rights movement influenced the Forum's orientation. This is clearly reflected in the Forum's 1964 manifesto, *The Community Development Project: A proposal for a Self-Help Project to Develop the Community by Strengthening the Family, Opening Opportunities for*

Youth and Making Full Use of Education. What is also apparent in the document is that one of the key lessons learned from the civil rights movement was not so much that to succeed political organization was necessary but rather that success required organization along ethnic lines (Lapp 1990: 304–305).

The Puerto Rican organizations that emerged during the early 1960s in New York City experienced a context in which participatory, grassroots democracy was normatively juxtaposed to representative government. Never before in the twentieth century had the suspicion of political elites and the rejection of political hierarchies been stronger than during this period of intense normative dissent. Emerging Puerto Rican leaders were not only shaped by this *zeitgeist* but, in addition, saw themselves as distinct and even alienated from the more traditional leadership within the community. This leadership was seen as island-centered and divorced from the people. In this context, what began as resentment of "an arm of the Puerto Rican government attempting to represent Puerto Ricans in New York" (Lapp 1990: 307) transformed into a general anti-establishment attitude. This led the new Puerto Rican leadership away from traditional political avenues and strategies.

By the mid-1960s, the signal feature of Puerto Rican organizational development was the rift between established and emerging elites. On the one hand, there was a strong, central organization, controlled and financed by the government of Puerto Rico, which was unable to live up to its own principles. On the other, there was a cadre of Young Turks that saw little value in hierarchical, centralized organization. As Lapp suggests, the rift was also cultural and generational: younger leaders wanted to make their mark and their ethnic identity was shaped more by New York than Puerto Rico. Neither group was able to initiate a compromise. For example, the Migration Division tried to adapt to the new environment by supporting demand-protest activities and encouraging the organization of autonomous groups. At one point the Division's director, Joseph Monserrat, declared that "if the only way people are going to listen is for us to start demonstrating, then we'll have to do it." The Division's overtures were publicly dismissed as "premature and ill-timed" and Monserrat was dubbed a "self-appointed spokesman." Lapp describes emerging community leaders as reluctant to take their lead from the Migration Division but the reality seems to be that their stance was strongly negative rather than merely ambivalent. The younger leadership could have worked in collaboration with the Division without following its lead; it simply refused to do so (Lapp 1990: 307, 310, 311).

The irony of this impasse, which is duly noted by Lapp, is that it coincided with a strategy of institutional development that was thoroughly dependent on federal anti-poverty funds. Furthermore, despite their formal allegiance to grassroots democracy, the Young Turks and their agencies quickly came to rely on centralized modes of operation that favored the expertise of trained professionals. The success of groups such as the Puerto Rican Community Development Project in gaining financial backing from the federal government, as well as Washington's willingness to fund organizations for the poor, combined to promote an explosion of organizational development which fostered the transformation of activists into bureaucrats presenting themselves as activists (Lapp 1990: 319, 320, 326–328).

On the margins of this process another drama unfolded which was reminiscent of the period best described by Lawrence Chenault in his 1938 classic, *The Puerto Rican Migrant in New York City*. In 1961, a small enclave of Puerto Ricans lived the colonial experience a little differently than most Puerto Ricans in the city. According to Vanguardia Betances, a group of politically active poets and intellectuals, 37 political prisoners whose only crime was to desire a free Puerto Rico, were in federal jails serving sentences totaling 7,172 years. In what would be a persistent theme of Puerto Rican politics in New York during the 1960s and well into the 1970s, Vanguardia asked the American people to "demand the immediate release of the Puerto Rican patriots."[4] In the documents "A Challenge to Remember, Puerto Rico – The Forgotten Nation," published in 1960, and "¡Abajo las caretas! Estados Unidos en el banquillo de los acusados" [Down with the Mask! The United States Stands Accused], published in 1961, Vanguardia members decried U.S. colonial intervention in Puerto Rico. In their view, the island was "desperately trying to survive under the twists and turns of foreign intervention, colonial exploitation and involuntary servitude."[5] In another document from 1961, titled "An Appeal to the World," Vanguardia refers to Puerto Ricans in the United States as "refugees [who] leave their country every year because they cannot earn a decent living in their own country."[6]

In an open letter to Adam Clayton Powell, Vanguardia protested Powell's position in favor of English-language instruction in Puerto Rico and in support of statehood for the island. Vanguardia told Powell, in so many words, to mind his own business, to focus on the fight for black rights if he wanted to earn the respect of Puerto Ricans. "Fight for them Mr. Powell," the group declared, "and don't forget that your honest and respectable people are exploited by the same tyrants that exploit the people of Puerto Rico."[7]

Two important books about the Puerto Rican experience in New York City were published in 1965, Oscar Lewis's *La Vida* and Patricia Cayo Sexton's *Spanish Harlem*. *La Vida* may be the best known assessment of Puerto Rican poverty in the United States. Cayo Sexton's book never received the same level of attention even though it provides a better analysis of Puerto Rican poverty. *La Vida* has been decried as deeply flawed by a whole generation of scholars but the fact is that it is not just a supply-side analysis of poverty. A careful reading of *La Vida* reveals the recognition that Puerto Rican poverty was more than a human capital problem and also involved limited employment opportunities. One of Lewis's findings was that unionization made a difference in the level of income of participants. Logically, if unionization had positive economic effects, its absence could only make economic advancement harder. Thus, this was an important exogenous factor in the cluster of causes associated with poverty status (Lewis 1965: xxxix).

Without exempting the poor from their share of responsibility for their status, Lewis pointed out how the culture of poverty was a consequence of unemployment, underemployment, and low wages and how it was also related to low levels of social, political, and economic organization. On the point about organization, Lewis's emphasis was unambiguously institutional: it was the failure of government to encourage or carry out the social, political, and economic organization of the poor that sustained the culture of poverty generated by poverty status (Lewis 1965: xliii). This institutional angle, however, was only a fleeting and general three-page elaboration in a book more than six hundred pages long.

Sexton's treatment of this angle was more extensive and direct. Subtitled "an anatomy of poverty," her book mapped out the terrain of Puerto Rican poverty in New York City, comparing the Puerto Rican case with the black and Italian experience and identifying politics as a crucial element in the fight against poverty. "Power makes the community's wheels spin, skid, or stop," wrote Cayo Sexton (1965: 93), while addressing the reasons why power was out of the Puerto Ricans' reach. Ethnic divisions and a basic failure to reach out to the emerging Puerto Rican electorate on the part of power holders were two reasons for the power vacuum within the community. The predominance of social workers in the political process was considered a discouraging factor given their paternalism and general dislike of mass organization and action. The church did not care to mobilize the poor either, instead preferring to emphasize their powerlessness. And then there was the distracting influence of social service agencies, focusing on small issues and keeping the poor away from the political process (Cayo Sexton 1965: 95, 97–98).

The failure of poor Puerto Ricans to influence and shape the power structure was a function of their relative absence from the polls. Low levels of participation were in turn related to literacy tests and cumbersome registration procedures. Fear was an additional factor that, according to Cayo Sexton (1965: 116), affected the Puerto Ricans' ability not just to vote but "to learn, to work, to stay sane and healthy, to venture out of their apartments or block.... Fear is a crippler in the slum." According to Sexton the community was essentially submissive and deferential.

Just as her book hit the stands, 620 Puerto Ricans gathered at a two-day convention to establish the National Association for Puerto Rican Civil Rights under the leadership of Gilberto Gerena Valentín. Also in 1965 Puerto Ricans created the National Association for Puerto Rican Affairs with Ramón Vélez at the helm, a group that claimed to have 10,000 members, 3,000 of these in the New York metropolitan area.[8] Two years later another contrary image came thundering along during the East Harlem Riot of 1967, one of the worst the city had seen and the first large-scale Puerto Rican riot in the community's history. In 1968, along with their black counterparts, Puerto Rican parents provided much of the time, energy, and resources that gave local school districts full authority over hiring and firing, curriculum, and spending in the wake of the school decentralization battles that began in Ocean Hill-Brownsville. These were hardly examples of a "submissive and deferential" community.

Four years after the publication of *La Vida* and *Spanish Harlem*, there were additional signs of change in the community. In January 1969, a group of students organized a series of protests at Queens College demanding the continuation of SEEK, a program designed to recruit and assist students from poor New York City neighborhoods. In February, just as the city council's president pledged his support for legislation to expand the council and to redraw electoral districts to increase black and Puerto Rican representation, Gerena Valentín, acting as chairman of the Puerto Rican Community Conference, vowed to increase the number of Puerto Rican registered voters from 250,000 to 300,000.[9]

In April, the Puerto Rican member of the city's Human Rights Commission, Dr. Sergio S. Peña, announced the foundation of the New Progressive Party to rally Puerto Rican voters. After denying any links to the pro-statehood, island-based party of the same name, Peña explained that the organization was necessary since the Democratic and Republican parties courted Puerto Ricans during election periods only to forget them shortly thereafter. A few days later, Bronx Borough President Herman Badillo announced his candidacy for mayor, presenting himself as the "only liberal candidate" and charging that his opponents were either conservatives or party regulars "terrified of a white backlash." In May, Badillo and Frank Espada, chairman of Aspira and vice president of the Urban Coalition, joined a group of black leaders to form the group Black Independent Voters, to endorse candidates, and to unify the city's black and Puerto Rican vote.[10]

By mid-July, Mayor John Lindsay had enough support to secure his reelection bid, and Badillo's candidacy was over. The voter registration drive promised by Gerena Valentín was actually led by H. Carl McCall and Frank Espada. While more than 60,000 new voters were added to the rolls, the campaign was considered a failure. The large number of blacks and Puerto

Ricans expected to register did not materialize, and there were charges of apathy, indifference, and even subversion of the effort on the part of the political parties. Blacks and Puerto Ricans were allegedly discouraged from registering by inspectors doing the bidding of local party leaders. As a result, McCall and Espada called for the abolition of the board of elections and for the placing of federal supervisors in districts where less than 50 percent of the voters were registered.[11]

In October, a second voter registration campaign opened in East Harlem and by then Badillo was urging Puerto Ricans to support the reelection of Lindsay.[12] While the mayor was expected to win in part because of an estimated surge in black and Puerto Rican support, from 35 percent in 1965 to 70 percent in 1969, none of the Puerto Rican officeholders—Badillo and Councilmen Roberto Lebrón and Carlos M. Rios—were expected to retain their offices. Of the five Puerto Rican candidates running, all were considered likely to lose.

Indeed, the year came to a close with an electoral reversal of fortune for Puerto Ricans. The loss of Badillo's seat to Robert Abrams and of the city council seats could have been avoided. Had Badillo run again, he would have gained reelection. All Lebrón had to do was secure his name on the ballot, which, incredibly, he failed to do, and Rios could have been reelected had it not been for the splitting of the vote by a Puerto Rican challenger. The defeat of the Puerto Rican candidates—none of whom had the support of the main parties—was not surprising. This was especially true of the candidacy of Jesús Colón, who ran under the banner of the Communist Party.[13]

By the end of 1969, the city's board of education had approved a plan to reorganize Manhattan's existing school districts in a way that would give Puerto Ricans a greater voice in local education. To maintain racial and religious harmony in Jewish neighborhoods with growing black and Puerto Rican populations, the mayor proposed the creation of a program to promote housing for old and new residents alike. Then, on December 31, Lindsay announced the appointment of Puerto Rican Amalia Betanzos as a mayoral assistant.[14]

These accomplishments somewhat compensated for earlier setbacks. The situation of Puerto Ricans in 1969 was dynamic, yet the pattern was similar to that noted by Cayo Sexton in 1965: political participation was low but the problem was not a failure to participate but rather a failure to succeed in ways that made a real difference. Lewis's generalizations were unwarranted, but his portrait was undeniably powerful. No criticism of the idea of a culture of poverty could deny that by the end of the decade the poverty rate for Puerto Ricans was more than double the city rate, that their unemployment level was unacceptably high, that the proportion of Puerto Rican women heading a household alone was twice the rate for the city, or that only 8 percent of Puerto Ricans were homeowners compared to 24 percent for New York. Sexton's account of the community's political life was accurate as far as it went, but it failed to render a lasting characterization. For their part, opinion leaders insisted on reducing the causes of Puerto Rican woes to their "laggard" pattern of participation.[15]

The 1970s: A Failure to Participate?

The 1970s were years of intense mobilization and unprecedented incorporation. Puerto Ricans mobilized to achieve community control of local institutions, to protest party endorsements that excluded them, and to fight against the termination of funding for antipoverty programs. School redistricting was another issue that caught their attention, especially when proposed plans were believed to violate the 1964 Civil Rights Act and to foster segregation. An enormous amount of time, energy, and resources was also spent on activities and campaigns in support of independence for the island. Even war veterans got into the act, protesting unemployment rates among them of over 60 percent and exclusion from employment training, educational, and housing programs. All of this took place in the context of the progressive decline of Puerto Rico's Migration Division—the community's leading institutional resource since 1948. In 1973, the agency was declared ineffectual by its own sponsors but they found relief in the existence of 600 Puerto Rican self-help organizations in the city that served as an alternative. While that figure seems inflated, the phenomenon of independent organizations substituting for the Commonwealth's office was real.[16]

Prominent expressions of mobilization included a work stoppage and hunger strike by inmates at Rikers Island where Puerto Ricans were 40 percent of the population in 1970; several protests in the East Village in that same year where looting and firebombings occurred; the 1971 incident at Attica State Correctional Facility where more than 1,000 Puerto Rican and black inmates took over the yard of Cellblock D, holding 32 guards as hostages; a slew of terrorist bombings executed by the Fuerzas Armadas de Liberación Nacional (FALN) beginning in 1974; the gathering of 20,000 supporters of independence for Puerto Rico at Madison Square Garden, also in 1974; rent strikes against slumlords in 1975; the "bicentennial without colonies" rally in Philadelphia in 1976; and the eight-hour occupation of the Statue of Liberty by a group of 30 *independentistas* in 1977.[17]

To achieve representation Puerto Ricans resorted to diverse tactics. For example, in 1970 the Williamsburg Community Corporation spearheaded a drive to create a majority-minority Assembly District in an area where 85 percent of the population was black and Puerto Rican. When participation threatened existing representatives they were not above mobilizing to *prevent* it, as in the case of the boycott sponsored by United Bronx Parents in the school board elections of March 1970.[18]

Despite many obstacles, which ranged from literacy tests to counterintelligence programs aimed at confusing and harassing pro-independence groups, Puerto Ricans did not cease to organize and the level of political incorporation increased during the decade. While voting among other ethnic groups was higher than their proportion of the city's population, in the Puerto Rican case it was lower by almost 50 percent. Yet rather than registering and voting at a consistently low level, their participation was punctuated by surges depending on electoral circumstances. When they voted, they overwhelmingly supported co-ethnics, but at times they gave their votes generously to outgroup candidates.[19]

Politically, the 1970s started with a bang. The creation of a Manhattan-Bronx-Queens district with a heavy concentration of Puerto Ricans—engineered by Republican leaders hoping to increase the reelection chances of Governor Rockefeller—was instrumental to the election of Herman Badillo to Congress in 1970.[20] In that year the state legislature agreed to enlarge the city council to expand black and Puerto Rican representation.[21] On the other hand, Mayor Lindsay went on the record opposing the extension of the Voting Rights Act (VRA) to Kings and Bronx counties where, in his view, there was no discrimination against Puerto Ricans.

In 1970, Puerto Rican representation was achieved within the New York City Housing Authority and the Board of Elections. In that year, for the first time since 1966, four Puerto Ricans—all from New York City—were elected to the state assembly. A three-day voter registration effort in October resulted in the addition of 141,618 voters to the rolls. Nevertheless, by the end of the year as many as 700,000 blacks and Puerto Ricans remained unregistered.[22]

Rather than rely exclusively on the decisions of politicians, Puerto Ricans formed groups to pressure elected officials, sometimes working in coalition with other Hispanics. For example, in 1971 the Puerto Rican Coordinating Committee for the Northeast was created, an organization headed by the President of the Puerto Rican Association for National Affairs, Dr. Francisco Trilla and Frank Espada. This group sought collaboration with Mexican-Americans to achieve greater recognition of Hispanic needs. Also in 1971, a group of Puerto Ricans in Brooklyn formed the Puerto Rican-Hispanic Democratic Caucus with one Gumersindo Martínez as chairman. The purpose of this organization was "to unite American citizens of Hispanic heritage in a political body to act on both the local and national levels."[23]

At the school level, underrepresentation was a serious problem in 1971 with only 11 percent of school board members being Puerto Rican in a system where 65 percent of students were Puerto Rican and black. At the same time, Candido de Leon became the first Puerto Rican college president in the United States when he assumed the helm of Hostos Community College in September of 1971. A month later, Luis Quero Chiesa was elected to head the Board of Higher Education, the ruling body of the City University of New York.[24] Another positive development was the 1971 ratification of the constitutional amendment granting eighteen-year-olds the right to vote; this was seen as potentially enlarging the Puerto Rican franchise.

In July 1972 school principal Luis Fuentes was appointed superintendent of School District 1 on the Lower East Side. In November, in an effort to appease critics, the chairman of the Temporary New York State Charter Revision Commission, which was charged with devising a more realistic power scheme in the city, appointed a Puerto Rican lawyer, Charles J. Carreras, as a member.[25]

In September 1973 the Puerto Rican Legal Defense and Education Fund scored a significant victory when a federal district judge ruled on a suit filed by the group, ordering the city's elections board to provide bilingual voting instructions and translators for the November election at all polling places in districts where 5 percent or more of the residents spoke Spanish. In that year's election, Puerto Ricans achieved representation on the city council after a three-year absence with the victories of Ramón Vélez from the Bronx's 11th District, and Luis Olmedo from Brooklyn's 27th. Velez's longtime feud over antipoverty funds with Louis Gigante, also elected in 1973 to represent the largely Puerto Rican 8th District, continued with a vow from both men to "destroy each other."[26] Abraham Beame's mayoral victory was followed by Puerto Rican demands for representation within his administration.

By March of 1974, Badillo had withdrawn his support of Beame, which was never more than reluctant to begin with, charging that his administration was stocked with "clubhouse people and civil servants" and not enough Puerto Ricans. Although publicly Beame refused to heed Badillo's pressure, his appointment of two Puerto Ricans to his cabinet and twelve others to various posts in the administration belied his declaration that "no one is dictating to me who to appoint." In November, voters had the opportunity to use bilingual ballots for the first time in New York City's history. In addition, Puerto Ricans were granted new protections when a federal district court declared that congressional and legislative districts in Manhattan, Brooklyn, and the Bronx were subject to review under the VRA for racial fairness. Unfortunately, the Spanish ballot was so full of mistakes that many feared Spanish-speaking electors would be wildly confused or misled. By the end of the year, a group of forty Puerto Rican leaders voiced their dissatisfaction with Beame, expressing dismay and anger not just at the small number of appointments in policy-making positions but also at the poor services for Puerto Ricans in virtually every critical policy area, from education to economic development.[27]

By the mid-1970s, operating expenses were rising rapidly in New York City. The recession of this period was driving more and more people to the welfare rolls while inflation was increasing costs and operating expenses across the board. Short-term borrowing increased dramatically to close the gap between expenses and revenues and inflationary pressures were pushing the costs of borrowing ever higher. Once the banks and the investor community lost confidence in the city's ability to manage its affairs and reduce expenses they refused to buy the city's bonds.

Cutbacks in city services, layoffs, the closing of community programs and schools, reduced funding and access to the City University of New York, the elimination of capital construction projects, and increases in taxes and fees in combination with a national downturn in economic activity and rising inflation squeezed the more vulnerable groups in the city. Relative newcomers such as Puerto Ricans were hit particularly hard.

There was more than enough blame to go around for this state of affairs; it would be heaped on the city's leadership, the financial community, the labor unions, the federal government, and the state, but the bottom line was that the residents of New York City found themselves paying more for fewer services, facing precarious prospects for continued employment, seeing needed capital infrastructure projects postponed or cancelled, and, overall, experiencing a decline in the quality of life. The impact of the city's fiscal crisis can be summarized as follows:

> Plans for all new subsidized housing and rehabilitation of existing projects were suspended for five years; aid to dependent children programs in basic nutrition and consumer education were eliminated; the city's cultural institutions shut their doors earlier, eliminated programs and many were forced to close down altogether; the City University severely limited its open admissions policy, designed to educate those who could not otherwise afford college. And there were the little things, services taken for granted by New Yorkers that all of a sudden began to vanish: closings of regional offices in which to pay traffic tickets, for example...; extra subway change booths were ordered closed; South Bronx model cities program security guards...found themselves sent to affluent Riverdale and middle-class Queens to replace the more than two thousand school crossing guards that were laid off; there were fewer ferries in the harbor and riders had to pay more for less. All of these lessened the quality of the city's life (Ferretti 1976: 366).

Rather than being immune to these developments, the Puerto Rican population of the city found itself disproportionately affected by them. Poverty, already high by any standard, skyrocketed among Puerto Ricans. In 1970 almost one-third of Puerto Rican residents had income levels that fell below the poverty line (see table 3).[28] By the end of the decade that figure increased to over 42 percent, a staggering number illustrative of the extent to which Puerto Ricans suffered disproportionately from the city's fiscal crisis. In contrast, for New York City residents as a whole, the poverty rate rose from 14 percent to 18 percent over the 1970–1980 period.

Table 3
POVERTY RATES IN NEW YORK CITY, 1970-1990
(in percent)

Year	% of Persons in Group Under Poverty Level	
	New York City	Puerto Ricans
1970	14.48	32.92
1980	18.34	42.04
1990	17.25	37.26

Source: See Table 1 above.

Unemployment pushed more and more Puerto Ricans into poverty. The national recession slowed economic activity, while manufacturing employment, which constituted almost 40 percent of Puerto Rican employment in the city in 1970, continued to fall as the trend of deindustrialization in the Northeast prevailed. By the end of the 1970s, unemployment among male and female Puerto Ricans in New York City rose to double-digit levels (to 11 and 12 percent, respectively; see table 4). Although unemployment was to rise in the city as a whole, it was particularly severe in Puerto Rican communities. This period also marks the expansion of Puerto Rican single-female headed households a group that has traditionally been over-represented among the poor. Between 1970 and 1980, the fraction of Puerto Rican female-headed households increased from one-quarter to one-third of the population (see table 5). Puerto Ricans suffered disproportionately during the fiscal crisis because they were relative newcomers to the city, and hence "last hired-first fired" applied particularly to them; manufacturing employment growth was on the wane; and the city's safety net for the poor was under considerable stress.

Table 4
MALE AND FEMALE UNEMPLOYMENT RATES IN NEW YORK CITY, 1970-1990
(in percent)

Year	Unemployment Rate	
	New York City	Puerto Ricans
Male Population		
1970	3.88	5.28
1980	7.04	11.45
1990	8.67	14.38
Female Population		
1970	5.00	6.42
1980	7.15	12.24
1990	8.08	13.13

Source: See Table 1 above.

Table 5
FEMALE-HEADED HOUSEHOLDS IN NEW YORK CITY, 1970-1990
(in percent)

Year	% of Female-Headed Households in Group	
	New York City	Puerto Ricans
1970	12.55	26.06
1980	15.67	33.20
1990	17.25	35.69

Source: See Table 1 above.

Puerto Ricans were also, by and large, a population with low home ownership. Only 10 percent of the Puerto Rican population in New York City owned their living quarters (see table 6), and the decline in investment in the city's aging housing stock as property taxes increased resulted in growing numbers of substandard housing units in Puerto Rican communities. Visions of dilapidated housing in the South Bronx, popularized by television and movies at the time, while exaggerated, were grounded in fact. In 1976, with one member out of nine, Puerto Rican representation in yet another charter revision commission was commensurate with their proportion of the city's population, which was then about 10 percent. This notwithstanding, a survey revealed that 56 percent of the city's residents were unhappy with Mayor Beame's performance. Of these, 40 percent blamed his administration for the city's fiscal crisis. Blacks and Puerto Ricans were the most negative of all respondents. In 1977, the electoral victory of Robert Rodríguez raised the number of Puerto Ricans on the city council to three, providing small compensation for the community's terrible plight.[29]

Table 6
OWNERSHIP OF LIVING QUARTERS IN NEW YORK CITY, 1970-1990
(in percent)

Year	% of Ownership of Living Quarters that they Own	
	New York City	Puerto Ricans
1970	23.56	7.91
1980	28.29	9.00
1990	32.89	11.32

Source: See Table 1 above.

Politically, three problems stood out during this decade: under-representation in governing bodies, infighting among Puerto Rican elites, and intergroup conflict. Early on these struggles took place within the community agencies, the case of the Puerto Rican Community Development Project being the most prominent. Conflict among the Project's board members over the direction of the agency led to an acrimonious and public division in 1965. In 1971, a controversy over control of a $2.8 million program led the New York City Council Against Poverty to withdraw an antipoverty contract from the agency. While Puerto Rican leaders charged the Council with trying to destroy the Project's ethnic base, the Council in fact remained committed to awarding the contract to another Puerto Rican group. The Project managed to survive additional blows but it was not able to overcome the state of siege imposed upon it by its internal and external enemies. One dramatic action took place in 1978 when councilman Gilberto Gerena Valentín led a sit-in demanding the dismissal of the Project's board of directors, halting the operations of the agency for a week. Shortly afterward, the city took over the

Project, charging misuse of millions of dollars; eventually it cut off its funds.[30]

In the public arena, Puerto Ricans fought each other for essentially small prizes: an assembly seat here, a school district superintendency there, the name Pedro Albizu Campos for Fiorello La Guardia School in East Harlem, Avenue of Puerto Rico for Graham Avenue in Williamsburg; in these battles the casualties were often Puerto Ricans themselves. One conflict pitted Board of Education President Joseph Monserrat against School District 1 Superintendent Luis Fuentes, with Monserrat calling Fuentes a racist in *El Diario-La Prensa* because he allegedly had asked two Jewish principals to change their name to Gonzales to avoid a challenge to their promotions from Puerto Ricans. At times it seemed that being a small minority was not enough for Puerto Rican officials. In addition, they appeared determined to turn their relationships into a zero-sum game.[31]

Between 1966 and 1976 there were at least forty-eight instances of conflict between Puerto Ricans and other groups reported in the *New York Times*. This is a clear indication that interethnic tension was widespread during the 1960s and 1970s. From the reports it is also obvious that such conflict was debilitating. Community life was rife with conflict. Puerto Ricans fought blacks over control of antipoverty agencies; had altercations with Italians over turf in Park Slope; confronted Hasidic Jews in the Lower East Side and Williamsburg over housing, community resources, or simply because they crossed paths with them; and had violent encounters with Poles in Greenpoint over grievances that were often hard to understand. In some cases, Puerto Rican–black conflict was criminal in nature and did not necessarily reflect the character of everyday relationships. But interethnic rivalries in the political arena were significant and prevented both the delivery of services to desperately needy people and the development of empowering coalitions. Of course, there were exceptions to this pattern, often within the very communities where conflict was particularly intense, but when collaboration occurred it was sometimes described as rudderless, fraught with conflict, and focused on the wrong battles even by the participants themselves.[32]

The 1980s: Continuity and Change

By 1980, the Puerto Rican population in the United States was viewed as a group for which the "American dream" was just that—a dream. All of the relevant socioeconomic indicators pointed to this reality. In the national context, Puerto Ricans had among the lowest income levels, highest poverty rates, low labor force participation and high welfare dependency, significant numbers of single female-headed households, and low educational attainment. Yet, given their high concentration in New York City and the calamity that befell that city from 1975 until 1984, when the municipal budget ran a surplus, could things really have been any different? By 1990 the picture that was emerging showed that positive changes were taking place.

While migration from Puerto Rico picked up compared to the previous decade, New York City was not the main area of destination for Puerto Ricans leaving the island. As table 7 shows, of the metropolitan statistical areas with the largest concentration of Puerto Ricans in the United States, New York City ranked last in terms of the fraction of its population that came from Puerto Rico in the five years prior to the survey date of 1990. In 1990, 63 percent of the Puerto Rican population of New York City had not moved in five years, while 33 percent had moved within the city or across municipal and state lines. Only 3.5 percent of the city's Puerto Rican population had moved directly from Puerto Rico in the previous five years. Puerto Ricans are an increasingly mobile population within the United States but the San Juan–New York City connection in 1990 was weaker than it had once been.

An opposite way of framing the previous point is that the Puerto Rican population of New York City is increasingly stable. This stability, certainly over the 1980s, was reflected in the population's income growth over that period. Table 8 compares mean income per capita in New York City and among its Puerto Rican residents, in 1980 and 1990. Puerto Rican mean income growth (per capita) certainly kept pace with that of the city in general, and the gap in mean income per capita closed somewhat by 1990. While the picture is not great, it is certainly different from what one might have expected if trends dating back to 1970 had been consistent.

The relevant question then, is what occurred during the 1980s that managed to create conditions for improvement in the socioeconomic status of Puerto Ricans in New York City? First, educational attainment increased among the Puerto Rican population of the city during the 1980s (see Table 9). The greatest change occurred at the postsecondary level, where the fraction of the population completing some college and beyond increased significantly. By 1990, 23 percent of the population had completed some instruction beyond a high school diploma, compared to only 13 percent ten years earlier. The education gap was certainly closing at the upper end, and educational attainment and income levels remain highly correlated.

In addition to educational attainment, income levels are influenced by the degree of participation in the labor market and one's occupation and sector of employment. While male labor force participation has remained at relatively high levels, it is participation among Puerto Rican women that has shown a dramatic rise over the years (see Table 10). The difference in labor force participation rates between Puerto Rican women in New York City and all women in New York City declined significantly between 1980 and 1990. If one compares the change in income levels of Puerto Rican men and women (ages 25 to 64) from 1980 to 1990 by educational attainment, in this case between those with less than a high school diploma and those with a high school diploma, the group with the highest income growth rates were female high school graduates (Rivera Batíz and Santiago 1994: 86). Thus, not only did increases in educational attainment have a positive impact on Puerto Rican income growth in New York City during the 1980s but it is particularly the rising labor force participation rate of Puerto Rican women that fueled this outcome.

Both the occupational and sectoral distribution of the Puerto Rican labor force shifted dramatically in New York City over the period 1970–1990 (see tables 11 and 12). The most significant change was the decline in manufacturing employment and the decline in the numbers of Puerto Ricans employed as laborers, fabricators, and operators within manufacturing. No other ethnic or racial group experienced the extent of decline in manufacturing employment as did Puerto Ricans. From 1970 to 1990 the decline in the share of Puerto Rican employment in manufacturing in New York City fell from 38 percent to 15 percent, while the decline went from 22 to 12 percent for the city as a whole. The Puerto Rican population was particularly affected by the de-industrialization of New York City. On the other hand, employment among Puerto Ricans increased in professional and managerial fields, as well as in sales, administrative support, and service occupations. The modest economic improvement experienced by Puerto Rican New Yorkers during the 1980s was offset by the fact that in 1990 they had lower socioeconomic status compared to the overall Puerto Rican population in the United States. The mean household income per capita of Puerto Rican New Yorkers was below the average for the overall Puerto Rican population by 5 percent. For Puerto Ricans in New York, the poverty rate in 1989 was 36.5 percent compared to 30.3 percent for Puerto Ricans in the country.

Continuity and change during the 1980s were evident not just in the socioeconomic status of Puerto Ricans in the city. A prominent example of troubling continuity concerned the outcome of the decentralization of New York City's public schools in 1970. When decentralization was accomplished, no one was truly satisfied, but all were hopeful. Ten years later, the results were mixed and the most enthusiastic supporters of "community control" were those who originally fought it bitterly. By 1980, the proportion of minority teachers and principals had increased significantly but performance continued to be far below national standards.[33]

Table 7
Percentage of Non-movers, Movers from Puerto Rico, and All Other Movers in Metropolitan Areas with Largest Puerto Rican Populations, 1990

Metropolitan Statistical Area	Non-Movers (%)	Movers from Puerto Rico (%)	All Other Movers (%)
Lawrence-Haverhill, MA	24.2	26.5	49.3
Worcester, MA	37.3	20.3	52.4
Waterbury, CT	29.3	16.1	54.6
Rochester, NY	29.3	11.1	59.6
Lancaster, PA	29.6	12.9	57.6
Tampa/St.Pete Clearwater, FL	31.0	15.4	53.6
Reading, PA	31.6	14.9	53.5
Springfield, MA	32.0	17.7	50.3
Miami, FL	33.7	12.4	53.9
Buffalo, NY	33.7	15.3	51.0
Boston, MA	35.8	11.5	52.6
Hartford, CT	35.9	14.5	49.6
Bridgeport, CT	38.0	9.6	52.4
Cleveland-Lorain-Elyria, OH	38.5	12.1	49.4
Allentown-Bethlehem-Easton, PA	39.9	11.7	48.4
Trenton, NJ	41.0	10.9	48.1
Chicago, IL	42.4	5.1	52.5
Los Angeles - Long Beach, CA	43.6	4.8	51.6
Newark, NJ	44.7	9.1	46.2
Philadelphia, PA	44.9	7.5	47.6
Lorain-Elyria, OH	47.4	5.3	47.2
Jersey City, NJ	50.6	5.7	43.7
New York City, NY	63.0	3.5	33.5

Source: U. S. Department of Commerce. 1990. U.S. Census of Population and Housing, 5% Public Use Microdata Sample (PUMS); authors' tabulations.

During the 1980s the legal provisions for ballot access in New York virtually guaranteed the exclusion of political outsiders. Election laws were full of hyper-technical requirements that, according to one New York judge, made them "a maze whose corridors are compounded by hurdles, to be negotiated by only the wariest of candidates." According to an expert on electoral systems, the New York laws were "the most restrictive in the nation" concerning access to the ballot. This was a serious problem for Puerto Ricans at the individual level, ten times more significant than apathy, as one Agustín Alamo found out the hard way. Seven times between 1980 and 1990, Alamo entered Democratic primaries in the South Bronx and seven times he failed, utterly stumped by stringent requirements.[34]

If one thing is clear about this period it is that changes in the rules of the game can make the difference between participation and alienation, between structural exclusion and political incorporation. Indeed, some of the political battles fought by Puerto Ricans during the 1980s revolved around such changes. This was the case in 1981 when district lines that reduced black and Hispanic representation on the city council were challenged by a host of groups that included the Black and Puerto Rican Legislative Caucus and the Puerto Rican Legal Defense and Education Fund (PRLDEF), with the latter leading the opposition to the district lines. According to PRLDEF, the new districts would preserve the status quo whereas a map that reflected the city's demographic reality could add between two and five minority members to the council.[35] The fact that the Justice Department sided with the challengers did not discourage the council's lawyers from inflicting harm under the guise of conformity with the Department's mandate. Thus the new plan threatened the incumbency of Robert Rodríguez, from the 8th District, and promised to pit Bronx incumbents Wendell Foster, a black Democrat from the 9th District, and Gilberto Gerena Valentín from the 11th, against each other in a redrawn district.

Table 8
MEAN HOUSEHOLD INCOME IN NEW YORK CITY, 1970-1990

	New York City			Puerto Ricans		
Year	Mean Household Income	Persons in Household	Mean Household Income Per Capita	Mean Household Income	Persons in Household	Mean Household Income Per Capita
1970	---	2.73	---	---	3.72	---
1980	$18,645	2.54	$7,352	$10,802	3.10	$3,490
1990	$42,043	2.56	$16,412	$24,028	3.03	$7,926

Source: See Table 1 above.

In the end, the council came up with a plan to create five black-Hispanic majority districts in Brooklyn, three in the Bronx, and three more in Manhattan, for a total of twelve seats that minorities could win, four more than the seats then held by Puerto Ricans and blacks. Mayor Koch promised to stay out of the redistricting battle but, at the request of Rodríguez, a fellow Democrat and supporter, he pleaded with the council to protect the Puerto Rican incumbent.[36]

While the revised plan was a victory for PRLDEF and its allies, the lawyers who brought suit against the council were guarded in their optimism. Favorable district configurations, they suggested, do not guarantee results. According to César Perales, PRLDEF's general counsel, "It's twelve on paper, but at best it may be ten, maybe only nine" minority seats.[37]

In 1981, another battle involved the city's election of two council members at-large from each borough. This system was instituted in 1963 to counter the overwhelmingly Democratic affiliation of council members elected by district. As partisans, Puerto Ricans could not complain about Democratic hegemony. But they could argue that the at-large scheme was detrimental to them because it was designed to safeguard the interests of minor parties. This, however, would not be a problem if there were opportunities for them within the Democratic Party. If not, they could take advantage of at-large opportunities by seeking the support of third parties. In theory, this was good for Puerto Ricans as far as it went. In practice, Puerto Ricans had been *sin la soga y sin la cabra* all along. Democratic affiliation was all but worthless because the party ignored them. On the other hand, their chances to profit from at-large opportunities through third parties were nil since that scheme had allowed for minority representation only once in nearly twenty years.[38]

Table 9
EDUCATIONAL ATTAINMENT OF THE POPULATION OF NEW YORK CITY, 1970-1990
(as a percent of persons 25 years of age and older)

Group	New York City			Puerto Ricans		
	1970	1980	1990	1970	1980	1990
Less than High School	52.83	35.77	29.69	78.93	61.92	53.43
High School	28.44	30.94	26.23	17.31	24.49	23.36
Some College	8.19	13.54	19.48	2.57	9.24	16.85
College or More	10.54	19.75	24.60	1.19	4.35	6.37

Source: See Table 1 above.

The challenge to the at-large system was based on a general claim: that by permitting the same number of members in boroughs with different population numbers it violated the principle of equal representation. Thus Staten Island, with fewer residents than Manhattan or the Bronx, was entitled to the same number of representatives. It so happened that the disparity was also racial and ethnic and this concern was reflected in the identity of the plaintiffs in the case.[39]

In September 1981, when Democrats in the state assembly, preoccupied with their own redistricting process, announced their willingness to eliminate the seats of white incumbents in order to protect black and Hispanic seats, the outcry was minor. The sole Republican assemblyman from the Bronx, Guy Valella, threatened to take the legislators to court for "discrimination against whites and Italians, and Republicans, the biggest minority in the city." But no one protested the idea of saving Robert García's district which, as a result of massive out-migration of Puerto Ricans from the Bronx, was the nation's smallest. Instead, Democrats and Republicans drew highly partisan redistricting plans, each hoping to outmaneuver the other.

In November 1981, a federal judge paid heed to the challenge to the at-large system, declaring the apportionment of seats in the council on this basis unconstitutional. In July 1982, ten months after the redistricting process began, the Justice Department approved a revised plan. The new scheme satisfied both partisan concerns and the Justice Department's original objection that the voting power of Hispanics should not be enhanced at the expense of blacks.[40]

Table 10
MALE AND FEMALE LABOR FORCE PARTICIPATION RATES IN NEW YORK CITY, 1970-1990
(in percent)

Year	Labor Force Participation Rate	
	New York City	Puerto Ricans
	Male Population	
1970	71.38	67.24
1980	70.48	65.79
1990	71.81	65.91
	Female Population	
1970	41.73	27.01
1980	47.80	33.98
1990	54.56	42.94

Source: See Table 1 above.

By 1982 representation within the city council had not increased; three Puerto Ricans—the same number as in 1977—held seats in district 8 (Bronx-Manhattan), the 11th (Bronx), and 27th (Brooklyn). Nearly a year after the city council appealed the at-large decision, the U.S. Supreme Court upheld it without opinion. In spite of favorable district lines, the elections of 1982 produced no new seats for Puerto Ricans. Insult was added to injury in that year when councilmen Rodríguez and Gerena Valentín were ousted as a result of a primary challenge. Coincidentally, an estimated two-thirds of Latinos, most of them Puerto Rican, had failed to register to vote.[41]

In April 1983 Puerto Ricans were elated with the appointment as school chancellor of Anthony Alvarado, one of the community's rising stars. In June a Charter Revision Commission designated by Mayor Koch recommended the abolition of the at-large system, an arrangement that, despite two court rulings declaring it unconstitutional, was still in effect. The proposal was submitted to the voters in November, and it was approved by a two-to-one margin. In that year a bill to eliminate runoff elections in New York City primaries, sponsored by Puerto Rican Assemblyman Angelo Del Toro, was killed in committee. In 1984, the Center for Constitutional Rights filed a federal class-action suit to overturn the law requiring runoff elections. Speaking on behalf of plaintiffs Calvin Butts, a black minister, and Digna Sánchez, a Puerto Rican activist and attorney for the Center, argued that the law "discriminates against black and Latin voters, it discourages black and Latin candidates, and the city has no compelling state interest for enforcing this statute." Under the law, he said, "it takes more votes to become a candidate than it does to win election to office." At this point, barely a year since his appointment, Anthony Alvarado's star had already fallen in one of the most infelicitous episodes of dashed hopes in the community.[42]

Table 11
OCCUPATIONAL DISTRIBUTION OF THE LABOR FORCE
IN NEW YORK CITY, 1970-1990
(in percent)

Group	New York City			Puerto Ricans		
	1970	1980	1990	1970	1980	1990
Managerial And Professional	16.06	24.64	28.80	4.25	10.19	14.73
Technical, Sales, and Administrative Support	40.90	36.34	34.85	28.12	32.12	36.54
Service Occupations	13.77	15.08	16.12	16.30	19.77	20.99
Farming, Forestry, and Fishing	0.09	0.51	0.43	0.16	0.62	0.61
Precision Producton, Craft, and Repair	9.61	8.33	7.70	10.68	9.38	8.40
Operators, Fabricators, And Laborers	19.58	15.00	12.09	40.49	27.92	18.74

Source: See Table 1 above.

The law called for a runoff if no candidate for the offices of mayor, city council president, or comptroller received more than 40 percent of the votes in a primary. Puerto Rican candidates for those positions had been historically scarce, and not necessarily because of the law, so this lawsuit could hardly make much of a difference to them as a group. But there was evidence that the runoff requirement had debilitated Herman Badillo's candidacy in 1973. The decision of a federal judge in 1985 to strike down the runoff law as unconstitutional was a welcome victory. Unfortunately, the law was upheld on appeal because, according to the court, "the record shows that [it] was never intended to deny minority voters—and does not have the effect of denying them—an equal opportunity to participate in the political process." Badillo was disappointed and called on the legislature to eliminate the requirement.[43]

In 1985, Mayor Koch appointed Manuel Bustelo, then a former publisher of *El Diario-La Prensa*, commissioner of the city's Department of Employment. At the same time, Angelo Del Toro failed to secure the presidency of the city council and Ismael Betancourt Jr. and José Serrano competed unsuccessfully for Bronx borough president. The biggest political fiasco of 1985 was Herman Badillo's truncated third attempt at winning the mayoral nomination, after a group of black leaders rejected him in favor of Herman D. Farrell.

By that year, about 200,000 Latinos, 10 percent of the total in New York City and its suburbs, were members of Protestant churches. Close to 40 percent belonged to Pentecostal groups and another 40 percent was affiliated with Evangelical denominations. In the opinion of Dr. Jaime Vidal, a theology graduate from Fordham University, Hispanics joined Protestantism out of feelings of uprootedness and abandonment. According to the *New York Times*, this was "a striking development in the Hispanic community."[44]

One important change during this decade was that the pull of island issues, which in the past had been strong, was less pronounced. During the 1970s, the passion of militants and the bombings of the FALN had captured the attention of a majority of Puerto Ricans but not their minds and hearts. After the disintegration of the Young Lords Party during the mid-1970s and the collapse of the Puerto Rican Socialist Party around 1983 (Morales 1998: 222, Velázquez 1998: 66), the status question became the exclusive concern of groups that, like the larger radical movement in the United States, were little more than living fossils. Now, in October 1985, the residents of El Barrio could think of nothing else about Puerto Rico but "la tragedia" [the tragedy]—the death of hundreds of people on the island and the homelessness of thousands in the wake of a devastating storm and the flooding and mudslides that followed. According to one resident, "the disaster has touched everybody in El Barrio," because most had friends or family on the island.[45]

In the 1980s there were Puerto Ricans in New York like Reinaldo Pacheco, a resident for thirty-four years who had never voted in the city's elections but who reacted with indignation at the thought of not being able to vote in a plebiscite to decide the island's political status. To people like him the issue had to do with identity, heritage, and/or economics. Those who had left Puerto Rico felt that migration did not make them any less Puerto Rican and that alone sustained their interest on the island. The ancestral connection of New York-born Puerto Ricans with the island was symbolic but equally powerful. And then there were those who worried about their families *al otro lado del charco*, and the implications that a change in status might have for their well-being. These were also concerned with their own economic situation and wondered what they would do if unable to go back when in a bind. When it came to the specific question of voting in a plebiscite, however, the response of nearly 40 percent of Puerto Ricans in the United States was indifferent.[46]

Table 12
INDUSTRIAL DISTRIBUTION OF THE LABOR FORCE
IN NEW YORK CITY, 1970-1990
(in percent)

Group	New York City			Puerto Ricans		
	1970	1980	1990	1970	1980	1990
Agriculture, Forestry, and Fisheries	0.24	0.31	0.87	0.33	0.28	0.38
Mining	0.10	0.08	0.06	0.00	0.01	0.05
Construction	3.36	3.08	4.57	1.89	2.38	4.57
Manufacturing	21.82	18.00	12.16	37.98	28.36	15.23
Transportation	5.65	6.15	6.08	5.52	4.99	6.49
Communications and Public Utilities	3.89	2.85	2.70	2.19	1.88	2.04
Wholesale Trade	4.87	4.69	4.24	3.98	4.26	4.33
Retail Trade	14.85	14.52	14.50	15.67	15.13	15.51
Finance, Insurance, and Real Estate	10.21	10.52	11.33	7.18	9.65	10.04
Business and Repair Services	5.38	6.51	6.46	4.05	5.36	6.35
Personal, Entertainment and Recreational Services	6.46	5.63	5.90	5.75	4.59	5.68
Professional and Related Services (Health, Education)	17.90	22.81	27.25	12.25	18.40	24.26
Public Administration	5.28	4.88	4.37	3.20	4.71	5.06

Source: See Table 1 above.

Still fresh from the debacle of his mayoral candidacy, Badillo struck out again in the 1986 race for state comptroller, which was won by Edward Regan. In that year, Governor Mario Cuomo caused a minor furor among Puerto Rican elites in New York and Puerto Rico after referring to Puerto Rican New Yorkers as welfare parasites. This type of characterization has been a constant feature of the Puerto Rican experience in the United States. Puerto Rican politicians such as Herman Badillo, José Serrano, and Israel Ruíz were quick to accept a halfhearted apology from the governor, while community leaders such as Diana Caballero from the National Congress for Puerto Rican Rights and Angelo Falcón from the Institute for Puerto Rican Policy were less forgiving and more critical. This was also emblematic of a pattern in terms of how Puerto Rican moderates and militants related to powerful figures within the political establishment. The following year, Mayor Koch named two Puerto Ricans to political positions: Luis Miranda as special adviser for Hispanic Affairs and Amalia Betanzos to the board of education. In addition, by October 1987, the Department of Puerto Rican Community Affairs's voter registration campaign had reportedly added 37,628 new Puerto Rican voters to the rolls.[47]

The most significant change in the rules of the game during this decade was the revision of the city's charter in 1989. After two years of deliberation, in August the fifteen-member Charter Revision Commission recommended a host of changes that included abolishing the Board of Estimate, redistributing its powers, creating several boards and commissions to deal with procurement, employment, and redistricting, increasing the size of the city council, and establishing a two-house city legislature.

The public reaction was far from unanimous. Interestingly, the opposition to the proposed changes included prominent minority leaders such as the former Manhattan Borough President, Percy Sutton, Democratic Party leader Herman Farrell Jr., and Bronx Borough President Fernando Ferrer. In a letter to the *Times*, councilman Hilton Clark, from Manhattan's 5th District, decried the notion that a mere increase in the size of the council would enlarge minority representation. He argued that by "lumping African-Americans, Puerto Ricans, Cubans, Dominicans and Mexican-Americans together, the commission might just possibly decrease the percentage and political clout of underrepresented ethnics in New York City."[48]

Borough presidents were accused of simply defending their power, which was tied to their position within the Board of Estimate. In their view, the real problem was the increased power the mayor would enjoy, the costs of the new arrangement, and the negative impact it would have on policy by complicating the decision-making process.[49] Noting that the city's immigrants were not "rushing to politics," the *New York Times* quoted Frank Bonilla, who argued that low rates of political participation were the consequence of "a new milieu, a sense of not having a great impact on outcomes and no figures around which to rally." Bonilla's analysis was interesting because it echoed the explanation offered by Dr. Jaime Vidal in 1985 for the growth of Protestantism among the city's Hispanics. Could it really be that the factors that were driving newly arrived Hispanics into the arms of Protestantism were also responsible for the electoral alienation of Puerto Ricans forty-four years after their large-scale arrival to New York? If such was the case, it was the best example of change and continuity within the Puerto Rican community during the 1980s.[50]

The divisive campaign over the charter culminated with a divided vote in November. Although New Yorkers approved the proposed revisions, more than 400,000 voters, or 45 percent, rejected the proposal that increased the size of the council from 35 to 51 seats and made it the final arbiter of budget, land use, and zoning matters. In December, the Justice Department approved the new charter, and the new municipal government became effective January 1, 1990.[51]

The impact of the revised charter on minority representation was immediate: of the fifteen members of a redistricting commission appointed in 1990 by Mayor David Dinkins, 46 percent were white, 26 percent were black, 20 percent were Hispanic, and 6 percent were Asian. These proportions reflected the demographics of the city, as required by the new law. In that year Dinkins also appointed Víctor Alicea, president of Boricua College and a commissioner of the New York State Energy Research and Development Authority, to his Appointments Committee; Sally Hernández-Piñero as deputy mayor for finance and economic development, and Carlos Rivera as fire commissioner. Two Puerto Ricans—Luis Reyes and Ninfa Segarra—were named by Manhattan Borough President Ruth Messinger and Bronx Borough President Fernando Ferrer respectively to the board of education.[52]

The mayoral appointments came about after tremendous pressure was put on Dinkins. Although his administration was heralded as the most diverse in the city's history, Puerto Ricans still complained about their small numbers among appointees. The fact of the matter was that, however important the appointments might be, they meant little to ordinary Puerto Ricans. The resignation in October 1990 of William Nieves, the director of the Mayor's Office of Latino Affairs, due to "limited resources and a lack of access to the Mayor" illustrated further the limitations of this type of access. The tension following Dinkins's characterization of Puerto Rican nationalists as assassins, only heightened the discontent prevailing among the Puerto Ricans in his coalition.[53]

In 1989, the city council consisted of 35 members serving four-year terms. Puerto Ricans were 8.5 percent of the council (3 out of 35) compared to 10.5 percent of the city's standard metropolitan statistical area. As a result of charter revision, those members served a two-year term. After a redrawing of district lines, the special ballot held in 1991 resulted in the election of eight Puerto Rican councilmen, a 166 percent increase from 1989. It is clear that there was a correlation between the *Atrévete* voter registration campaign organized by the Department of Puerto Rican Community Affairs in the United States—which reportedly yielded over 200,000 new voters nationally—changes effected by charter revision, redistricting, and increased Puerto Rican representation at the city council. The precise weight of each factor is unknown but it is unlikely that the level of representation would have changed without the opportunities created by charter revision and redistricting.[54]

Increasing representation on the council through charter reform was easy compared to the troubles Puerto Rican candidates and incumbents faced throughout the decade. In some cases the difficulties were the result of competition, with white candidates winning over Puerto Rican voters. In others, too many Puerto Rican candidates dividing the ballots or low turnout allowed whites to dominate the process. According to Herman Badillo, part of the problem was that Puerto Ricans were unwilling to play hardball. Referring to the relationship of Robert García and José Serrano to the political establishment he said: "García and Serrano get their tails kicked and they say 'Thank you.' García endorses Koch and when they reorganize the Mayor's cabinet, there's not a single Hispanic in it. Serrano endorses Simon [Stanley Simon, Bronx Borough President in 1982] and when Simon names his Board of Education member, it's not a Hispanic. Those guys are satisfied too easily."[55]

As early as 1982 observers noted that increases in black and Puerto Rican representation were unlikely to significantly increase their influence over policy. Loyalty to party leaders, small numbers among legislators—even after winning new seats on the city council—and persistent factionalism were cited as reasons for the gap between representation and responsiveness. According to Brooklyn Councilman Luis Olmedo: "If there were more of us and we were together, they would have to listen to us. But now, we don't have that power." This was the case throughout the 1980s. While Puerto Ricans were no less inclined to work with other groups than their black and white counterparts, they did not seem more inclined to do so either.[56]

The end of the decade witnessed what many considered a regression in the state of race relations in the city. Ethnic conflict between Puerto Ricans and other ethnic groups was part of a pattern of racial relations in which competition was persistent and collaboration rare.[57] A decade that began with images of the Bronx as a haven for crime, drug addiction, and prostitution came to a close with efforts to rebuild the community from the ashes of devastating corruption and political scandals. Throughout the decade the performance of Mayor Koch vis-à-vis Puerto Ricans was erratic. His on-again-off again relationship with the community was defined by patronizing attitudes, insignificant initiatives, and overall incoherence. Just at the time that Puerto Ricans were believed to have lost their faith in government, political leaders Fernando Ferrer and José Serrano began to gain wider recognition both for the challenges they faced and for their promise.[58]

By the end of 1991, Puerto Ricans were 12 percent of the city's population and 16 percent of city councilmen. Yet it is hard to put a positive spin on a decade that was bracketed by the 1981 release of *Fort Apache, The Bronx*, a movie that wrote off the South Bronx as hopelessly mired in poverty and degradation, and the 1990 resignation under charges of conspiracy, extortion, bribery, and receipt of illegal gratuities of Congressman Robert García. Among other things, these events illustrated the urban plight of Puerto Ricans and the problematic nature of their political leadership.[59] To be sure, the title of the 1969 *New York Times* article by Alfonso Narvaez, "Puerto Rican Prospect: 10% of Population, 0% of Political Power," no longer described the community's reality. In the aftermath of Wedtech—a scandal that not only destroyed Garcia's career but also drove one more nail in the coffin of federal urban policy—the question was whether its political leaders would be able to make headway in narrowing the divide between political representation and policy responsiveness.[60]

The Leadership Factor

While the preceding account shows that the determinants of socioeconomic and political status are multiple and the dynamic that leads to specific outcomes complex, it is also evident that these outcomes are in large part the result of agency factors. This is also apparent in the various explanations of the Puerto Rican predicament in New York City that analysts have offered over the years, from Sherrie Baver's (1984) argument that the slow growth of the community's leadership stratum impaired its political impact, to Antonia Pantoja's (1989) emphasis on the Puerto Rican leadership's ethical lapses, to Michael Lapp's (1990) thesis that the unwillingness of the leadership of the Migration Division of the Commonwealth's Department of Labor to rock the political boat explains in part the community's inferior political and socioeconomic status.

For some the structural setup of the postwar period relegated Puerto Ricans to their subordinate position. According to James Jennings (1984: 87), during this period, the Democratic Party was in a position that allowed it to ignore the electoral potential of Puerto Ricans. In an addendum to this explanation, José R. Sánchez (1996: 287–288) argues that Puerto Ricans were unable to make themselves recognized because they lacked the leverage that social and economic power provides. From this vantage point it is easy to fall into the position that the only way to surmount systemic obstacles is to effect systemic change, a position embraced by many within Puerto Rican intellectual and political circles.[61] This chapter suggests that it is possible, although not easy, to alter structural conditions even in the absence of systemic transformation. In the promotion of such change Puerto Ricans played a role despite their second-class citizenship and socioeconomic disadvantage. They did so against at-large council seats and runoff elections, during redistricting battles, and on the streets. The challenge of participation consisted of matching what Puerto Ricans were able to do with what the systemic setting allowed, a challenge that the political leadership of the community met inconsistently. In some cases, systemic forces were indeed overpowering, but in others failure was a function of leadership quality and style.

Countless individuals in New York City have altered the flow of events by creating organizations to pursue social, economic, and political agendas. No discussion of the National Puerto Rican Forum or Aspira can exclude the role played by Antonia Pantoja in the establishment of these organizations. Similarly, the history of the Institute for Puerto Rican Policy, a New York City–based advocacy group that merged with the Puerto Rican Legal Defense and Education Fund in 1998, is inextricably tied to the figure of Angelo Falcón, its founder and President for over ten years. Many individuals, from Cesar Perales in the 1970s to Juan Figueroa in the 1980s, have been responsible for sustaining the Puerto Rican Legal Defense and Education Fund through thick and thin.

In 2001, Puerto Rican nonprofit organizations in the Northeast made up more than one-fifth of the twenty-five largest Latino nonprofit agencies in the country. These Puerto Rican groups had expenses totaling $55.1 million, almost a quarter of the expenses of the twenty-five top Latino institutions. With $26 million in expenditures the Aspira Association ranked number one in the pool of twenty-five. The Puerto Rican Family Institute, based in New York City, ranked fifth, and the Congreso de Latinos Unidos from Philadelphia was tenth on the list. By the criterion of institutional development—and these are only a few out of hundreds of examples—the performance of Puerto Rican leaders was outstanding.[62]

In terms of effectiveness in improving the socioeconomic condition of Puerto Ricans, the story is quite different. Puerto Rican community and political leaders have been instrumental in improving the lives of many individuals. Unfortunately, their impact on the collective well-being of the community has been less impressive.[63] The contribution of Puerto Rican political leaders in particular remains to be spelled out in detail. What role have they played in the enactment of redistributive policies? A significant number serve at the school board level; do they make a difference in issues of curriculum and governance? Do they contribute in any way to improved teacher performance or student achievement?

Good research on the aspects of political leadership that relate to policymaking and policy impact has yet to be carried out. At this point it is safe to say that the inability to significantly reduce the incidence of Puerto Rican poverty in the city is the most glaring shortcoming of the Puerto Rican political elite. This is true of the record of all officials elected during the period covered in this chapter—from Herman Badillo to Nydia Velázquez.

Is it fair to say that these officials have been incapable of dealing with the issue of poverty? Perhaps not, but the question is still pertinent. The problem could be that elected officials have no idea how to tackle the issue of persistent poverty. But this is unlikely since the available evidence suggests that they have their policy priorities right. A national survey of Puerto Rican elected officials conducted in 1992 revealed that their top public policy issues were education, housing, economic development, health care, crime prevention, and civil rights.[64] Anyone who knows that these issues are of critical importance also knows what conditions need to be improved to lift Puerto Ricans out of poverty. In 1996, the group Boricua First! developed a public policy agenda highlighting measures that needed to be taken regarding these and other issues. This knowledge never crystallized into a strategy focused on carrying out those proposals.

At the national level some have suggested that the crucial obstacle a poverty-focused policy agenda faces is the absence of political will on the part of legislators (McFate 1991). Others argue that since public policy is not a dominant factor in the causation of poverty, it makes no sense to think of public policy as the centerpiece of an antipoverty strategy (Teitz and Chapple 1998: 59). Research has shown that as a link between voter interests and public policy, electoral politics matter, even though the ways in which representation translates into responsiveness are contingent and complex. In some cases, to produce results, descriptive representation is not as important as the quality of the interaction between elected officials and administrators.[65] Further, to catch the attention of policymakers, constituencies must be demographically strong and public opinion must favor the direction of desired policies, a factor that is in part determined by the demographic strength of interested parties (Browning, Marshall, and Tabb 1984: 52, 250–253).

Other research on how political leaders negotiate the relationship between representation and responsiveness suggests the influence of an array of mediating factors. A working environment poisoned by hostility and suspicion among players is not conducive to responsiveness. A focus on ideological principles in total disregard of pragmatic considerations does not help. Further, business antagonism and/or the inability to win the favor of the economically and socially powerful (e.g., corporations and the media) can keep political leaders from hitting their stride. Leaders who know how to win elections but know little about the policy process tend to be less effective than those who take the trouble of knowing as much as possible about both. Similarly, brokered representation in the agenda-setting or policymaking process increases the chances that important priorities might be overlooked. A lack of knowledge about the precise degree of affinity between political leaders is another negative variable. To the extent that these conditions result in an environment of uncertainty, unpredictability, and flux, it is more difficult for leadership to be effective. Conversely, the more control leaders have over these variables, the more likely it is that they will move beyond representation into responsiveness (Cruz 1998: 176–196).

Leadership performance cannot be judged in a vacuum. The balance of structural constraints and personal qualities among Puerto Rican leaders needs to be established more systematically. It is clear, however, that in the struggle against poverty Puerto Rican political leaders have yet to make their mark. The failure of Puerto Rican political leaders must be understood in the context of the general lack of political will within the policy establishment to tackle the issue of poverty. This absence of political will is the result of the view that, at best, public policy plays a minimal role in the reduction of poverty. Since political will and policymaking are interdependent variables, this view is nefarious.

This predicament nevertheless highlights the importance of political leadership in the battle against Puerto Rican poverty. Puerto Rican elected officials are saddled with a dual responsibility: they must insist that public policy can break the cycle of poverty and they must help gather the political will to turn that conviction into a sustained program. The fact that during the 1980s progress and stagnation in labor market performance occurred in the context of economic growth, gains in human capital, and policy retrenchment suggests the following: in the absence of public policies that target Puerto Rican needs, some Puerto Ricans will experience increases in earnings and move out of poverty in tandem with increases in economic activity and higher educational and skill levels, while others will continue to experience economic and social disadvantage.

The implications of this are clear: political leaders must set their sights on two kinds of public policies—policies aiming at promoting economic growth and policies that enable individuals to take advantage of improved economic environments. Ideally, Puerto Rican elected officials should pursue both types of policies. A more realistic strategy is for them to take the lead in the formulation and adoption of policies that enhance the productivity potential of Puerto Ricans while working with others in support of policies that increase economic opportunities in general.

By 1990, Puerto Ricans in New York City were older in terms of age structure than in 1960, better represented, but not more powerful. Registration and turnout levels were still low and the increase in elected officials was due more to charter revision than to greater or better mobilization efforts. Residential stability and higher educational attainment were two notable features whose political impact had not been fully felt. Between 1960 and 1990, Puerto Ricans in the city were pretty much in sight but in terms of policy initiatives almost completely out of mind.

In January 1990, José Serrano worried about the implications of the Wedtech scandal. "When you walk down the street," he said, "there will always be that percentage that looks at you and feels you're no good and that you're up to no good. It's probably the same percentage that will never give Garcia credit for the good work he did, who will only remember the end of Garcia's career." In September, Bronx Borough President Fernando Ferrer joined Henry Cisneros, the former mayor of San Antonio, Texas, Mayor Federico Peña of Denver, and a host of officials and leaders of Hispanic organizations from across the country to establish the National Hispanic Agenda. Seeking to "speak with one voice across the differences that divide the Hispanic community," this organization was a hopeful sign for Puerto Ricans in New York and elsewhere in the United States. A month later, some within the Dinkins coalition began to realize that they would not be empowered by proxy. "I guess you have to fight city hall anyway," said Elizabeth Colón, director of the Association of Puerto Rican Executive Directors, "rather than wait for the Mayor to do the right thing."[66] Thus, Puerto Rican leaders in New York City entered the 1990s with apprehension, hope, and a fighting spirit. It is impossible to know whether these feelings were echoed within the community. Given the high rates of poverty, unemployment, female-headed households, low household income and meager levels of educational attainment that marked the relative socioeconomic status of the group in 1990, political leaders would need all the energy and resources that they could muster to make things better for all.

REFERENCES

Anuario Hispano, Hispanic Yearbook 1997–98. 1998. McLean, VA: TIYM Publishing.

Baver, Sherrie. 1984. "Puerto Rican Politics in New York City: The Post–World War II Period," in *Puerto Rican Politics in Urban America*, James Jennings and Monte Rivera, eds. Pp. 43–59. Westport, CT: Greenwood Press.

Browning, Rufus P., Dale Rogers Marshall, and David H. Tabb. 1984. *Protest Is Not Enough: The Struggle of Blacks and Hispanics for Equality in Urban Politics*. Berkeley: University of California Press.
Cayo Sexton, Patricia. 1965. *Spanish Harlem, An Anatomy of Poverty*. New York: Harper and Row.
Cruz, José E. 1993. *1993. Directory of Puerto Rican Elected Officials in the United States*. Washington, D.C.: National Puerto Rican Coalition.
_____. 1998. *Identity and Power, Puerto Rican Politics and the Challenge of Ethnicity*. Philadelphia: Temple University Press.
Directory of Puerto Rican Organizations. 1992. Washington, DC: National Puerto Rican Coalition.
Ferretti, Fred. 1976. *The Year the Big Apple Went Bust*. New York: G. P. Putnam's Sons.
Flores, Juan. 1999. "Pan-Latino/Trans-Latino, Puerto Ricans in the 'New Nueva York'," in *Identities on the Move*, Liliana R. Goldin, ed. Pp. 107–132. Albany, NY: Institute for Mesoamerica Studies.
The Green Book: Official Directory of the City of New York. 1989–1990. New York: Department of General Services.
_____. 1990–1991. New York: Department of General Services
Hernández-Alvarez, José. 1976 [1967]. *Return Migration to Puerto Rico*. Westport CT: Greenwood Press.
Jennings, James. 1984. "Puerto Rican Politics in Two Cities: New York and Boston," in *Puerto Rican Politics in Urban America*, James Jennings and Monte Rivera, eds. Pp. 75–98. Westport, CT: Greenwood Press.
_____. 1999. "Persistent Poverty in the United States, Review of Theories and Explanations," in *A New Introduction to Poverty, The Role of Race, Power, and Politics*, Louis Kushnick and James Jennings, eds. Pp. 13–38. New York: New York University Press.
Kerr, Brinck, and Kenneth R. Mladenka. 1994. "Does Politics Matter? A Time-Series Analysis of Minority Employment Patterns." *American Journal of Political Science* 38: 4 (November): 918–943.
Koch, Edward I. 1985. *Politics*. New York: Simon and Schuster.
Lapp, Michael. 1990. "Managing Migration: The Migration Division of Puerto Rico and Puerto Ricans in New York City, 1948–1968." Ph.D. dissertation, Johns Hopkins University.
Lewis, Oscar. 1965. *La Vida, A Puerto Rican Family in the Culture of Poverty—San Juan and New York*. New York: Random House.
McCraken, Paul W. 1972. "Economic Policy and Lessons of Experience," in *The Battle Against Unemployment*, Arthur M. Okun, ed. Pp. 171–179. New York: W. W. Norton.
McFate, Katherine. 1991. *Poverty, Inequality and the Crisis of Social Policy*. Washington, DC: Joint Center for Political Studies.
Morales, Iris. 1998. "¡Palante, Siempre Palante! The Young Lords," in *The Puerto Rican Movement: Voices from the Diaspora*, Andrés Torres and José E. Velázquez, eds. Pp. 210–227. Philadelphia: Temple University Press.

National Association of Latino Elected and Appointed Officials. 1989. *1989 National Roster of Hispanic Elected Officials*. Washington, DC: NALEO Educational Fund.

Pantoja, Antonia. 1989. "Puerto Ricans in New York: A Historical and Community Development Perspective." *Centro de Estudios Puertorriqueños: Bulletin* 2: 5 (Spring): 20–31.

_____. 2002. *Memoir of a Visionary: Antonia Pantoja*. Houston: Arte Público Press.

Rivera-Batiz, Francisco, and Carlos E. Santiago. 1994. *Puerto Ricans in the United States: A Changing Reality*. Washington, DC: National Puerto Rican Coalition.

_____. 1996. *Island Paradox: Puerto Rico in the 1990s*. New York: Russell Sage Foundation.

Sánchez, José R. 1996. "Puerto Rican Politics in New York: Beyond 'Secondhand Theory'," in *Latinos In New York: Communities In Transition*, Gabriel Haslip-Viera and Sherrie L. Baver, eds. Pp. 259–301. Notre Dame, IN: University of Notre Dame Press.

Santiago, Carlos E. 1992. *Labor in the Puerto Rican Economy: Postwar Development and Stagnation*. New York: Praeger Publishers.

Shefter, Martin. 1992. *Political Crisis, Fiscal Crisis: The Collapse and Revival of New York City*. New York: Columbia University Press.

Sternberg, William, and Matthew C. Harrison, Jr. 1989. *Feeding Frenzy*. New York: Henry Holt.

Teitz, Michael B., and Karen Chapple. 1998. "The Causes of Inner-City Poverty: Eight Hypotheses in Search of Reality." *Cityscape* 3 (3): 33–70.

Torres, Andrés, and José E. Velázquez, eds. 1998. *The Puerto Rican Movement: Voices from the Diaspora*. Philadelphia: Temple University Press.

Velázquez, José E. 1998. "Coming Full Circle, The Puerto Rican Socialist Party, U.S. Branch," in *The Puerto Rican Movement: Voices from the Diaspora*, Andrés Torres and José E. Velázquez, eds. Pp. 48–68. Philadelphia: Temple University Press.

NOTES

1. In the top twenty-five cities with Puerto Rican concentrations in the United States, New York City ranks first in terms of Puerto Ricans who did not move five years prior to the census date of 1990 with 63 percent of the population and ranks last in terms of Puerto Rican migrants (3.5 percent) and all other movers (33.5 percent) to the city. See table 7. See also Rivera-Batíz and Santiago (1994).
2. For a discussion of the political dimensions of New York City's financial crisis see Shefter (1992).
3. Estado Libre Asociado de Puerto Rico, Departamento del Trabajo, División de Migración, *Informe Anual, Año Fiscal 1964–65*, p. 107. Centro Archives, Migration Division Collection, Annual Reports, Box 2.
4. "Tragedia Hispanoamericana, Presos Políticos de Puerto Rico en Carceles de Estados Unidos," 1961, p. 3. Centro Archives, Graciany Miranda Archilla Papers, Series III, Box 5, Folder 8. All quotations from Vanguardia documents translated from the Spanish by José E. Cruz.

5. "A Challenge to Remember, Puerto Rico—The Forgotten Nation," 1960, p. 1. Centro Archives, Graciany Miranda Archilla Papers, Series III, Box 5, Folder 8.
6. "An Appeal to the World," 1961, p. 9. Centro Archives, Graciany Miranda Archilla Papers, Series III, Box 5, Folder 8.
7. "Cuestion de Honor, Carta Abierta a Mr. Clayton Powell," 1962, p. 4. Centro Archives, Graciany Miranda Archilla Papers, Series III, Box 5, Folder 9.
8. Edward C. Burks, "Campaign Begun by Puerto Ricans," *New York Times*, March 6, 1965, p. 10; "Puerto Ricans Open Office," *New York Times*, May 3, 1965, p. 34.
9. Arnold H. Lubasch, "Campus Officers Upset in Queens," *New York Times*, January 7, 1969, p. 29; Seth S. King, "Smith to Support a Larger Council," *New York Times*, February 5, 1969, p. 27; "Parley Planned by Puerto Ricans," *New York Times*, February 21, 1969, p. 46.
10. Peter Kihss, "Lindsay Appointee Founds Hispanic Political Party," *New York Times*, April 1, 1969, p. 37; Clayton Knowles, "Badillo Joins Race as 'Only Liberal,'" *New York Times*, April 4, 1969, p. 1; "Negro Unit Seeks Power of Ballot," *New York Times*, May 11, 1969, p. 37. In February, Frank Espada was identified in a *New York Times* report as executive director of the Urban Coalition.
11. "Badillo Rejects a Mayoral Race; May Back Lindsay," *New York Times*, July 15, 1969, p. 1; Richard Reeves, "Democratic Group Endorses Lindsay at Unruly Session," *New York Times*, July 17, 1969, p. 1; "The Anti-Registration Drive," *New York Times*, August 25, 1969, p. 34; Peter Kihss, "Special Drive for Registration Fails to Draw Minority Voters," *New York Times*, August 26, 1969, p. 33; "Civic Body Scores Voter Drive Here," *New York Times*, September 5, 1969, p. 35.
12. "Registration Drive Is Held in Harlem," *New York Times*, October 3, 1969, p. 30.
13. Richard Reeves, "Analysis of Recent Voting Patterns Illustrate Reasons for Changes in Lindsay's Reelection Strategy," *New York Times*, October 6, 1969, p. 38; Alfonso A. Narvaez, "Puerto Rican Prospect: 10% of Population, 0% of Political Power," *New York Times*, October 15, 1969, p. 30. According to Narvaez, Colon ran for council president. A November *New York Times* report has him running for "controller."
14. Leonard Buder, "School Shift Set For Manhattan," *New York Times*, December 17, 1969, p. 1; Martin Tolchin, "Lindsay Pledges Stabilization in Changing Sections," *New York Times*, December 18, 1969, p. 53; "Head of Puerto Rican Unit Named an Aide to Lindsay," *New York Times*, December 31, 1969, p. 22.
15. Peter Kihss, "Suburb Vote Key to Governor Race," *New York Times*, October 18, 1970, p. 75.
16. John Sibley, "Service Reduced in Health Center," *New York Times*, January 28, 1970, p. 27; "Six East Harlem Residents Protest Liberals' Candidate," *New York Times*, May 5, 1970, p. 45; Michael Stern, "U.S. Investigating Complaint That Lower East Side School Districting Fosters Segregation," *New York Times*, June 5, 1970, p. 15; Will Lissner, "Poverty Agency Faces Fund Loss," *New York Times*, September 4, 1970, p. 24; Francis X. Clines, "City Moves to Review Poverty Fund Cuts," *New York Times*, September 11, 1970, p. 83; Peter Kihss, "Migrant Division Held Ineffective," *New York Times*, September 23, 1973, p. 56; Alfonso A. Narvaez, "Puerto Rican Veterans Here Seek Aid," *New York Times*, November 25, 1973, p. 76; Peter

Kihss, "20,000 Rally Here for Puerto Rican Independence," *New York Times*, October 28, 1974, p.35; Leonard Buder, "3,000 in Brooklyn Protest Feared Student Transfer," *New York Times*, March 19, 1975, p. 51; John Kifner, "2 Counterrallies In Philadelphia," *New York Times*, July 5, 1976, p. 18. Also see Torres and Velázquez, eds.(1998: passim).

17. "Police in Harlem Pelted by Bricks," *New York Times*, July 23, 1967, p. 23; Homer Bigart, "Disorders Erupt in East Harlem; Mobs Dispersed," *New York Times*, July 24, 1967, p. 1; Gene Roberts, "U.S. Troops Sent into Detroit; 19 Dead; Johnson Decries Riots; New Outbreak in East Harlem," *New York Times*, July 25, 1967, p. 1; Rudy Johnson, "Protest Is Ended on Rikers Island," *New York Times*, March 17, 1970, p. 67; "Violence Recurs in East Village," *New York Times*, July 27, 1970, p. 56; Fred Ferretti, "Convicts Revolt at Attica, Hold 32 Guards Hostage," *New York Times*, September 10, 1971, p. 1; Will Lissner, "Terrorists Here Set Off 5 Bombs at Business Sites," *New York Times*, October 27, 1974, p. 1; Peter Kihss, "20,000 Rally Here..."; C. Gerald Fraser, "Clean Up Is Begun by Rent Strikers," *New York Times*, January 26, 1975, p. 44; John Kifner, "2 Counterrallies..."; Mary Breasted, "100,000 Leave New York Offices as Bomb Threats Disrupt City; Blasts Kill One and Hurt Seven," *New York Times*, August 4, 1977, p. 1; Mary Breasted, "30 in Puerto Rican Group Held in Liberty I. Protest," *New York Times*, October 26, 1977, section 2, p. 3.

18. Leonard Buder, "Voter Turnout Is 14.5% for City School Election," *New York Times*, March 23, 1970, p. 1; Clayton Knowles, "Williamsburg District Plan Is Gaining," *New York Times*, December 14, 1970, p. 46.

19. Peter Kihss, "Ethnic Division in Vote Is Noted," *New York Times*, June 19, 1969, p. 1; Peter Kihss, "Poor and Rich, Not Middle-Class, the Key to Lindsay Reelection," *New York Times*, November 6, 1969, p. 37.

20. Richard L. Madden, "Republican Accord Is Near on Redistricting for State," *New York Times*, January 8, 1970, p. 1; Clayton Knowles, "Creation of a New 'Puerto Rican' District Stirs Controversy," *New York Times*, January 22, 1970, p. 24; Fred P. Graham, "High Court Ruling Due on School Aid," *New York Times*, November 7, 1972, p. 1; Steven R. Weisman, "New York City, Mississippi: Surprising Pair," *New York Times*, January 13, 1974, section 4, p. 4; John M. Crewdson, "Levi Reveals More Harassment by F.B.I.," *New York Times*, May 24, 1975, p. 1; Frank Lynn, "The Status of This Year's Democratic Convention Is More Quo than Quota," *New York Times*, April 12, 1976, p. 23; Linda Greenhouse, "280,000 New Voters Registered in New York State," *New York Times*, August 17, 1976, p. 27; Frank Lynn, "Ratio of Blacks and Puerto Ricans Was Heavy in Primary Balloting," *New York Times*, September 22, 1976, p. 81.

21. Thomas F. Brady, "Lindsay Opposes Extension of Voting Rights Act Here," *New York Times*, March 11, 1970, p. 21; William E. Farrell, "Assembly Favors a Bigger Council to Aid Minorities," *New York Times*, April 19, 1970, p.1; Warren Weaver, Jr., "Court Rules Districting in 3 Boroughs Is Subject to Racial Fairness Test, *New York Times*, January 5, 1974, p. 1.

22. "Lindsay Appoints a Puerto Rican to Housing Panel," *New York Times*, February 7, 1970, p. 14; Peter Kihss, "Registration Dip Indicated in City," *New York Times*,

October 8, 1970, p. 43; "Local Electoral Reform," *New York Times*, November 13, 1970, p. 36; Alfonso A. Narvaez, "4 Puerto Ricans Will Take Seats In Legislature at Opening Jan. 6," *New York Times*, December 6, 1970, p. 51; Edward Ranzal, "Council Names 4 to Board of Elections," *New York Times*, December 25, 1970, p. 33.

23. Will Lissner, "Coalition Sought by Puerto Ricans," *New York Times*, September 30, 1971, p. 43; "Latins in Brooklyn in Democratic Caucus," *New York Times*, December 12, 1971, section 15, p. 24.

24. "Revision Urged in City System of Picking Local School Boards," *New York Times*, April 11, 1971, p. 58; "Candido de Leon, Now Hostos Dean, Will Head College," *New York Times*, September 29, 1971, p. 37; Andrew H. Malcolm, "Puerto Rican Heads the City U. Board," *New York Times*, November 23, 1971, p. 36.

25. "Lower East Side Board Hires Principal Ousted in Brooklyn," *New York Times*, July 21, 1972, p. 32; Ronald Smothers, "Puerto Rican Brooklyn Lawyer Is Named to City Charter Panel," *New York Times*, November 27, 1972, p. 39.

26. John Darnton, "Gigante vs. Velez in Ring of Slum Politics," *New York Times*, November 19, 1973, p. 37.

27. Glenn Fowler, "Beame Names Irizarry, Puerto Rican Banker, as City's Finance Administrator," *New York Times*, January 27, 1974, p. 42; John Darnton, "Badillo, Beame Clash Over Jobs," *New York Times*, March 25, 1974, p. 1; "Two More Puerto Ricans Get City Posts In Wake of Protest," *New York Times*, March 31, 1974, p. 40; Harriet Heyman and Jack Schwartz, "Badillo Ends Period of Grace," *New York Times*, March 31, 1974, section 4, p. 6; "12th Puerto Rican Named by Beame," *New York Times*, April 4, 1974, p. 25; Murray Illson, "Judge Orders City to Run Bilingual Elections Nov. 6," *New York Times*, September 28, 1973, p. 1; Linda Greenhouse, "Bilingual Ballot Errs in Spanish," *New York Times*, September 10, 1974, p. 82; "Puerto Ricans Seek More High Posts," *New York Times*, November 4, 1974, p. 41.

28. The poverty rate indicates the fraction of the population that falls below a federally designated income level associated with a given standard of living.

29. "New York Council Expected to Clear New District Lines," *New York Times*, December 30, 1976, p. 42; Frank Lynn, "Carey Tops Beame in Poll On Finances," *New York Times*, October 26, 1976, p. 1; Glenn Fowler, "Council Gets New Look: More Women And Minorities," *New York Times*, November 9, 1977, section 2, p. 5.

30. Edward C. Burks, "Split Emphasized by Puerto Ricans," *New York Times*, March 16, 1965, p. 22; Alfonso A. Narvaez, "Puerto Rican Body Loses A City Poverty Contract," *New York Times*, July 3, 1971, p. 28; Charles Kaiser, "Goldin Blocks Mayor on Patronage Move," *New York Times*, December 2, 1977, p. 21; Peter Kihss, "Sit-In Group Demands Ouster of Directors of Puerto Rican Project," *New York Times*, March 7, 1978, p. 39; John Kifner, "Puerto Rican Poverty Agency Accused of Wasting 'Millions,'" *New York Times*, March 25, 1978, p. 23; John Kifner, "Bronx Poverty Corporation Loses City Funds in Fraud Investigation," *New York Times*, April 26, 1978, section 2, p. 3; Charles Kaiser, "Ex-Officials of Puerto Rican Poverty Agency Indicted," *New York Times*, June 28, 1978, section 2, p. 3; "Funds Are Cut Off for Work Project," *New York Times*, July 21, 1978, section 2, p. 2.

31. Ronald Smothers, "Monserrat Calls Fuentes 'Racist,'" *New York Times*, August 5, 1972, p. 29; Alfonso A. Narvaez, "2 Puerto Ricans See Hope in G.O.P.," *New York*

Times, October 31, 1972, p. 37; Maurice Carroll, "Puerto Ricans Here Termed Their Own Worst Political Enemies," *New York Times*, June 3, 1974, p. 24; Linda Greenhouse, "Senators Already Seeking a Zaretzki Replacement," *New York Times*, September 12, 1974, p. 33; "La Guardia School," *New York Times*, April 20, 1976, p. 34; Edward Ranzal, "Beame Upheld in Council on Street Name Change," *New York Times*, June 9, 1976, p. 43.

32. "13 Injured, 2 Held as 2 Two Ethnic Groups Fight in the Bronx," *New York Times*, August 29, 1966, p. 38; Joseph Novitski, "Mott Haven Leaders Meet in Bronx with City Aides in Wake of 4 Slayings," *New York Times*, July 19, 1968, p. 10; "Melee Follows Rites in Brooklyn," *New York Times*, September 25, 1968, p. 30; Andrew H. Malcolm, "3 Die, 3 Wounded in Shootings; One Killed in Quarrel in a Bus," *New York Times*, July 27, 1969, p. 39; Charlayne Hunter, "Friction Slows Harlem Model Cities Program," *New York Times*, August 22, 1970, p. 1; Peter Kihss, "Antipoverty Program Is Found to Aggravate Ethnic Tensions," *New York Times*, December 3, 1972, p. 86; Michael T. Kaufman, "Feud Keeps Park Slope on Guard," *New York Times*, June 29, 1973, p. 39; John T. McQuiston, "Park Slope Talks Yield Agreement," *New York Times*, June 30, 1973, p. 34; "Hispanics and Poles Clash in Brooklyn," *New York Times*, July 2, 1973, p. 54; "Ethnic Fighting in Greenpoint Ends as 2 Sides Talk," *New York Times*, July 3, 1973, p. 29; Steven R. Weisman, "Housing for Jews Upheld by Court," *New York Times*, September 13, 1973, p. 93; Michael T. Kaufman, "7 Seized in June Riot After Appeals in Park Slope," *New York Times*, November 1, 1973, p. 47; Iver Peterson, "'Conciliators' to Aid in Policing Election at District 1 Schools," *New York Times*, May 11, 1974, p. 45; Emanuel Perlmutter, "Hasidic Groups File Suit to Bar Redistricting As 'Gerrymander,'" *New York Times*, June 12, 1974, p.27; "42 Prisoners Hurt as 'Racial Fracas' Erupts on Rikers," *New York Times*, June 18, 1976, section 2, p. 18; "Hasidic Jews Protest Housing Plan," *New York Times*, December 21, 1976, p. 37; Frank Lynn, "Continuing Split in Ethnic Vote," *New York Times*, September 13, 1977, p. 20; Sheila Rule, "Influence and Power of Minority Caucus Doubted in Albany," *New York Times*, May 29, 1978, p. 1.

33. Edward B. Fiske, "Community Run Schools Leave Hopes Unfulfilled," *New York Times*, June 24, 1980, p. 1.

34. Martin Gottlieb with Dean Baquet, "A Perennial Maze: New York's Election System," *New York Times*, October 18, 1990, p. 1.

35. Joseph P. Fried, "Court Bars City's Primaries in Suit on Council Districts; Appeal is to be Filed Today," *New York Times*, September 9, 1981, p. 1; Maurice Carroll, "A Close-Up of Map Making for Those Councilmanic Districts," *New York Times*, September 20, 1981, section 4, p. 6.

36. Maurice Carroll, "U.S. Rejects Plan for Redistricting New York Council," *New York Times*, October 28, 1981, p. B5; Michael Goodwin, "Tentative New District Lines Drawn to Follow U.S. Order," *New York Times*, November 5, 1981, p. B1; Joyce Purnick, "A Council Panel Offers New Plan on Redistricting," *New York Times*, December 31, 1981, p. B3; Michael Goodwin, "Koch Seeks to Have City Council District Redrawn," *New York Times*, February 25, 1982, p. B10.

37. Joyce Purnick, "A Council Panel Offers New Plan on Redistricting," New York Times, December 31, 1981, p.B3.
38. Douglas Muzzio, "Faulty Arguments on City Council Redistricting," *New York Times*, March 15, 1982, p. 16.
39. Joseph P. Fried, "City Council Faces New Court Attack," *New York Times*, September 27, 1981, p. 39.
40. E. J. Dionne Jr., "New York Legislature Begins Redistricting Task," *New York Times*, September 29, 1981, p. B3; E. J. Dionne Jr., "Questions on State Reapportionment," *New York Times*, February 13, 1982, section 2, p. 29; Jane Perlez, "New Redistricting by New York State Is Approved By U.S.," *New York Times*, July 4, 1982, p. 1.
41. Michael Goodwin, "Democrats Gain Seat on City Council," *New York Times*, November 4, 1982, p. B14; Maurice Carroll, "Hispanic-Voting Study Finds 'Sleeping Giant,'" *New York Times*, August 29, 1982, p. 39.
42. Joyce Purnick, "Alvarado Chosen to be Chancellor of City's Schools," *New York Times*, April 29, 1983, p. 1; "Excerpts From Decision Ruling At-Large Seats in Council Unconstitutional," *New York Times*, November 18, 1981, p. B2; Clyde Haberman, "Appeal of Ruling Indicated by Council," *New York Times*, November 19, 1981, p. B3; "Liability to Pay Medical Bills of Criminal Suspects," *New York Times*, October 5, 1982, p. 27; "The City; Koch Seeks to End At-Large System," *New York Times*, April 28, 1983, p. B3; David W. Dunlap, "Council At-Large Posts Nearly at End," *New York Times*, June 14, 1983, p. B5; Frank Lynn, "New York's Voters Give Approval to $1.25 Billion State Bond Issue," *New York Times*, November 9, 1983, p. 1; "A Bill to End Runoffs in City Primaries Dies," *New York Times*, June 3, 1983, p. B3; "Suit Seeks to End City Primary Law," *New York Times*, October 21, 1984, section 1, part 2, p. 55; "Alvarado Story Moved Fast From Start," *New York Times*, March 26, 1984, p. B4.
43. William G. Blair, "New York Runoffs Are Called Biased," *New York Times*, June 4, 1985, p. B5; Arnold H. Lubasch, "Runoffs in New York's Primaries Barred by U.S. Judge in Bias Suit," *New York Times*, August 14, 1985, p. 1; Arnold H. Lubasch, "City Runoff in Primaries Is Upheld," *New York Times*, December 14, 1985, p. 29.
44. "Employment Post Is Filled by Mayor," *New York Times*, March 14, 1985, p. B6; Frank Lynn, "Del Toro Announces Plans to Run for President of City Council," *New York Times*, January 11, 1985, p. B3; Frank Lynn, "Betancourt Declares Candidacy for Bronx Borough President," *New York Times*, March 8, 1985, p. B3; Frank Lynn, "Farrell Seeking Suport of Hispanic Democrats," *New York Times*, February 10, 1985, p. 36; Sam Roberts, "Coalition Maneuvers," *New York Times*, February 13, 1985, p. B1; Jeffrey Schmalz, "Endorsement of Farrell Splits Minority Caucus," *New York Times*, February 18, 1985, p. B1; Frank Lynn, "Serrano Asserts Hispanic Voters Lost Franchise," *New York Times*, September 27, 1985, p. B3; Larry Rohter, "Protestantism Gaining Influence in Hispanic Community," *New York Times*, January 12, 1985, p. 23.
45. Larry Rohter, "El Barrio Residents Worry and Wait," *New York Times*, October 10, 1985, p. B16.

46. Mireya Navarro, "U.S. Puerto Ricans Debate Right to Vote on Island's Future," *New York Times*, June 5, 1990, p. B1; David Ortiz, "Let Islanders Decide Puerto Rico's Fate," *New York Times*, August 4, 1990, p. 22.
47. Lydia Chavez, "Badillo's Run Highlights Lack of Hispanic Gains," *New York Times*, October 12, 1986, section 4, p. 9; Jesus Rangel, "Cuomo Clarifies Ethnic Remark in an Apology," *New York Times*, October 17, 1986, p. B3; "Hispanic Adviser Named," *New York Times*, May 20, 1987, p. B8; Jane Perlez, "Hispanic Woman to Fill School Board Vacancy," *New York Times*, December 8, 1987, p. B5; David E. Pitt, "Puerto Rico Expands New York Voter Drive," *New York Times*, October 14, 1987, p. B5. Also see Baver's discussion (1984) of Puerto Rican politics in New York from 1950 to the early 1980s.
48. Todd S. Purdum, "Black and Hispanic Officials Are Cool to 2-House Plan," *New York Times*, May 1, 1989, p. B1; Hilton B. Clark, "More Minority Voices on the City Council?," *New York Times*, September 5, 1989, p. 18.
49. Todd S. Purdum, "On Ballot, a Charter Is Distilled to 276 Words," *New York Times*, September 10, 1989, p. 41; Alan Finder, "Coalition Opposing Charter Revision Starts Its Campaign," *New York Times*, September 28, 1989, p. B1.
50. Sam Roberts, "New York's Immigrants Aren't Rushing to Politics," *New York Times*, July 22, 1989, p. 27.
51. Alan Finder, "Puzzled About New Charter? There Are 2 Basic Questions," *New York Times*, October 17, 1989, p. B1; Alan Finder, "The 1989 Elections: Charter; Overhaul of New York City Charter is Approved, Polls Show," *New York Times*, November 8, 1989, p. B1; Alan Finder, "New York City Charter Revision Approved by Justice Department," *New York Times*, December 14, 1989, p. 1.
52. Sam Roberts, "Now It's the Law, But New Charter Still Riles Koch," *New York Times*, April 23, 1990, p. B1; Todd S. Purdum, "Dinkins Appoints Advisers on Drugs and Top Positions," *New York Times*, January 24, 1990, p. B1; Todd S. Purdum, "Dinkins Wanted an Unusual Group to Run His City, And Here It Is," *New York Times*, April 1, 1990, section 4, p. 20; Joseph Berger, "School Board Gets 2 New Hispanic Members," *New York Times*, June 29, 1990, p. B3.
53. David González, "Hispanic Aide's Departure Signals Growing Tensions," *New York Times*, October 21, 1990, p. 32; Todd S. Purdum, "Praising Mandela, Dinkins Shakes Fragile Coalition," *New York Times*, June 16, 1990, p. 23.
54. See *The Green Book: Official Directory of the City of New York* (1989-1990, 1990-1991); "Congresswoman Nydia M. Velázquez 12th Congressional District," Online. Available: <http://www.nydems.org/elected/velazquez.html>; National Association of Latino Elected and Appointed Officials (1989: 61); and José E. Cruz (1993: 35–36).
55. Ronald Smothers, "Strong Races in Bronx Fade as Primary Nears," *New York Times*, September 5, 1981, section 2, p. 24; Maurice Carroll, "Influence and Numbers Swell New Wave in Hispanic Politics," *New York Times*, January 24, 1982, section 4, p. 7; E. J. Dionne Jr., "Minorities Gain in City Primary, But Only a Little," *New York Times*, September 28, 1982, p. B1.
56. Michael Goodwin, "Role of Minorities on City's Council," *New York Times*, May 9,

1982, p. 40; Frank Lynn, "Borough Chief Contest Splits Hispanic Politicians in Bronx," *New York Times*, March 25, 1987, p. B5; Sam Howe Verhovek, "Garcia is Battling Energetic Rival in the Bronx," *New York Times*, September 13, 1988, p. B1; Todd S. Purdum, "Dinkins Appoints Advisers on Drugs and Top Positions," *New York Times*, January 24, 1990, p. B1; Todd S. Purdum, "Dinkins Wanted an Unusual Group to Run His City, and Here It Is," *New York Times*, April 1, 1990, section 4, p. 20.

57. Maurice Carroll, "Black-Hispanic Coalition Pressing for 2 Borough Presidencies in City," *New York Times*, January 27, 1981, p. B4; Sheila Rule, "Minority Divisiveness Seen in Brooklyn Races," *New York Times*, July 25, 1982, p. 24; Wayne King, "Coalitions of Black and Hispanic Voters Still Rare," *New York Times*, January 5, 1984, p. B10; Crystal Nix, "Attack in Bronx Hurts 2 Youths; Bias Is Charged," *New York Times*, July 30, 1986, p. B3; Crystal Nix, "200 Officers Sent to Bronx After New Ethnic Violence," *New York Times*, August 5, 1986, p. B3; Barry Weisberg, "No Reason for Optimism About Race Relations," *New York Times*, July 14, 1987, p. 26; Frank Lynn, "Ethnic Tension Marks Bronx Race for Garcia Seat," *New York Times*, March 12, 1990, p. B3.
58. Bruce Lambert, "Man in the News; New Bronx Chief Hopes to Restore 'Faith': Fernando Ferrer," *New York Times*, April 16, 1987, p. B1; Frank Lynn with Michael Oreskes, "In Bronx Politics, Signs of City's Future," *New York Times*, June 15, 1987, p. 1; Sam Howe Verhovek, "Ferrer Emerges as Strong Voice for Bronx," *New York Times*, February 11, 1988, p. B1. Also see Koch (1985: 169–176).
59. Molly Ivins, "Council Rejects Call for Boycott of 'Fort Apache,'" *New York Times*, February 27, 1981, p. B3; Lydia Chavez, "Mayor's Response to Report on Hispanic Concerns Criticized," *New York Times*, March 10, 1987, p. B3; William Glaberson, "Garcia and Wife Are Found Guilty in Extortion Case," *New York Times*, October 21, 1989, p. 1; Frank Lynn, "Facing Sentencing, Rep. Garcia Quits," *New York Times*, January 3, 1990, p. 1; Frank Lynn, "Serrano and Molinari Elected in Special Congressional Races," *New York Times*, March 21, 1990, p. B1.
60. Wedtech was a South Bronx company subsidized by the federal government. The scandal involved large-scale corruption among its executives and the government officials that supported the company. The full story is chronicled by Sternberg and Harrison in *Feeding Frenzy* (1989).
61. See for example, Jennings (1999: 32); Flores (1999: 121)); and José Serrano, "Taking Exception with Chavez," *New York Newsday*, October 23, 1991, pp. 83, 86.
62. "Nonprofits: The Money Behind the Mission," *Hispanic Business*, September 2001; see *Directory of Puerto Rican Organizations* (1992) and *Anuario Hispano, Hispanic Yearbook 1997–98* (1998) for a wider snapshot of institutional development.
63. Antonia Pantoja referred to Aspira as "the most important work of my life" because in thirty-six years the agency "touched the lives of approximately 36,000 young people." For Aspira and for those it helped, this is a significant record. For the community, it represents a humble accomplishment at best. See Pantoja (2002: 106).
64. The main purpose of this survey was to compile a directory of Puerto Rican

elected officials in the United States. A total of 143 officials were identified and 105 or 73.4 percent provided additional information, including a ranking of public policy concerns.
65. See Kerr and Mladenka (1994: 918) who focus on this issue at the municipal level.
66. Kevin Sack, "For the Likely Successor to Garcia, an Eloquent Pride," *New York Times*, January 8, 1990, p. B1; "Heads of Hispanic Groups Seek One Political Voice," *New York Times*, September 27, 1990, p. 14.

CHAPTER TWO
Commentary

October 26, 1977 cover page of the *San Juan Star* reporting on the takeover of New York's Statue of Liberty by Puerto Rican radicals. (*Centro Library and Archives. Center for Puero Rican Studies, Hunter College, CUNY*)

Commentary

From Civil Rights to the "Decade of the Hispanic": Boricuas in Gotham, 1960–1990

Angelo Falcón

In "The Changing Socioeconomic and Political Fortunes of Puerto Ricans in New York City, 1960–1990, "political scientist José E. Cruz develops a much-needed and sweeping interpretation of the post–Great Migration Puerto Rican experience in New York City (also see Cruz and Santiago 2001). These are thirty years that encompass major changes in American society, New York City, and Puerto Rico in the years before the last decade of the twentieth century. From the peak of the civil rights movement and the War on Poverty to the dominant neoliberalism of the end of the 1980s, Puerto Ricans have had to navigate and attempt to change social and economic policies and structures that worked to disadvantage them as a community, but which also offered possibilities for change (for a general overview of this period, see Schulman 2002). These were the years during which a young community came to mature politically and socially.

However, Cruz's chapter can at best be described as a comprehensive "first draft" of a chronicling of the Puerto Rican experience in New York City during this turbulent era. It lays out events that occurred during this period and provides some commentary on their connections and their meaning, but more in the form of "Post-It™ notes" that require much further examination. Cruz is extremely uneven in his interpretation, which makes it unclear which of these events were important and which were not. Many key developments are omitted or insufficiently developed, leaving gaping holes in his historical narrative and producing a rather thin interpretation of events and players.

A major problem with this chapter is Cruz's almost total reliance on the *New York Times* as the source of his historical reconstruction. Perhaps it would have been more accurate to add to his chapter title the qualifier, " ... According to the *New York Times*." This approach is highly problematic given the ongoing critique of the *New York Times*'s coverage of the Puerto Rican community, especially during the period that Cruz covers. This critique includes the complaint that the paper historically seems always to stress negative developments in this community, which the Cruz chapter certainly documents.

The *New York Times*'s historical social distance from the Puerto Rican community has also resulted in a selective inattention where important concerns and debates within the Puerto Rican community were hardly ever reflected on its pages. Viewing the Puerto Rican experience from the prism of the *New York Times*'s pages is like viewing oneself in a fun house mirror. While in many ways producing an intriguing interpretation of the Puerto Rican reality during this 1960–1990 period, the reliance on this single source is a major flaw, especially when many others in both Spanish and English are so readily accessible. This is especially baffling given Cruz' participation in the SUNY-Albany team that researched the excellent and well-documented Stateside Puerto Rican history in Acosta-Belén, et al. (2000).

IDENTIFYING KEY EVENTS, ISSUES, AND THEMES FOR THE 1960–1990 PERIOD

By revisiting each of the historical periods he discusses, critical themes and issues will be outlined here that will highlight oversights (or what might be called underdeterminations) in Cruz's treatment. In so doing, perhaps a wider and more critical discussion can be generated on the questions that an analysis of the 1960–1990 period should be addressing in future research.

The 1960s: From Civil Rights to Revolution

This decade was most interesting because of the leftward shift in American and Puerto Rican politics that it witnessed. For Puerto Ricans it was a period in which this community asserted itself both in terms of New York politics and the politics of Puerto Rico. As part of the civil rights movement, a number of Puerto Ricans emerged as politically committed professionals, primarily social workers and educators. Individuals such as Antonia Pantoja and others began forming and developing institutions like the Puerto Rican Forum (in 1957), Aspira (1961), the Puerto Rican Family Institute (PRFI) (1963), and the Puerto Rican Community Development Project (PRCDP) (1964). In

1969, the Museo del Barrio was founded in an East Harlem public school. Aspira, for example, was significant as the first Puerto Rican agency to be the recipient of private foundation support, indicating a certain level of community development in terms of first-time linkages to New York's philanthropic world. In 1962, Joe Ripal began a venture that became another important Puerto Rican business institution, Valencia Bakeries.

At the same time, more grass-roots efforts, such as those led by labor organizer Gilberto Gerena Valentin and others, started to build a hometown clubs movement and other organizations like the National Association for Puerto Rican Civil Rights and the United Bronx Parents (UBP) that made direct links to the growing civil rights movement in the sixties. These included promoting Puerto Rican participation in such mobilizations as the 1964 school boycotts, the 1968 school decentralization battle in Ocean Hill-Brownsville, and the Poor People's March on Washington, DC. The role of Puerto Ricans in the civil rights movement was, however, viewed as problematic by many Black leaders (see, for example, Robinson, Graham, and Cunningham 1962, and *New Pittsburgh Courier* 1963).

On the political front, the early part of this decade witnessed the first major entrée of Puerto Ricans into citywide politics. As a result of a major internal battle for control of the Democratic Party under Mayor Robert F. Wagner, Puerto Rican political activists such as John Carro and Herman Badillo became significant players in city politics (Carter Hannigan 1962). This was the beginning of Badillo's pioneering career in politics, and serious Puerto Rican engagement, largely as reformers, within the Democratic Party. The election of Carlos Rios in 1961 as a Democratic Party district leader in Manhattan's El Barrio was part of this Puerto Rican reform movement within the party (in contrast to the machine-controlled election of Tony Mendez in 1953 as the first Puerto Rican district leader in the party, who was viewed as simply a party operative).

The election of Republican John V. Lindsay as mayor (and Badillo as Bronx borough president) in 1965 also presented Puerto Ricans with an opening as a result of a reform election (Gotsch 1966), culminating symbolically in a major citywide conference, sponsored by the mayor and coordinated by Marta Valle, entitled, "Puerto Ricans Confront Problems of the Complex Urban Society: A Design for Change" held on April 15–16, 1967 at the High School of Art and Design in Manhattan (City of New York 1967). The link between such "deviating elections" and the access of communities of color, such as Puerto Ricans to significant government posts, was discussed by some at the time, but appears to have been a phenomenon limited to the 1950s and 1960s. Also discussed at the time was the disproportionate affiliation with Protestantism among the more prominent Puerto Rican politicians, despite

Puerto Ricans being overwhelmingly Catholic.

The institution building of the early part of this decade became the basis for Puerto Rican participation in the War on Poverty. As Cruz points out, by the middle of the decade, the Puerto Rican Forum and others had developed a major citywide antipoverty agency called the Puerto Rican Community Development Project (PRCDP). This was an important development because it drew Puerto Ricans into the politics of President Lyndon Baines Johnson's Great Society programs.

It also represented a break with the efforts of the Commonwealth of Puerto Rico to market Puerto Ricans as benign hardworking migrants in contrast to Blacks, who were increasing their demands on American society as an oppressed racial minority. It was an inner-city Puerto Rican reality also made accessible to the American public with the publication of Piri Thomas's bestseller, *Down These Mean Streets,* in 1967, a major corrective of the parodies of the Puerto Rican poor in the 1955 film *The Blackboard Jungle,* the musical play and film of the early 1960s *West Side Story,* and the fatalistic "culture of poverty" and sensationalist Puerto Rican images popularized in the 1966 release of Oscar Lewis's book, *La Vida* (see Morales 2002: 56–59).

The PRCDP proposal, written largely by sociologist Frank Bonilla under the direction of social worker and former Aspira of New York founding director Antonia Pantoja, documented the high number of Puerto Ricans living in poverty and began articulating demands for change (see Puerto Rican Forum 1980 [1964]; for contrasting interpretations of this project's history, see Fitzpatrick 1971: 67–69 and Fitzpatrick 1996: 57–58, and Pantoja 2002: 109–121). However, it was not the increasingly nationalist Black model of development that was articulated, but rather the assimilationist, yet ethnically based model of the Jewish community. The publication of Glazer and Moynihan's influential *Beyond the Melting Pot* in 1963 had already articulated such a position for Puerto Ricans. The other important aspect of the PRCDP proposal was its ambitiousness—it reflected a strong faith in the possibilities of social engineering and planning, which were the hallmarks of the government bureaucrats of Puerto Rico at the time, such as Teodoro Moscoso, the major architect of Operation Bootstrap working off the New Deal legacy of former Puerto Rico Governor Rex Tugwell and others.

The PRCDP episode, along with the establishment of Aspira, was significant in other ways. These were perhaps the first experiences by Puerto Ricans in running their own nonprofit organizations with boards of directors and professional staff, which required some adjustment and opened up space for conflict at a different level. They were also explicitly ethnically based programs that ran against the more universalistic and bipolar Black-White race relations rhetoric of the time's public policy environment. Finally, these programs were not geographically based because the Puerto Rican population was relatively dispersed and had not achieved the level of concentration in particular neighborhoods as Blacks had in Harlem and Bedford-Stuyvesant. Within the city's antipoverty program Puerto Ricans began advocating for "citywide" programs that were not geographically, but rather ethnically, based. This created a different pattern of organizational development from that of the city's Black population.

The late sixties brought together a confluence of forces, from the growing movement against the war in Vietnam to the rise of the Black Power movement. The country's move to the political right with the election of Richard Nixon as president in 1968 had its counterpart in Puerto Rico with the first election of a pro-statehood government in Puerto Rico in that same year that was also more conservative. This last development resulted in the movement of a significant number of pro-*independentista* intellectuals and activists to New York, many of whom found homes in exile in the newly established Puerto Rican studies, Open Admissions and SEEK programs in the City University of New York, and in similar programs on other campuses. These new programs were the direct result of activism by Puerto Rican students like the 1969 takeover of the City College campus and the establishment in 1968 of new institutions such as the City University's Eugenio Maria de Hostos Community College in the South Bronx.

The late sixties saw the rise of radical organizations like the Young Lords (an offshoot from a Chicago-based organization), the U.S. branch (or, as they referred to themselves, "U.S. Zone") of the Puerto Rican Socialist Party (PSP), *El Comité* on Manhattan's West Side, the Puerto Rican Student Union (PRSU), and other groups, including those pursuing armed struggle like MIRA. This gave expression to a revitalized and reconfigured nationalist/left movement in the Puerto Rican community. The Young Lords were at the time viewed as a very dangerous organization, as it emulated Black power groups like the Black Panther Party and linked itself up to radical organizations, including those advocating violence, like the Weather Underground. A recent book by one of its members has revealed that the group had, in fact, been organizing an underground network of armed cells (Meléndez 2003).

Puerto Rican politicians like Badillo, on the other hand, were asserting what they considered as their rightful place as representatives of New York's Puerto Rican community against what they saw as interference from the government of Puerto Rico in their affairs. (This was also the case with the growing group of Puerto Rican professionals in the city who were creating institutions like Aspira and the PRCDP.) These local Puerto Rican politicians also saw themselves as outsiders within the Democratic Party and fashioned themselves as reformers (see Jennings 1977).

This New York Puerto Rican assertion of independence from what they saw as a paternalistic Commonwealth of Puerto Rico took on a new dynamic in the 1960s that presaged a stateside-island tension that exists today. In 1967, a plebiscite was held in Puerto Rico on the political status of the island, and there was a movement by Puerto Ricans in New York to be allowed to participate in this vote to the consternation of Commonwealth officials, who mistakenly believed at the time that stateside Puerto Ricans would support statehood for the island (see Montserrat 1968). This demand for participation was something that continued to grow and took on greater significance with the plebiscites on status that were held in the 1990s, especially as stateside Puerto Rican advocacy on issues like the removal of the U.S. Navy from Vieques and presidential clemency for Puerto Rican political prisoners in the late 1990s and early twenty-first century, made this island-stateside relationship more complex (see Falcón 1993, Morales 2002: chapter 9 and Perez 2002).

It was in Black and Puerto Rican participation in the 1968 teachers' strike over community control of the schools and the vote that year on the unsuccessful proposal for a civilian complaint review board for the Police Department (Rogowsky, Gold, and Abbott 1972), that Blacks and Puerto Ricans began to be seen together as the city's "minorities." Blacks and Puerto Ricans were later to be viewed as the "native minorities" (compared to the "new minorities" emigrating from Third World countries) trapped in a world of an urban underclass and a self-defeating victimology. What was never made clear was the source of this change, especially if adoption of the immigrant model promised the many material and social rewards Glazer and Moynihan described in their writings.

Toward the end of the decade, local War on Poverty fights for federal funding and power between Blacks and Puerto Ricans and between Puerto Rican factions revealed the ugly side of these developments. The low point was the August 6, 1969, killing of a Ramon Velez opponent, Edwin Rivera, over the allocation of Model Cities funding, a crime that some attributed to Velez, although it was never solved (Jonnes 2002: 185–188). Rivera's death strangely paralleled the social death that the South Bronx began rapidly experiencing from that point on, until its comeback in the 1990s.

This political convergence of Puerto Ricans as outsiders from both the left and liberal ranks of the political spectrum became linked to the Black Power movement and the growing independence movement that opposed the surge in pro-statehood sentiment on the island. These movements included those calling for the community control of the public schools, open admissions at the City University, and civilian oversight of the police. On the other hand, the coming to power of a conservative Republican administration in Washington, DC, would begin to shape a politics of lowered expectations in the decades to follow.

The 1970s: From Potential Immigrant to Racial Minority

The beginning of this decade witnessed the unraveling of American liberalism. The antiwar movement disintegrated as the military draft was terminated and the Vietnam War came to an end. Many Puerto Rican organizations on the political left disappeared during this period and the Republican administration in Washington and the New York fiscal crisis of 1975 eroded many of the gains that were made during the relatively brief Great Society period of the previous decade.

However, the institution building of the 1960s in the Puerto Rican community continued at a different level in the early 1970s. Private philanthropic institutions, especially the Ford Foundation, provided resources in 1968 for Aspira of New York to expand nationally in the early 1970s to become Aspira of America (currently known as the Aspira Association). The Puerto Rican Forum also went national during this period, but with the support of federal funding and its association with the Republican Party. In the early 1970s, institutions like the Center for Puerto Rican Studies (El Centro) of the City University of New York, the National Conference of Puerto Rican Women (NaCoPRW), the Nuyorican Poets Cafe, the Puerto Rican Legal Defense and Education Fund (PRLDEF), and Boricua College were established.

The opening of the doors of the Nuyorican Poets Cafe in 1973 in the Lower East Side (Loisaida) represented, in a sense, the institutionalization of the new New York Puerto Rican aesthetic of the "Nuyorican." The poetry of the First Poets, Pedro Pietri, and many others; the theater of a Miguel Piñero; the music of a Willie Colón: all came together in ways to create a new cultural sensibility/invention from the streets of Puerto Rican New York that would endure to the present and impact on Puerto Ricans on the island and throughout the United States.

Puerto Ricans started to make some inroads in the media in this decade. Magazines like *New York* began to acknowledge Puerto Ricans in a new light in their "Big Mango" issue (1972), and publications on the Puerto Rican experience like *Latin New York* (1971), *The Rican* (1972), and the *Revista Chicano-Riqueña* (1973) began to emerge. In 1972, a group of Puerto Rican activists that included Dylcia Pagan, Lou De Lemos, and others agitated for and wound up producing *Realidades* on the local public television station, WNET-TV, the first bilingual television public affairs program in the country (it was syndicated nationally in 1975 by the Public Broadcasting System).

Puerto Rican characters and themes began to emerge in television programs. These included Freddie Prinze in *Chico and the Man* (1974), the *Tony Orlando and Dawn Show* (1974), Erik Estrada in *CHiPS* (1978), and in PBS's *Oye Willie* mini-series (1979). Then there were highly controversial films like *Badge 373* featuring Felipe Luciano (1972), and the play and film of Miguel Piñero's *Short Eyes* (1974). In 1972, Geraldo Rivera made a name for himself as a television journalist when he exposed the deplorable conditions for the mentally handicapped in the Willowbrook Developmental Center in Staten Island.

Later in the decade, in 1976, the U.S. Commission on Civil Rights issued an important report, *Puerto Ricans in the Continental United States: An Uncertain Future*. It documented the high incidence of poverty in Puerto Rican communities throughout the country and became the basis for the creation in 1977 of the first Washington-based Puerto Rican advocacy organization, the National Puerto Rican Coalition. Louis Nuñez, a Republican who was staff director of the Civil Rights Commission under President Reagan, went on to become the NPRC's first executive director, a post he held into the 1990s.

In the electoral arena, Puerto Ricans continued to break new ground (Falcón 1994). In 1970, Badillo was elected to the United States House of Representatives, the first Puerto Rican to achieve this distinction. He ran for mayor in 1969, 1973, and 1977 and went on to become the first Puerto Rican deputy mayor of New York in 1978, a post he resigned from in 1979. In the New York State Assembly, José Serrano began to come into prominence, and Robert Garcia replaced Badillo as the congressman from the South Bronx.

The new Puerto Rican Legal Defense and Education Fund (PRLDEF) scored a number of landmark legal victories on behalf of the Puerto Rican community in New York during the early part of this decade. These included, in 1974, the introduction of bilingual ballots in school board and general elections, and the Aspira Consent Decree mandating transitional bilingual education programs to Puerto Rican and other Latino students in the public school system, as well as changes in the hiring requirements in the police and other government jobs that had been obstacles to the employment of Puerto Ricans. The legal argument for bilingual ballots, while based on the specific situation of Puerto Ricans on the island voting in Spanish as U.S. citizens and not being able to do so when they migrated stateside, was an important factor in the adoption of bilingual ballots for Latinos and other language minorities nationally.

Through the mayoralties of John Lindsay, Abraham Beame, and Ed Koch in this decade, Puerto Ricans remained outsiders but received a level of recognition, even if largely symbolic, that they had not achieved before. However, with the decline in Badillo's political fortunes throughout this decade, Puerto Ricans were not able to develop a strong citywide political leadership and were focused on the more local politics of the South Bronx, El Barrio and the Lower East Side of Manhattan, and the Williamsburg section of Brooklyn. Badillo's move from the Congress to city hall in this period was seen by many as a pivotal and negative point in the history of Puerto Rican political leadership in the city.

Puerto Rican left organizations, such as the Young Lords, witnessed a decline toward the middle of this decade as some deformed into highly sectarian political cults and disappeared, due both to internal (the inexperience of youth) as well as external factors (e.g., government infiltration programs like the FBI's counterintelligence programs (COINTELPRO). Lopez (1996–1997: 7) summarized the fate of the Young Lords in New York in the following terms: "[W]hat happened to the Young Lords is ironic and irritating. Long before they morphed into the limping self-parody that was the Puerto Rican Revolutionary Workers Organization (PRRWO) in the mid-1970s, the Young Lords had abandoned their own political linkage to Puerto Rico, ... were barely visible in our communities, and had joined the political fratricide of the U.S. left."

The independence movement achieved a certain momentum as the statehood movement became more significant, with all the major parties on the island—those supporting commonwealth, statehood, and independence—reaching a consensus before the United Nations in the early part of the decade that Puerto Rico was indeed a "colony." On October 27, 1974, more than 20,000 persons packed Madison Square Garden on the "National Day of Solidarity with the Independence of Puerto Rico" organized by the Puerto Rican Socialist Party (PSP) (Velázquez 1998: 53–54). In 1975, the Fuerzas Armadas de Liberación Nacional (FALN) took credit for planting a bomb in Manhattan's Fraunces Tavern, killing 4 and injuring 53.

Despite the lack of majority support in the Puerto Rican community, these movements had a profound impact on the political and cultural sensitivities of the Puerto Rican leadership and youth in New York and elsewhere. Opinion surveys indicated that by the 1980s, a significant portion of Puerto Rican leaders supported the independence of Puerto Rico, although the large majority of the community supported the status quo of commonwealth (Falcón 1993).

In the late 1970, as a concrete expression of this sensitivity, South Bronx Congressman Garcia openly took up, to great fanfare in the Puerto Rican community, what became the successful campaign to free from federal prisons Lolita Lebron and the other Puerto Rican Nationalists who had attacked the U.S. Congress and President Truman's residence in the early 1950s. Normally, this would have made him a target of anti-Communist forces both from Puerto Rico and the United States in the 1950s and early 1960s, (as was the case earlier with Congressman Vito Marcantonio, and activists Gilberto Gerena Valentin and Ted Velez of the East Harlem Tenants Council, but it did not.

In addition, as Glazer and Moynihan noted between the first and second editions of their influential book, *Beyond the Melting Pot*, Puerto Ricans underwent a fundamental transformation in how they viewed their place in American society. In the 1963 edition, Glazer and Moynihan predicted that Puerto Ricans would "leapfrog" Blacks in socioeconomic status because they appeared to be rejecting a self-defeating identification as a "racial minority" by adopting the more individualistic immigrant model. However, by their 1970 edition, Glazer and Moynihan were lamenting the fact that Puerto Ricans had by then embraced, because of the "resurgence of ethnicity," the Black model of a racial minority oppressed by American society. This racialization of Puerto Rican identity in the American consciousness was captured nicely in the 1969 movie, *Popi*, starring Alan Arkin, in which a hardworking Puerto Rican single father from El Barrio in New York City concocts a convoluted scheme to pass off his two sons as Cuban refugees in Miami as a way to assure a better future for them. Here you have the interesting case of a major studio film revealing how Puerto Ricans had by the late sixties been widely identified as a racial minority group in contrast to another Latino group (Cubans), whose arrival at the time (pre-Mariel) was more valued and not racially stigmatized.

However, within this framework, the continued growth of Puerto Rican community organizations was accompanied in the 1970s by important changes in their funding. The Nixon administration had tightened its control of federal funding for community programs with the abolition of the Office of Economic Opportunity (OEO) in 1974, eliminating the freedom that many Puerto Ricans and other city leaders and advocates enjoyed under the Great Society of the Democrats.

Those few Puerto Rican organizations that had relied largely on private funding in the past became increasingly dependent on government grants in the 1970s. This initiated a transformation in the politics of these community-based organizations that narrowed the scope and independence of their political agendas and refashioned them more and more as extensions of government. The militant advocacy and social movement ideology of the 1960s gave way to a more conservative bureaucratic-managerial culture among the larger Puerto Rican community-based organizations.

In addition, large businesses whose consumer base was the Puerto Rican population began to move out; one such business was Goya Foods. Founded in 1936 in New York City, it moved to Secaucus, New Jersey, in 1974 as a result of the city's weakened economic position. New public institutions that focused on the Puerto Rican community, like the PRCDP and Hostos Community College in the Bronx, came under attack (see Meyer 2003 and Jiménez 2003 on Hostos) as a result of the city's fiscal crisis at the time. The seventies were a period where the role of government and the Puerto Rican relationship to it was being challenged by the right.

In the early 1970s, the Catholic Church took a more serious view of the need to reach out to the Puerto Rican community. Díaz-Stevens (1996: 170ff.) discusses the Hispanic National Encounters that started in this period, but that in New York City resulted in a postconciliar reorganization that utilized the broad framework of "Hispanos" or "Spanish-speaking" to the detriment of focusing directly on Puerto Ricans and other Latino subgroups. By the end of the decade, and following this broad approach, the Archdiocese of New York (1980) had published a two-volume study, *Hispanics in New York: Religious, Cultural and Social Experience*, which was the first extensive study of Latino religiosity in the city. To many in the Puerto Rican community, it looked more like a marketing study by the Catholic Church, which saw its traditional White ethnic base shrinking while a potentially large pool of potential Latino Catholic consumers needed to be reeled in more systematically. The Catholic Church, however, remains, to the present day, aloof from the Puerto Rican community in New York City.

It was also in the 1970s that the rise of Protestantism among Puerto Ricans in New York began to be noted seriously; the phenomenon had grown significantly in the Puerto Rico of the 1960s. As some observers had pointed out before, a significant number of important Puerto Ricans leaders were Protestants. These included Herman Badillo, Robert Garcia ,and Carlos Rios, among others. By the mid-1970s, Puerto Rican and other Latino Pentecostal churches had formed a short-lived citywide federation, the Civic Action Commission, which sought government funding for social programs in a kind of precursor to the faith-based initiatives being developed today (Briggs 1975). In 1992, the Latino Pastoral Action Center was established to provide programs for the Protestant clergy. However, while Protestantism is a significant factor in the city's Puerto Rican politics today, it is not dominant.

All in all, the 1970s became the decade in which the Puerto Rican presence politically and organizationally began to grow nationally, beyond New York City. Within the city, this growing national network of Puerto Rican politicians and advocates did not, however, generate sufficient power to allow this community to play a bigger role in local politics. This was partially a result of the fiscal crisis the city found itself and the neoliberalism it engendered. In 1977, President Jimmy Carter made his famous symbolic but ultimately useless visit to the South Bronx to highlight the area's deterioration, while in 1979, Mayor Koch dismantled the Puerto Rican Community Development Project with relatively little fanfare or opposition. At the same time, the beginning of a significant reverse migration to Puerto Rico and the greater competitiveness of party politics on the island in the 1970s began to complicate the political relationship between island and New York–based Puerto Rican.

The 1980s: The "Decade of the Hispanic" and Other Humorous Notions

By the middle of the 1980s, New York City had become, for the first time in its history, a "majority minority" city. Blacks, Latinos and Asians together constituted the majority of its population and more than three-quarters of the students in the public school system. By the end of the decade, New York had elected its first African American mayor, David N. Dinkins. This was also the decade during which the economy's post-industrial transformation became complete as the service sector became dominant. The Puerto Rican population in the city continued to grow, but its socioeconomic and political progress began to stall.

Politically, Puerto Ricans began to make greater but still limited inroads in state-level politics with the election of Democrat Mario Cuomo as governor of New York in 1982; they remained the most underrepresented group in state government employment throughout his three terms in office, with Latinos making up less then 3 percent of state workers while being 13 percent of the state's population. Locally, in 1983, Anthony Alvarado became the first Puerto Rican to hold the post of schools chancellor (and in a 1985 report by Aspira of New York, he was confronted by the fact that Puerto Ricans and other Latinos had the highest dropout rates in the public school system, a problem that persists to the current day).

Fernando Ferrer became Bronx borough president in 1987, appointed by the city council to replace Stanley Simon, who was convicted in the municipal scandals of the time), finally restoring a position to Puerto Ricans that Badillo had given up almost twenty years earlier. As with the 1961 Robert Wagner-Carmine DeSapio break, this disruption among political elites caused by the scandals created openings for Puerto Ricans to advance. Ferrer, for example, confided to this author at the time that the Simon conviction accelerated his political career by at least five years.

In 1980, South Bronx Congressman Garcia attracted national attention for his co-sponsorship of the Kemp-Garcia Bill, which created urban enterprise zones in the inner cities, a progenitor to today's urban neo-liberal policy of tax incentives rather than direct federal government intervention. But by the end of the decade, Garcia was forced to resign from Congress as a result of the Wedtech scandal (he was acquitted of all charges years later, but it effectively ended his political career). José Serrano replaced him in the Congress in 1990.

The number of Puerto Rican elected officials in New York City during the 1980s at all levels peaked at no more than twelve, and Puerto Ricans continued to be underrepresented in the state and city government bureaucracies (Falcón 1992). However, in the early 1980s, the Puerto Rican Legal Defense and Education Fund achieved some success in using the Federal Voting Rights Act to defend the rights of Puerto Rican voters in the redistricting process.

This was a process, along with the 1989 U.S. Supreme Court ruling that the city's government structure was unconstitutional, that began having a payoff in the early 1990s as other groups, including the Institute for Puerto Rican Policy and the Commonwealth of Puerto Rico, got involved in redistricting, resulting in the number of Puerto Rican elected officials in the city increasing significantly at all levels of government.

Puerto Rican organizations began to see the gains they had made erode as the community's political progress seemed to dissipate. With the dismantling of the Puerto Rican Community Development Project in 1979, the Koch administration established a watered-down replacement in 1981 called the Puerto Rican Organization for Growth, Research, Evaluation and Social Services (PROGRESS), with a fraction of its budget and a much narrower mandate to provide technical assistance to smaller community-based organizations.

By the end of this decade, the Association of Puerto Rican Executive Directors (APRED), the only citywide federation of Puerto Rican agencies, established in 1981, closed its doors. It was replaced at the beginning of the 1990s by a more pan-ethnic United Way of New York City creation, the Hispanic Federation of New York City, currently known simply as the Hispanic Federation, which is largely run by Puerto Ricans.

The shift from APRED to the Hispanic Federation of New York City represented a response to demographic changes within the city's Latino community that affected Puerto Rican visibility in important ways. With the dramatic growth of the city's Latino immigrant population, particularly Dominicans, Colombians, Ecuadorians, and, in the 1990s, Mexicans, the focus of much of the policy debate and media attention on Latinos shifted to immigration and these newer communities.

Puerto Ricans, who up until this point had been the focus of attention when it came to Latino matters in the city, began to feel invisible despite representing the majority of the Latino population. These demographic changes also began to change the clients and constituents of the Puerto Rican social agencies and institutions in ways that began to strain their original missions. By the mid-1990s these changes spawned a national Boricua First! Campaign to assert the importance of the Puerto Rican community within a new Latino reality (Colón 1996).

In the 1980s, leading and longstanding Puerto Rican nonprofit organizations like Aspira of New York and the National Puerto Rican Forum began to fall on hard economic times. In 1984, the relatively young and high-profile Puerto Rican Legal Defense and Education Fund had a major internal crisis that led to the unionization of its employees and its declining influence during the rest of the decade.

New initiatives, like the Institute for Puerto Rican Policy, the Puerto Rican Research Exchange, Los Pleneros de la 21, Teatro Pregones, and the Committee for Hispanic Children and Families emerged in the early 1980s, but these entities were largely dependent at the time on volunteers and limited funds from private sources. In 1984, a National Puerto Rican/Hispanic Voter Participation Project was created through the National Puerto Rican Coalition in Washington, DC, to mobilize Puerto Rican voters in the Northeast. This was an attempt to replicate successful voter mobilization organizations in other parts of the country, specifically the Southwest Voter Registration Education Project and the Midwest Voter Registration and Education Project (now called the United States Hispanic Leadership Institute). However, this Puerto Rican initiative was short-lived because of limited financial support and internal divisions. By 1985, the AIDS crisis reached the point in the Puerto Rican community that the Hispanic AIDS Forum was established, and the Latino Commission on AIDS followed in 1990.

The film *Fort Apache, The Bronx* was released in 1981 and sparked a movement of Puerto Rican activists, led by Richie Pérez and others, who organized to hold the media more accountable for its images of the community. This effort continued beyond this film with media advocacy groups such as the Latino Coalition for Fair Media (now defunct) and the New York Chapter of the National Hispanic Media Coalition, created in 1986 and currently led by Marta García.

The Comité Noviembre, a voluntary coalition of organizations, was established in 1987 to promote November as Puerto Rican Heritage Month, which continues to function today and has spawned similar efforts in New Jersey and elsewhere. However, it was the publication of Virginia Sanchez Korrol's dissertation, *From Colonia to Community*, and the *Memorias de Bernardo Vega*, both in 1983, that played the role among Puerto Ricans that the TV mini-series and book, *Roots* had played for the African American community in presenting their history in this country in a new light.

The relationship between Puerto Ricans in New York and Puerto Rico began to deepen, as exemplified by a major conference by the Puerto Rican Family Institute, "The First Forum on the Human Rights of the Puerto Rican Migrant Family," held in San Juan, Puerto Rico on November 28–30, 1983 (Puerto Rican Family Institute 1983). In the middle of this decade, the island government under *Popular* Governor Rafael Hernandez Colon took the bold move of turning its Migration Division in New York into a cabinet-level Department of Puerto Rican Affairs in the United States, which the governor placed under the leadership of Nydia Velazquez, who was to become the first Puerto Rican women elected to the U.S, House of Representatives at the beginning of the next decade.

In 1987, this new entity launched, among other initiatives, the ambitious Atrevete voter registration program in Puerto Rican communities throughout the United States. This development was largely related to the status politics of the island and the Commonwealth party's efforts to court stateside Puerto Rican support to their cause. Under the pro-statehood government of Pedro Rosselló of the following decade, this cabinet-level department was dismantled, replaced by the Puerto Rico Federal Affairs Administration, an office with no cabinet status.

By the end of the decade, the Puerto Rican and Black vote began to come together as an important force in city politics, as its had in the late 1960s, particularly in support of African American political empowerment at both the local and national levels (Falcón 1989 and1992). However, the relationship was strained in 1985, when a citywide group of Blacks, the Coalition for a Just New York, rejected the nomination of Badillo for the mayoralty, supporting instead a weak Black candidate, Herman "Denny" Farrell. This prompted Badillo, in retaliation, to endorse Ed Koch instead. Despite this, Puerto Rican support for Jesse Jackson's presidential campaign became a critical part of its success in 1988, and the following year it was crucial to the election of David N. Dinkins as the first African American mayor of the city (Institute for Puerto Rican Policy 1989, and Falcón 1992).

The stage appeared set for these communities to turn their numbers into the political, economic, and cultural power that would make them real partners in the governing of the city. The future, at least for Puerto Ricans in New York City, had different plans. The media's dubbing of the 1980s as the "Decade of the Hispanic" was, by the end of this decade, a bit of a joke, as Puerto Ricans found themselves increasingly invisibilized by this new broad Hispanicity. In retrospect, the 1980s turned out not to be the right decade for such a triumphal pronouncement...certainly not in the Puerto Rican case.

CONCLUSION

As this broad overview of the issues and themes facing Puerto Ricans in

New York illustrates, the Cruz chapter ignores or minimizes many of the landmark events that influenced the evolution of this community in the years from 1960 to 1990. The type of sweeping review of three decades that Cruz undertook should have yielded much broader questions than what he produced. He also fell into the familiar trap of focusing largely on Puerto Rican poverty conditions at the expense of a more expansive view of the Puerto Rican experience that would examine much more deeply the development of the Puerto Rican professional-managerial class, island-stateside interactions, the role of culture, and so on.

For example, Cruz's discussion of the impact of the Migration Division on the politics of the Puerto Rican community in the 1960s is curiously narrow. He presents this as solely a function of a clash of two interest groups without reference to broader forces at work in the society. At other points he singles out groups like Vanguardia Betances in 1961, without establishing their significance within the overall community.

His treatment of the literature on the Puerto Rican in New York is also very uneven and narrow. While he discusses Oscar Lewis (but seems to miss the essence of his "culture of poverty" thesis), he makes no mention of the equally influential *Beyond the Melting Pot*, by Glazer and Moyhihan. Nor does he make note of other important books of the period such as Fitzpatrick's *Puerto Rican-Americans: The Meaning of Migration to the Mainland*, Thomas's *Down These Mean Streets*, Lopez's *The Puerto Rican Papers: Notes on the Re-Emergence of a Nation*, the *Memorias de Bernardo Vega*, the Centro's *Labor Migration Under Capitalism*, Rodriguez's *Puerto Ricans: Born in the USA*, James Jennings's *Puerto Rican Politics in New York City*, and Rosa Estades's *Patterns of Political Participation of Puerto Ricans in New York City*.

Still discussing the 1960s, Cruz argues, "The failure of poor Puerto Ricans to influence and shape the power structure was a function of their relative absence from the polls." While trying to illustrate the institutional obstacles that Puerto Ricans specifically faced in voting, he makes no mention of the more general problem of the low participation of the poor in American elections in contrast to the situation in Puerto Rico, where socioeconomic status does not affect voter participation levels (for an early discussion of this, see Falcón 1983).

Cruz's reliance on the *New York Times* as his main historical source often leads him to come to unwarranted conclusions. Discussing Puerto Rican relations with other racial-ethnic groups he observes,

> Between 1966 and 1976 there were at least forty-eight instances of conflict between Puerto Ricans and other groups reported in the *New York Times*. This is a clear indication that interethnic tension was

widespread during the 1960s and 1970s. From the reports it is also obvious that such conflict was debilitating. Community life was rife with conflict. Puerto Ricans fought Blacks over control of antipoverty agencies; had altercations with Italians over turf in Park Slope; confronted Hasidic Jews in the Lower East Side and Williamsburg over housing, community resources, or simply because they crossed paths with them; and had violent encounters with Poles in Greenpoint *over grievances that were often hard to understand.* [my emphasis] In some cases, Puerto Rican–Black conflict was criminal in nature and did not necessarily reflect the character of everyday-life relationships. But interethnic rivalries in the political arena were significant and prevented both the delivery of services to desperately needy people and the development of empowering coalitions. Of course, there were exceptions to this pattern, often within the very communities where conflict was particularly intense, *but when collaboration occurred it was sometimes described as rudderless, fraught with conflict, and focused on the wrong battles even by the participants themselves.* [my emphasis]

As this passage indicates, Cruz simply reproduces the world according to the *New York Times,* giving credibility to accounts that have been consistently criticized within the Puerto Rican community. In doing so, he reinforces an image of Puerto Ricans as irrational and irresponsible, underestimating the obstacles they faced and the sacrifices made to empower their community in an often-hostile environment that devalued and worked at all turns to thwart their efforts.

It is also interesting that, while relying on the *New York Times* for his historical reconstruction of this period, Cruz neglects to use the many Puerto Rican analysts of this period in his reconstruction. Puerto Rican writers like Luis Fuentes, Clara Rodríguez, Alfredo Lopez, Richie Perez, Pablo Guzman, James Jennings, and others who have written about important aspects of this period are not utilized to provide some dimensionality to the events covered. This is curiously reminiscent of Richard Rodríguez's similar but more wholesale blotting out of Latino writers in his most recent book, *Brown: The Last Discovery of America.* This seems like a needless squandering of a relatively rare resource, the motivation of which is not particularly clear to me.

Cruz's treatment of many issues and developments is also too incomplete and could be misleading. He introduces players like David Dinkins without pointing out that he was the first African American mayor elected in New York City and without noting the special role that Puerto Ricans played in his election. He mentions Puerto Rico's Department of Puerto Rican Affairs in the United States without explaining its genesis or purpose. He discusses the disastrous effects of the Wedtech scandal on former Congressman Robert Garcia's career but never explains that the charges against him were eventually dropped.

Despite these criticisms, Cruz's chapter represents an important and unfortunately all-too-rare starting point for the analysis of this recent period of Puerto Rican community development in New York City. It lays out some benchmarks in terms of chronologically arraying some of the critical events of this thirty-year period and isolates some of the important themes and debates that need to be further developed. His approach, however, is seriously flawed on a number of fronts, resulting in his laying out a terrain full of factual and theoretical weeds and dead ends that need to be traversed with great care. However, the rewards of attacking the subject with the rigor it deserves are extremely promising and make this a long-overdue task. Cruz had the largely thankless task of being among the first to tackle these problems in analyzing this period of Puerto Rican history, which he did in a way that should provoke, as it has in this commentary, a lively discussion on its nature and meanings.

REFERENCES

Acosta-Belén, Edna, Margarita Benítez, José E. Cruz, Yvonne González-Rodríguez, Clara E. Rodríguez, Carlos E. Santiago, Azara Santiago-Rivera, and Barbara R. Sjostrom. 2000. *"Adiós, Borinquen querida": The Puerto Rican Diaspora, Its History, and Contributions.* Albany: Center for Latino, Latin American, and Caribbean Studies, State University of New York at Albany.

Archdiocese of New York. 1980. *Hispanics in New York: Religious, Cultural and Social Experience*, 2 vols. New York: Office of Pastoral Research, Archdiocese of New York.

Briggs, Kenneth A. 1975. "Pentecostalism Rises Like a Phoenix from the Slums." *New York Times*, February 20, p. 70.

Carter Hannigan, Janet. 1962. "Puerto Rican Political Leaders." Unpublished paper, Seminar in American Politics, Columbia University (spring).

City of New York. 1967. "Puerto Ricans Confront Problems of the Complex Urban Society: A Design for Change," April 15–16 Conference Proceedings, Office of the Mayor, City of New York.

Colón, Israel. 1996. "Memories of *Boricua First!* A Personal Perspective." *Crítica: A Journal of Puerto Rican Policy and Politics* 22–23 (March–April): 1, 15–17.

Cruz, José E., and Carlos E. Santiago. 2001. "The Changing Socioeconomic and Political Fortunes of Puerto Ricans in New York City, 1965–1990." Unpublished paper, Annual Meeting of the American Political Science Association, San Francisco (September 1).

Díaz-Stevens, Ana María. 1996. "Aspects of Puerto Rican Religious Experience: A Sociohistorical Overview," in *Latinos in New York: Communities in Transition*,

Gabriel Haslip-Viera and Sherrie L. Baver. eds. Pp. 147–186. Notre Dame, IN: University of Notre Dame Press.

Falcón, Angelo. 1983. "Puerto Rican Political Participation: New York City and Puerto Rico," in *Time for Decision: The United States and Puerto Rico*, Jorge Heine, ed. Pp. 27–53. Lanham, MD: North-South Publishing.

———. 1989. "Puerto Ricans and the 1989 Mayoral Election in New York City." *Hispanic Journal of Behavioral Sciences* 11: 3 (August): 245–258.

———. 1992. "Puerto Ricans and the 1988 Election in New York City," in *From Rhetoric to Reality: Latino Politics in the 1988 Elections*, Rodolfo O. de la Garza and Louis DeSipio, eds. Pp. 147–170. Boulder, CO: Westview Press.

———. 1993. "A Divided Nation: The Puerto Rican Diaspora in the United States and the Proposed Referendum," in *Colonial Dilemma: Critical Perspectives on Contemporary Puerto Rico*, Edwin Meléndez and Edgardo Meléndez, eds. Pp. 173–180. Boston: South End Press.

———. 1994. "The Puerto Rican Activist Stratum in New York City 1978." New York: Institute for Puerto Rican Policy Reprint.

Fitzpatrick, Joseph P. 1971. *Puerto Rican Americans: The Meaning of Migration to the Mainland*. Englewood Cliffs, NJ: Prentice-Hall.

———. 1996. *The Stranger is Our Own: Reflections on the Journey of Puerto Rican Migrants*. Kansas City, MO: Sheed and Ward.

Glazer, Nathan, and Daniel Patrick Moynihan. 1970 (1963). *Beyond the Melting Pot: The Negroes, Puerto Ricans, Jews, Italians, and Irish of New York City*. Cambridge: MIT Press.

Gotsch, John Warren. 1966. "Puerto Rican Leadership in New York," MA thesis, New York University.

Institute for Puerto Rican Policy. 1989. *Towards a Puerto Rican-Latino Agenda for New York City, 1989*. New York: Institute for Puerto Rican Policy.

Jennings, James. 1977. *Puerto Rican Politics in New York City*. Washington, DC: University Press of America.

Jiménez, Ramón J. 2003. "Hostos Community College: Battle of the Seventies." *Centro Journal: Centro de Estudios Puertorriqueños*, 15: 1 (spring): 98–111.

Jonnes, Jill. 2002. *South Bronx Rising: The Rise, Fall, and Resurrection of an American City*. New York: Fordham University Press.

López, Alfredo. 1996–1997. "The Rise and Fall of the Young Lords Party: Reflections on 'Pa'lante, Siempre Pa'lante.'" *Critica: A Journal of Puerto Rican Policy and Politics* 31–32 (December–January): 1, 5–8.

Meléndez, Miguel (Mickey). 2003. *We Took to the Streets: Fighting for Latino Rights with the Young Lords*. New York: St. Martin's Press.

Meyer, Gerald. 2003. "Save Hostos: The Struggle for a College." *Centro Journal: Centro de Estudios Puertorriqueños*, 15: 1 (Spring): 72–97.

Montserrat, Joseph. 1968. "Symposium on Puerto Rico in the Year 2000." *Harvard Law Journal*, 15: 1 (fall): 12–27. Reprinted in Kal Wagenheim and Olga Jiménez de Wagenheim, eds. 1994. *The Puerto Ricans: A Documentary History*. Pp. 321–323. Princeton, NJ: Marcus Weiner Publishers.

Morales, Ed. 2002. *Living in Spanglish: The Search for a Latino Identity in America*. New

York: St. Martin's Press.
New Pittsburgh Leader. 1963. "Puerto Rican Fence-Sitting Role in Rights Fight Hit by Leaders." *New Pittsburgh Courier* (New York edition), vol. 4, no. 22, September 14, p.1.
Pantoja, Antonia. 2002. *Memoir of a Visionary.* Houston: Arte Publico Press.
Pérez, Marvette. 2002. "The Political 'Flying Bus': Nationalism, Identity, Status, Citizenship and Puerto Ricans." *Critique of Anthropology,* 22: 3 (September): 305–322.
Puerto Rican Family Institute. 1983. "The First Forum on the Human Rights of the Puerto Rican Migrant Family: Official Proceedings, November 28–30, San Juan, Puerto Rico." New York: Puerto Rican Family Institute.
Puerto Rican Forum. 1980. "A Study of Poverty Conditions in the New York Puerto Rican Community" (1964), in *Regional Perspectives on the Puerto Rican Experience,* Carlos E. Cortés, ed. New York: Arno Press.
Robinson, Major, Alfredo Graham, and Evelyn Cunningham. 1962. "Are Puerto Ricans Cooperating, Freedom Fighters Ask Leaders: Negroes Question Role of Spanish-Americans in Social Revolution." *New Pittsburgh Courier* (New York edition), vol. 4, no. 21, September 7, p. 1.
Rogowsky, Edward T., Louis H. Gold, and David W. Abbott. 1972. "Police: The Civilian Review Board Controversy," in *Race and Politics in New York City: Five Studies in Policy-Making,* Jewell Bellush and Stephen M. David, eds. Pp. 59–97. New York: Praeger.
Schulman, Bruce J. 2002. *The Seventies: The Great Shift in American Culture, Society, and Politics.* New York: The Free Press.
Velázquez, José E. 1998. "Coming Full Circle: The Puerto Rican Socialist Party, U.S. Branch" in *The Puerto Rican Movement: Voices from the Diaspora,* Andrés Torres and José E. Velázquez, eds. Pp. 48–68. Philadelphia: Temple University Press.

CHAPTER THREE

Puerto Rican Day Parade, 1990. (Records of the Office of the Commonwealth of Puero Rico. *Courtesy: Center for Puerto Rican Studies, Hunter Collge, CUNY*)

CHAPTER 3

PUERTO RICAN NEW YORKERS IN THE 1990S: A DEMOGRAPHIC AND SOCIOECONOMIC PROFILE

Francisco L. Rivera-Batíz

The Puerto Rican population of New York has been declining sharply in recent years, both in relative size when compared to other Latino groups and in absolute numbers. Between 1990 and 2000, the number of Puerto Ricans in New York dropped by more than 100,000 persons. What explains this demographic shift? What factors account for the drop in the Puerto Rican population of New York?

Using data recently released by the 2000 U.S. Census of Population and Housing, this chapter begins by describing and analyzing the major demographic changes occurring among Puerto Rican New Yorkers in the 1990s. Shifts in migration patterns between Puerto Rico and the United States are discussed as well as the demographic changes in the population of Puerto Ricans in the city. The chapter then examines the key socioeconomic changes that occurred in the last decade. Despite gains in some areas, Puerto Ricans in New York, on average, were not significantly better off in the year 2000 than in 1990. What explains this lagging economic performance? Using Current Population Surveys as well as 1990 and 2000 U.S. Census of Population and Housing information, the chapter describes the changing socioeconomic status of Puerto Ricans in New York and examines the major forces explaining the sluggish economic growth. The analysis explores the role played by patterns of employment and labor demand in New York City, labor force participation among men and women, educational attainment, family structure, and migration.

Despite the diminishing population and difficult economic conditions, the nearly 800,000 Puerto Ricans in the city are by far its largest Latino group and a powerful ethnic bloc. Their influence on New York City culture, politics, and economics continues to be significant and, despite fears to the contrary, is unlikely to decline over the next decade.

The Shifting Demographics of the Puerto Rican Population in New York

Table 1 shows the changes in the Puerto Rican population of New York since 1920. The period of great expansion occurred from 1940 to 1970, when the Puerto Rican population of the city grew by close to 750,000 people. By 1960, more than 80 percent of all Latinos in New York were Puerto Rican. This period of expansion slows down in the 1980s and ends in the 1990s, when the Puerto Rican population of New York declines from 896,763 to 789,172. By the year 2000, Puerto Ricans accounted for just above one-third of all Latinos in the city. What explains this major demographic shift?

TABLE 1

THE PUERTO RICAN POPULATION OF NEW YORK CITY, 1920-2000

Year	Puerto Rican Population	Percentage of the Hispanic/Latino Population of New York City
1920	7,370	17.9%
1930	44,908	40.7
1940	61,431	45.8
1950	246,306	--
1960	612,574	80.8
1970	811,843	67.5
1980	860,552	61.2
1990	896,763	50.3
2000	789,172	36.5

Sources: Haslip-Viera (1996) and U.S. Bureau of the Census, Census of Population and Housing, 1980, 1990, 2000a.

The reduction in the Puerto Rican population of New York in the 1990s is explained by three major forces: a drop in the level of migration of Puerto

Ricans to the mainland United States, an increase in the net migration of Puerto Ricans out of the city, and an aging population and consequent increased mortality rate among Puerto Rican New Yorkers.

The slowdown in the migration of Puerto Ricans to the mainland United States is part of a gradual reversal of the Great Migration period between 1940 and 1970. Table 2 shows the pattern of net emigration of persons from Puerto Rico to the mainland United States in the twentieth century. The largest net outflow of people from Puerto Rico occurred in the 1950s, when close to half a million Puerto Ricans emigrated to the United States. Since then, however, the out-migration has displayed a negative long-run trend. Recent estimates constructed by the U.S. Bureau of the Census show a net migration of 43,926 persons from Puerto Rico to the U.S. mainland occurring between 1990 and 1999, the smallest out-migration from the island since the 1930s (see U.S. Department of Commerce 2000b). This long-term migration pattern closely follows the demographic transition in Puerto Rico, where fertility rates and population growth have sharply declined since the 1970s. It was the massive explosion of the labor force in the Island during the 1940s through the 1960s that fed a significant portion of the migration to the United States. However, as fertility rates dropped and labor force growth slowed down, so did migration to the mainland United States.

TABLE 2

NET MIGRATION FROM PUERTO RICO TO THE MAINLAND U.S., 1990-1999

Period	Net Number of Migrants:
1900-20	13,000
1920-30	42,000
1930-40	18,000
1940-50	151,000
1950-60	470,000
1960-70	214,000
1970-80	65,817
1980-90	116,571
1990-99	43,926

Sources: The figures for 1900-1970 are from Vazquez-Calzada (1979); those for 1970-1990 are from Rivera-Batiz and Santiago (1996: 45). The 1990-1999 figure is an estimate provided by U.S. Department of Commerce (2000b).

Relative economic conditions in Puerto Rico and the U.S. have also influenced migration flows. The huge wage gaps between the Island and the mainland were the engine behind the Great Migration period. Indeed, in 1952, average hourly earnings in Puerto Rican cigar factories were less than 30 percent of the wages that could be found in New York or other American factories (Gutierrez (1977: Table A-1). In the apparel industry, the earnings differentials were even higher. The expanding American economy in the post–World War II years, and the booming New York City manufacturing sector in particular, was able to absorb the migrants, offering employment opportunities at high wages when compared to Puerto Rico. These wage differences gradually narrowed over the years. By the late 1960s, the average hourly earnings in many manufacturing industries in Puerto Rico were close to 70 percent those in the mainland United States. The 1990s in particular were years of substantial economic growth in the Island, with unemployment rates declining sharply relative to those in New York City and income per capita increasing as well. As relative economic conditions changed, the out-migration rates from the Island to the mainland declined.

A second factor behind the diminishing Puerto Rican population in New York is the increase in the number of Puerto Rican New Yorkers moving out of the city, to Puerto Rico, into suburban areas, and elsewhere in the mainland United States. This pattern began in the 1980s. As the New York City Department of City Planning (1994: 9) concluded in its report of Puerto Rican migration in the 1980s: "Between 1985 and 1990, New York city had 51,402 Puerto Rican in-migrants and 138,089 out-migrants for a net loss of 86,687 Puerto Ricans." The 1990s saw a continuation of this trend. The explanations given by the out-migrants as reasons for their move are partly economic (to get a better job or higher pay), but a large share of the migrants give noneconomic reasons, including a desire to be close to the amenities provided by suburban locations and the warmer temperatures supplied by Puerto Rico and southern areas of the U.S. In a recent *New York Times* article, Navarro (2000: B7) presents the view given by Hildamar Ortiz, a Puerto Rican lawyer who moved from New York to the Island in 1996: "[Ms. Ortiz] said she moved partly to honor her late father's dreams of retiring in Puerto Rico. But she said she always wondered what it would be like to be Puerto Rican in Puerto Rico."

The changing migration patterns have led to a dramatic shift in the geographical distribution of Puerto Ricans away from New York City. In the year 2000, the total population of Puerto Ricans in the continental U.S. was 3,406,178; New York Puerto Ricans accounted for just 23 percent of this population, down from proportions that back in the 1940s and 1950s were as high as 80 percent.

TABLE 3

THE POPULATION OF NEW YORK CITY, 1990 - 2000

Population Group	1990 Population	% of NYC Population	2000 Population	% of NYC Population
New York City	7,322,564	100.0%	8,008,278	100.0%
Non-Hispanic White	3,163,125	43.2	2,801,267	35.0
Non-Hispanic Black	1,847,049	25.2	1,962,154	24.5
Latino/Hispanic	1,783,511	24.4	2,160,554	27.0
Asian and Pacific	489,851	6.6	783,058	9.8
Other	39,028	0.6	301,245	3.7

Latino/Hispanic Group	1990 Population	% of Latino Population	2000 Population	% of Latino Population
Total Population	1,783,511	100.0%	2,160,554	100.0%
Puerto Rican	896,763	50.3	789,172	36.5
Dominican	332,713	18.7	555,000	25.7
Mexican	61,722	3.5	125,150	5.8
Other Latino/Hispanic	492,313	27.5	691,232	32.0

Source: The 1990 data are from the population count of the U.S. Department of Commerce, *1990 United States Census of Population and Housing;* the figures for 2000 are from the count of the U.S. Census of Population and Housing (2000b). The figure for the Dominicans population in 2000 is an estimate based on Hernandez and Rivera-Batiz (1997).

The third major force behind the shrinking Puerto Rican population in New York is time itself. Puerto Rican New Yorkers have been gradually aging as a group. The median age in 1980 was twenty-four, in 1990 it was twenty-eight, and by 2000 it had increased to thirty-two years. The migrants who moved to New York as part of the Great Migration between 1940 and 1970 are now reaching age groups with high mortality rates. Workers who were twenty to thirty years of age in 1950 would be seventy to eight years of age in the year 2000. The higher mortality rates, combined with the migration patterns just discussed, have led to a sharp reduction in the number of Puerto Ricans who were born in the Island itself and who still live in New York City. In the year 2000, it was estimated that about 272,000 Puerto Ricans residing in New York had been born in the Island. This represents about one out of every three Puerto Rican New Yorkers, and it is a sharp drop compared to the corresponding figure of more than 50 percent for 1980.

Although important, the demographic changes described here should not be overemphasized. Despite the significant contraction in population, Puerto Ricans remain the largest Hispanic or Latino group in New York. Table 3 shows the composition of the resident population of New York City on the basis of race and ethnicity, as determined by the 1990 and 2000 U.S. Census of Population. Out of the 8,008,278 persons living in New York in 2000, a total of 2,160,554 were Latino/Hispanic. This constitutes about 27 percent of the population of the city. Table 3 also shows that Latinos have overtaken Black Americans as the largest minority in the city, with an addition of close to 400,000 Latinos to the population of New York since 1990.

TABLE 4

THEPUERTO RICAN POPULATION OF NEW YORK: BY BOROUGH

Borough	Puerto Rican population	Percentage of the total
New York City Total	789,172	100.0%
Bronx	319,240	40.5
Brooklyn	213,025	27.0
Manhattan	119,718	15.2
Queens	108,661	13.8
Staten Island	28,528	3.5

Source: 2000 U.S. Census of Population.

Table 3 breaks down the Latino/Hispanic population in New York into its major subgroups. Puerto Ricans continue to be the largest Hispanic subgroup. The 2000 Census of Population counted 789,172 Puerto Ricans residing in New York City, compared to about 555,000 Dominicans, the second largest Hispanic subgroup, and 125,150 Mexican/Chicano/ Mexican Americans, the third largest subgroup. Thus, despite a rapidly growing influx of other Latinos to the city, Puerto Ricans continue to be the city's largest Latino group.

The Puerto Rican population has become much more dispersed within New York City. Back in the 1950s and 1960s, most of the population was concentrated in certain areas of Manhattan and Brooklyn. Puerto Rican migrants came to these neighborhoods because of their previously established economic and social networks. As early as 1926, 60 percent of the Puerto Ricans in New York were residing in the East and East Central Harlem area later referred to as El Barrio. (Sánchez Korrol 1994: 58). In Lower Manhattan, where about 10 percent of the Puerto Rican population lived, many workers were employed in the cigar factories described by Bernardo Vega in his *Memoirs* (Vega 1984: 12). In addition, 25 percent of the population resided in Brooklyn, pulled to the area by the employment available in the bustling factories and the Brooklyn Navy Yards. It was only in the 1970s that a process of wide diversification occurred, shifting large parts of the population to the Bronx—particularly the South Bronx—and other parts of the city.

Table 4 shows the location of Puerto Ricans within New York City, as counted by the 2000 U.S. Census of Population. The largest concentration is in the Bronx (where 40 percent of Puerto Rican New Yorkers were residing), followed by Brooklyn (27 percent), Manhattan (15 percent), Queens (14 percent), and Staten Island (4 percent). In all of these boroughs, there are also growing numbers of other Latino groups, whether Dominicans in Manhattan and the Bronx or Colombians, Mexicans, and other Latinos in Queens and Brooklyn.

The Socioeconomic Status of Puerto Ricans in New York

What is the current socioeconomic status of the Puerto Rican population in New York? How did it change in the 1990s? How does it compare with that of the overall population of New York?

In comparing the socioeconomic status of populations, economists and other social scientists often use average household (or family) income as a basis for comparing the average standard of living in the group. However, using household (or family) income to compare the socioeconomic status of groups has the problem that the number of people residing in a household may vary across the various groups considered. Because of this variability, two households with identical income may have widely different standards of living: if one household has ten persons living in it while the other has only three persons, the standard of living is much higher in the latter. In order to adjust for differences in household size, economists usually divide household income by the number of persons in the household to compute per capita household income.

Table 5 displays the changes in the average annual per capita household income of the Puerto Rican population residing in New York during the 1990s. All the figures are adjusted for inflation and are expressed in 2000 dollars. As can be seen, Puerto Ricans had lower income per capita than most of the other major racial/ethnic groups. In 1999, the average annual income per person for Puerto Rican New Yorkers was $11,893, compared to $22,993 for New Yorkers overall, $15,513 for the non-Hispanic Black population, and $33,588 for non-Hispanic White Americans. Of the major groups considered here, only the Dominican and Mexican populations had lower per capita income than Puerto Ricans.

TABLE 5

HOUSEHOLD INCOME PER CAPITA IN NEW YORK

1989-1999 - All Households

Population Group	Household Income Per-Capita			
	1989	1993	1996	1999
New York Overall	$21,807	$17,653	$19,753	$22,993
Non-Hispanic White	30,767	24,304	28,075	33,588
Non-Hispanic Black	14,452	11,240	11,721	15,513
Asian	18,037	17,465	19,853	21,132
Hispanic	11,419	9,586	10,222	11,866
Puerto Rican	10,737	9,997	10,917	11,893
Dominican	8,587	6,505	7,179	9,069
Mexican	–	–	–	8,584
Other Hispanic	14,187	11,928	13,102	14,333

Source: Author's tabulations of 1990 Census data, Current Population Surveys (CPS) and 1999 NYC Housing and Vacancy Survey. The figures for 1993 and 1996 are an average of March CPS data for three years, with the midpoint year as stated. The figures for 1999 represent the average of the CPS for the three years with a 1999 midpoint plus the 1999 NYC Housing and Vacancy Survey data. All income numbers have been adjusted for inflation and expressed in 2000 dollars. No data are available for the Mexican population before 1999 due to small sample sizes. The "other Hispanic" category does not include the Mexican population in any year.

The per capita income of Puerto Ricans in 1999 was only slightly higher than it was in 1989. The lack of income growth reflects in large part the lack of economic growth overall in New York City during the 1990s. This result appears surprising, given the impressive record of growth displayed by the U.S. economy in the second half of the 1990s. However, what must be remembered is that New Yorkers had comparatively high income per capita in 1989, and this tumbled sharply in the years to follow, a product of one of the severest recessions to hit the city in the twentieth century. Table 5 shows the changes occurring between 1989 and 1999. The city hit rock bottom in 1993 when overall per capita income dropped to $17,653, down from the $21,807 level in 1989. This constituted a decline of close to 20 percent in four years. Since that time, there has been a recovery, with average income per capita rising from $17,653 to $22,993. But in 1999, the city was just recuperating to the income levels prevailing in the late 1980s, displaying no substantial net growth over the period.

TABLE 6

COMPARATIVE POVERTY OR PUERTO RICANS IN NEW YORK: ALL PERSONS, 1989-1999

Population Group	Poverty rate 1989	1999
New York City, Overall	16.9%	19.3%
Non-Hispanic White	8.2	9.1
Non-Hispanic Black	22.6	26.2
Asian	14.3	15.8
Hispanic	31.0	30.0
Puerto Rican	36.5	33.1
Dominican	36.3	37.9
Other Hispanic	–	20.7

Source: The poverty rate is the percentage of persons in the group residing in households whose income is below the poverty level. The data sources are the same as those in earlier Tables. The poverty level for 1989 is from the 1990 U.S. Census; for 1999 it is a combination of the March CPS for 1999, 2000 and 2001.

Poverty levels among Puerto Ricans in New York have not fared much better than income levels. Following the Census Bureau guidelines, a household of four (two adults, two children) is under the poverty level if it receives less than $16,665 as annual income. Table 6 shows changes in poverty levels in New York between 1989 and 1999. The proportion of Puerto Ricans living in households with income below the poverty line declined from 36.5 percent in 1989 to approximately 33.1 percent in 1999. Again, this sluggish decline in poverty is associated with the lack of a net economic expansion in the city during the 1989–1999 period. Overall, poverty in New York City *rose* between 1989 and 1999. In 1989, the poverty rate in New York was 16.9 percent, but in 1999 it was 19.3 percent. The largest increase in poverty occurred among Blacks and Hispanics, and the lowest among Asian and White Americans.

This dismal picture of poverty among New Yorkers has been confirmed by other recent research. A study released by the Community Service Society in October 1999 described the overall poverty picture in the city, concluding that "despite the strongest economy in years, nearly one out of four New York City residents had incomes below the Federal Government's threshold last year, a rate that has barely dipped since the last recession and that is twice as high as the national average" (Bernstein 1999).

The economic situation of Puerto Ricans in New York is also significantly worse than that of Puerto Ricans in the rest of the nation. While Puerto Rican New Yorkers had average annual household income per capita equal to $11,893 in 1999, the corresponding figure for Puerto Ricans outside New York City was $13,896. Of course, the situation of Puerto Ricans outside New York varies by location, with metropolitan areas such as Orlando, Florida, Bergen-Passaic in New Jersey, and Los Angeles, California displaying income above New York's. But cities like Hartford, Connecticut, and Springfield, Massachusetts, exhibit lower income per person.

TABLE 7

UNEMPLOYMENT RATES IN NEW YORK CITY, 1990 - 1999

Persons 16 years of age or older in the labor force

Population Group	Unemployment Rate (%)			
	1990	1994	1997	2000
New York, overall	8.3%	9.0%	9.9%	5.7%
Non-Hispanic White	5.3	6.9	7.3	3.1
Non-Hispanic Black	12.2	11.1	16.7	8.9
Asian	6.0	7.3	4.6	4.2
Hispanic	13.1	13.0	12.2	8.2
Puerto Rican	13.7	12.5	13.0	9.0
Dominican	17.3	18.0	18.6	10.9
Other Hispanic	10.1	9.8	9.2	6.8

Source: Data for 1990 are from the 1990 U.S. Census of Population; data for 1994-2000 are from the CPS, calculated on the basis of a three-year average, with the midpoint as stated. Data for 2000 also incorporates the 1999 NYC Housing and Vacancy Survey data.

Explaining the Socioeconomic Status of Puerto Ricans in New York

The dire economic situation of Puerto Rican New Yorkers can be explained by major shifts occurring in the New York City economy and labor market during the 1990s. These changes impacted more negatively on the employment and earnings of the Puerto Rican population, than on other groups in the city.

TABLE 8

FEMALE-HEADED HOUSEHOLDS IN NEW YORK CITY

All persons in the population group

Population Group	Proportion of the Population Residing in Female-Headed Households, 2000
New York, overall	23.8%
Non-Hispanic White	9.3
Non-Hispanic Black	45.3
Asian	9.4
Hispanic	32.0
Puerto Rican	37.0
Dominican	42.9
Mexican	16.3
Other Hispanic	22.1

Source: Data from the 1999, 2000 and 2001 CPS.

The comparatively high unemployment rates in New York City in the 1990s represent the most significant barrier to economic progress among Puerto Ricans as well as other ethnic and racial minorities. The U.S. recession of 1989–1993 not only had a deep impact on the New York City labor market but also left deep scars that have not healed so quickly. Unemployment in New York climbed from 4.5 percent in May 1988 to 11.6 percent in September 1992. Since that time, unemployment dropped, but only slowly, to 10 percent in July 1997, to 6.8 percent in June 1999 and to 4.9 percent in May 2001. Throughout this time period, the city's unemployment rate remained significantly higher than that in the rest of the nation.

Table 7 presents the behavior of unemployment rates in New York City from 1990 to 2000, broken down by race and ethnicity. The unemployment rate among Puerto Ricans was more than 13 percent in the early 1990s and remained at that level for most of the decade, declining only after 1997. In the year 2000, the Puerto Rican unemployment rate hovered around 9 percent, which is substantially higher than the 6 percent overall unemployment rate in the city, and drastically higher than that among White New Yorkers, which had about 3 percent unemployment at the time. The deep economic recession in New York thus had a long-lasting impact on Puerto Ricans, wiping out any significant economic gains during the decade. As Solidelle Wasser, a senior economist with the Bureau of Labor Statistics has noted, "an analysis of payrolls in New York city between 1992 and 1996 ...supports the idea that the recession here disproportionately hurt those at the bottom while the recovery disproportionately benefited those at the top" (Bernstein 1999: B1).

The aggravated impact of the recession on the Puerto Rican labor force reflects two forces: the disproportionate impact on the manufacturing sector and the negative effect on workers with low educational attainment. Puerto Rican workers have been historically overrepresented in the manufacturing sector of the city. Indeed, manufacturing was the predominant type of employment in the 1950s and 1960s, but even as late as 1980, close to one-third of the Puerto Rican labor force remained employed in the manufacturing sector. The restructuring of the New York economy in the 1970s and 1980s drastically reduced manufacturing employment opportunities. In 1967, close to 900,000 workers were employed in the manufacturing sector in New York. This dropped to 350,000 workers by 1987. This deindustrialization of the New York City economy partly accounts for the sluggish economic progress of Puerto Ricans in the city over the years.

The 1989–1992 recession had a further devastating effect on manufacturing, reducing employment in that sector by an additional 100,000 jobs. Puerto Ricans were deeply affected by these developments. Although manufacturing was no longer the leading sector of employment, it was a significant source of jobs. In 1990, about 15 percent of Puerto Rican workers were employed in manufacturing, making it the third leading sector of employment. As the recession developed in the early 1990s, so did unemployment among Puerto Rican workers laid off from manufacturing firms closing city operations. Factories owned by Swingline (producing staplers), Leslie Fay (apparel), Campbell's (a cannery), M&W Sewing (manufacturing blouses and dresses), ACE Metal Fabricators (alarm boxes and door covers), Hickory Hills (children's sportswear), and so on left New York City in these years, stranding thousands of Puerto Rican workers with no employment.

Although important in recent years, the deindustrialization of New York is not the only or even the most significant factor affecting the employment situation of Puerto Ricans in the 1990s. Puerto Rican workers have generally had higher unemployment rates than other major racial and ethnic groups for many decades, even before deindustrialization became a force. For instance, Glazer and Moynihan (1970: 117) note, "The Census of 1950 showed, for men, 7 per cent of the non-Puerto Rican whites, 12 percent of the Negroes and 17 percent of the Puerto Ricans unemployed; for women, 5 per cent of the non-Puerto Rican whites, 8.5 per cent of the Negroes, and 11 per cent of Puerto Ricans."

TABLE 9

THE EDUCATIONAL STATUS OF NEW YORKERS, 1990, 1999

Persons 25 years of age or older

Population Group	Percentage of the Population with Four Years of College	
	1990	1999
New York overall	30.0%	31.4%
Non-Hispanic White	41.5	45.0
Non-Hispanic Black	15.6	18.9
Asian	37.5	38.5
Hispanic/Latino	10.9	13.7
Puerto Rican	9.1	11.1
Dominican	7.9	10.5
Mexican	–	6.7
Other Hispanic/Latino	13.2	17.6

Source: 1990 data from the 1990 US Census of Population; data for 1999 from the 1999 NYC Housing and Vacancy Survey.

A wide array of factors explains the persistence of high unemployment among Puerto Rican workers. One of the key forces is the comparatively low educational attainment compared to other racial and ethnic groups, including Black Americans. Education has become an increasingly important determinant of employment success. This is partly due to a growing demand for skilled labor arising from technological changes in the economy. But it also responds to the rising importance of credentialism, which requires workers to acquire more education in order to compete more effectively with the rising level of schooling of others in the labor force.

The recession in the early 1990s had a more severe impact on workers with low levels of schooling because unskilled-labor-intensive sectors were hit the hardest and because most industries would lay off first workers with lower levels of schooling. Because of the low educational attainment of the Puerto Rican labor force, the recession had a disproportionate effect on Puerto Rican workers. And the sluggish demand for unskilled labor in the city meant that unemployment among Puerto Ricans remained high throughout the mid-1990s.

The New York City economy did finally display a boost of economic activity in the late 1990s and very early 2000s. But the resulting improvement in the employment situation of the Puerto Rican labor force was short-lived and came to a sudden halt in the summer of 2001. A slowdown of the national economy began to show itself in the city in June and July of that year. The slump worsened in the aftermath of the terrorist attacks on September 11. By late 2001, the city was suffering again from a collapsing economy, losing more than 100,000 jobs from October through December. By the end of the year, the unemployment rate had climbed back up from less than 5 percent in May to close to 7 percent.

As in earlier recessions, the economic slump in 2001–2002 affected Puerto Rican workers more severely. The brunt of the short-term adjustments made by many service, transportation, and commerce sectors in New York after September 11 were borne by relatively unskilled laborers. A study released in November 2001 showed that the top seven occupations affected by the recession after September 11 included waiters and waitresses, cleaning and maintenance workers, retail sales persons, food preparation workers, cashiers, housekeeping workers, and fast-food servers (as reported by Eaton and Wyatt 2001). This was followed by smaller losses in more-skilled occupations, such as general managers, top executives, sales supervisors, and service supervisors. The comparatively low educational attainment of Puerto Rican New Yorkers made Puerto Rican workers more prone to be laid off or fired.

The unemployment problem confronting the Puerto Rican population in the 1990s was more severe among women. In March–April 1999, the unemployment rate among Puerto Rican women was 10.9 percent, compared to 7.7 percent among men. This is a pattern that holds as well for the overall New York City economy, where the unemployment rate for the same time period was 5.6 percent among men and 7.5 percent among women. It is not a pattern reproduced at the national level, where male and female unemployment rates are virtually identical.

The unemployment crisis facing Puerto Rican women, combined with lower relative earnings, is one of the key factors linked to Puerto Rican economic distress. A rising fraction of the Puerto Rican labor force now consists of women. The labor force participation rates among Puerto Rican women rose sharply in the 1990s while those of men shrunk. In 1990, Puerto Rican women had a labor force participation rate of 43.3 percent, which rose to 47.6 percent by 1999. Among Puerto Rican men, however, the labor force participation rate dropped from 67.4 percent to 63.7 percent during the same time period. This gender pattern of changes in labor force participation rates cuts across racial and ethnic lines and holds for the overall New York City economy as well.

The higher female unemployment rates in the New York labor market has a magnified impact on the status of Puerto Ricans because of the major importance of female-headed households (where a woman is the head of household, with no male present) among this population. Table 8 shows that in the year 2000, close to 37 percent of all Puerto Ricans in New York City were living in female-headed households. Although this remains below the rate for the Dominican population (which was about 43 percent), it is substantially above that for other groups in the population. For instance, only 9.3 percent of non-Hispanic White New Yorkers resided in female headed households in the year 2000.

Because of the relatively high proportion of female-headed households among Puerto Ricans, the adverse labor market conditions facing female workers in New York City in the 1990s had a disproportionately negative impact on Puerto Rican New Yorkers. The average annual household income per capita among female-headed households in New York was $11,359 in the year 2001. Among other households, the per capita income was $27,295. Similarly, the poverty rate among female-headed households in New York in the year 2001 was 34.2 percent, compared to 12.9 percent among other households. These inequities cut across racial and ethnic lines. For instance, among White New Yorkers, female-headed households had an average annual per capita income of $19,194, but other households had an income per capita of $36,113.

The Role of Education and Experience in Economic Progress among New Yorkers

The Puerto Rican labor force was more deeply affected by the labor market situation in New York during the 1990s because of its comparatively low educational attainment. With labor demand for college graduates and professionals expanding rapidly, and rates of return to higher education increasing in the 1990s, Puerto Rican workers lagged in both employment and earnings.

Table 9 shows the proportion of Puerto Rican New Yorkers twenty-five years of age or older with a college diploma or greater in 1999, compared to other racial and ethnic groups in the city. Approximately 11 percent of Puerto Ricans twenty-five years of age or older had a college degree in 1999, compared to about 32 percent among New Yorkers in general and 45 percent among White Americans. The educational attainment of the Puerto Rican population did increase significantly in the 1990s. The proportion with a college degree or more rose from less than 7 percent in 1990 to close to 11 percent in 1999. But the educational gap between Puerto Ricans and the White population has grown. The proportion of Puerto Ricans with a college degree rose by close to 4 percentage points in the 1990s but the non-Hispanic White population completing college rose by more than 11 percentage points.

TABLE 10

EARNINGS AND EDUCATION IN NYC AND US, 2000

Full-time workers

Population Group	Annual Earnings in 2000 dollars	
	New York	United States
Less than high school	20,998	19,789
High school degree	28,517	27,654
Some college education	33,826	32,756
College degree	50,205	50,802
More than college degree	87,158	72,663
Average Earnings in 2000	42,843	37,052

Source: Data from the March 2001 CPS.

The rising gap in educational credentials is crucial in determining the lower socioeconomic status of Puerto Rican New Yorkers. Table 10 shows the rate of return to education in New York City and in the United States. The table presents the average annual pay received by full-time workers in the year 2000. Among New Yorkers with less than a high school diploma, the average earnings were $20,998, while for persons with more than a college education (professional or postgraduate degrees), the earnings were $87,158, on average. By comparison, in the United States overall, the earnings of those with more than a college degree were $19,789, while those with more than a college education received $72,663. The rates of return to levels of education above high school are generally higher in New York than elsewhere.

The economic returns to labor market experience are also greater in New York, which also helps explain the lower socioeconomic status of Puerto Ricans in the city, a population that is relatively young. In 2000, the average age of Puerto Ricans in New York was thirty-two, compared to thirty-six for the city overall, and forty-one for the non-Hispanic White population. Since workers with more experience also have higher earnings and lower unemployment rates, this shortfall in age accounts for part of the lower socioeconomic status of Puerto Ricans compared to other groups in New York City. On the other hand, as was noted earlier, the age differentials between Puerto Ricans and the rest of the city population have been diminishing over time and can only account for a small portion of the earnings gap.

Summary and Conclusions
The 1990s represented a decade of major demographic changes for Puerto Ricans in New York. For the first time since Puerto Rico became a territory of the United States, the Puerto Rican population residing in New York City declined. As a proportion of the Latino or Hispanic population in New York, the Puerto Rican population declined from 50.3 percent in 1990 to 36.5 percent in 2000. The reduction in the number of Puerto Rican New Yorkers is explained by three major forces: a gradual drop of Puerto Rican migration to the United States in the last three decades, massive migration of Puerto Ricans out of the city (to suburbs, to other states of the mainland, and back to the Island), and higher mortality rates associated with an aging of the Puerto Rican population that moved to New York as part of the Great Migration that occurred between 1940 and 1970.

Despite the declining population, Puerto Ricans continue to be the largest Hispanic/Latino group in New York. Furthermore, the visibility of the population in the city is greater, as Puerto Ricans are gradually becoming more dispersed among the five boroughs of New York. In 2000, a total of 40 percent of Puerto Rican New Yorkers lived in the Bronx, 27 percent in Brooklyn, 15 percent in Manhattan, 14 percent in Queens, and 4 percent in Staten Island. The impact of Puerto Ricans in New York City culture, politics, and economy thus remains undiminished.

The overall economic situation of Puerto Ricans in New York did not improve to a significant extent in the 1990s. Household income per capita remained more or less the same in 1999 as it was in 1989. Adjusted for inflation, the income per capita among Puerto Ricans grew slightly, from $10,737 to $11,893 during the period. This lack of significant economic progress reflects the overall economic situation of New York City in the

1990s. Although there was an economic boom in the period after 1996, the accelerated pace of employment creation was a mirage, as it involved mostly a recovery from what was a devastating and persistent recession in the early and mid-1990s (income per capita in New York fell by close to 20 percent between 1989 and 1993, a result of the 1988–1993 recession). The sluggish economic recovery meant that poverty rates among Puerto Ricans did not appreciably change over the decade, although they did drop from 36.5 percent in 1989 to 33.1 percent in 1999.

The unemployment rate among Puerto Rican New Yorkers in the labor force declined between 1990 and 2000, reflecting the economic recovery of the city from one of its most severe recessions of the twentieth century. The Puerto Rican unemployment rate dropped from 13.7 percent in 1990 to 9 percent in 2000, but this only happened after 1997. Before that year, the unemployment rate among Puerto Ricans hovered around 13 percent.

The socioeconomic situation facing Puerto Rican women became more difficult in the 1990s. Although Puerto Rican female labor force participation rates increased (while male rates declined), unemployment rates among women also became substantially higher than those for men, a pattern that occurred citywide. Because the proportion of female-headed households is higher among Puerto Ricans (37 percent of all Puerto Ricans resided in female-headed households in 2000), the deteriorating labor market status of women in New York had a disproportionate impact on Puerto Rican women and their households.

The comparatively low educational attainment of Puerto Rican New Yorkers is also a major factor explaining the sluggish economic progress in the 1990s. The proportion of the Puerto Rican population twenty-five years of age or older with a college degree rose from about 7 to 11 percent between 1990 and 2000. This gain of 4 percentage points, however, is dwarfed by the gain of close to 12 percentage points by the corresponding non-Hispanic White population. The lagging educational credentials have had a significant impact on employment and earnings, because schooling is closely connected to performance in the labor market.

As Puerto Rican New Yorkers encountered the new century, a national economic recession, magnified by the aftermath of the September 11 terrorist attacks, tainted the prospects for future growth in the city. If one were to predict the socioeconomic impact of this economic slump on the Puerto Rican population of New York based on the previous recession in the early 1990s, the effects would be severely negative. Such predictions, however, are subject to large potential errors. If the national and international economic scenes prevailing in late 2001 and early 2002 turn around for the better, it might then be possible for Puerto Ricans to profit from sustained economic development in New York. Policy measures that provide incentives for the economic revitalization of low-income areas of the city, and greater investments in quantity and quality of education will be essential in accelerating economic progress.

Appendix: Data Sources
The research described in this chapter is based on a combination of sources. The information for 1989 and 1990 is taken from the 1990 U.S. Census of Population, with demographic data from the Census counts and economic data obtained from the 1990 Public Use Microdata Samples (PUMS). Demographic information for 2000 is from the 2000 U.S. Census of Population. Because of the limited availability of 2000 Census data, some of the figures for 1999 or 2000 are based on a combination of samples from the 1999–2001 March Current Population Surveys (CPS) and the 1999 New York City Housing and Vacancy Survey. Similarly, the data for intercensus years, say 1997, was obtained by pulling data for three consecutive years, with the midpoint represented by the year in question; so, for unemployment in 1997, the CPS data on unemployment for 1996, 1997, and 1998 was pulled together. This was carried out to increase sample sizes and reduce confidence intervals.

The 1990 PUMS data consist of a random sample of five percent of the population in New York City, with 339,789 persons in the sample. The March CPS includes a random sample of about 5,000 observations for New York City. The New York City Housing and Vacancy Survey is based on a random sample of 15,417 households, with about 50,000 persons included. Note that, even when we combine the 1999–2001 March CPS and NYC Housing surveys, the resulting sample is substantially smaller than the 1990 Census PUMS. Still, the U.S. Department of Commerce routinely uses the CPS to provide public information about the population and socioeconomic status of Americans between each decennial Census. And the 1999 NYC Housing and Vacancy Survey included a substantial sample of New Yorkers. An analysis of the two data sets (the Census versus the combined CPS/NYC Housing and Vacancy surveys) shows that they provide similar profiles. As a result, we are confident of the analysis presented in this chapter. However, we must warn that the confidence interval around each economic variable calculated for 2000 or 1999 is higher than for Census-based data.

REFERENCES

Bernstein, Nina. 1999. "Poverty Rate Persists Despite Boom." *New York Times*, October 7, p. B1.

Eaton, Leslie, and Edward Wyatt. 2001. "Attacks Hit Low-Pay Jobs the Hardest." *New York Times*, November 6, p. B-1.

Glazer, Nathan, and Daniel P. Moynihan. 1970 [1963]. *Beyond the Melting Pot: The Negroes, Puerto Ricans, Jews, Italians, and Irish of New York City*. Cambridge: The MIT Press.

Gutierrez, Elias. 1977. *Factor Proportions, Technology Transmission and Unemployment in Puerto Rico*. Rio Piedras: University of Puerto Rico Press.

Haslip-Viera, Gabriel, and Sherrie L. Baver, eds. 1996. *Latinos in New York: Communities in Transition*. Notre Dame, IN: University of Notre Dame Press.

Hernández, Ramona, Francisco L. Rivera-Batíz, and Roberto Agodini. 1995. *Dominican New Yorkers: A Socioeconomic Profile*. New York: Dominican Research Monographs, CUNY Dominican Studies Institute.

Hernández, Ramona, and Francisco L. Rivera-Batíz. 1997. *Dominican New Yorkers: A Socioeconomic Profile, 1997*. New York: Dominican Research Monographs, CUNY Dominican Studies Institute.

Hispanic Federation. 1999. *Hispanic New Yorkers: A Profile of the Puerto Rican Community, Seventh Annual Hispanic Federation Survey*. New York: Hispanic Federation.

Kershaw, Sarah. 2000. "Led by Staten Island, New York City Grew in 1999, Census Reports." *New York Times*, March 9, pp. B1, B12.

Lemann, Nicholas. 1991. "The Other Underclass." *Atlantic Monthly*, December, pp. 96–110.

Massey, Douglas, Rafael Alarcón, Jorge Durand and Humberto González. 1987. *Return to Aztlán: The Social Process of International Migration from Western Mexico*. Berkeley: University of California Press.

Meléndez, Edwin. 1996. "Hispanics and Wage Inequality in New York City," in *Latinos in New York: Communities in Transition*, Gabriel Haslip-Viera and Sherrie L. Baver, eds. Pp. 189–210. Notre Dame, IN: University of Notre Dame Press.

_____. 1998. "The Economic Development of El Barrio," in *Borderless Borders: US Latinos, Latin Americans and the Paradox of Interdependence*, Frank Bonilla, Edwin Meléndez, Rebecca Morales and María de los Angeles Torres, eds. Pp. 105–127. Philadelphia: Temple University Press.

Navarro, Mireya. 2000. "Puerto Rican Presence Wanes in New York." *New York Times*, February 28, pp. A1, B7.

New York City Department of City Planning. 1994. *Puerto Rican New Yorkers in 1990*, DCP 94-09. New York (September).

_____. 1995. *Population Projections for the Year 2000*. New York (March).

_____. 1996. *The Newest New Yorkers, 1990–1994*, DCP 96-19. New York (December).

_____. 1999a. *1998 Annual Report on Social Indicators*, NYC DCP 99-05. New York.

_____. 1999b. *The Newest New Yorkers, 1995–1996*, DCP 99–08. New York (September).

New York City Department of Housing Preservation and Development. 1999. *1999 New York City Housing and Vacancy Survey*. New York: New York City Department of Housing Preservation and Development.

Powers, Mary G., and John J. Macisco, Jr. 1982. *Los Puertorriquenos en Nueva York: Un Analisís de su Participacion Laboral y Experiencia Migratoria*. Rio Piedras: Centro de Investigaciones Sociales, Universidad de Puerto Rico.

Rivera-Batíz, Francisco L. 1992. "Quantitative Literacy and the Likelihood of Employment Among Young Adults." *Journal of Human Resources* 27: 2 (spring): 313–328.

_____. 1994. "The Multicultural Population of New York City: A Socioeconomic Profile of the Mosaic," in *Reinventing Urban Education: Multiculturalism and the Social Context of Schooling*, Francico L. Rivera-Batíz, ed. Pp. 23–67. New York: IUME Press, Teachers College, Columbia University.

_____. 2002a. "The Socioeconomic Status of Hispanic New Yorkers: Current Trends and Future Prospects." Pew Hispanic Center Study, University of Southern California Annenberg School for Communication. Los Angeles, CA (January).

_____. 2002b. "The Impact of Education and Experience on Labor Market Outcomes: The Case of New York City." Mimeo, Program in Economic Policy Management, Columbia University. New York (March).

Rivera-Batíz, Francisco L. and Carlos E. Santiago. 1994. *Puerto Ricans in the United States: A Changing Reality*. Washington, DC: National Puerto Rican Coalition.

_____. 1996. *Island Paradox: Puerto Rico in the 1990s*. New York: Russell Sage Foundation.

Rodríguez, Clara E. 1979. "Economic Factors Affecting Puerto Ricans in New York," in *Labor Migration Under Capitalism: The Puerto Rican Experience*, Centro de Estudios Puertorriqueños, History Task Force, ed. Pp. 197–221. New York: Monthly Review Press.

_____. 1989. *Puerto Ricans: Born in the U.S.A.* Boston: Unwin Hyman.

Sánchez Korrol, Virginia E. 1994. *From Colonia to Community: The History of Puerto Ricans in New York City*. Berkeley: University of California Press.

Scott, Janny. 2001. "Sociologist Offers New Estimates of City Hispanic Census Groups." *New York Times*, July 6, p. B1.

Sullivan Mercer. 1993. "Puerto Ricans in Sunset Park, Brooklyn: Poverty Amidst Ethnic and Economic Diversity," in *In the Barrios: Latinos and the Underclass Debate*, Joan Moore and Raquel Pinderhughes, eds. Pp. 1–25. New York: Russell Sage Foundation.

Suro, Roberto. 1998. *Strangers Among Us: How Latino Immigration is Transforming America*. New York: Alfred A. Knopf.

Tienda, Marta. 1989. "Puerto Ricans and the Underclass Debate." *Annals of the American Academy of Political and Social Science* 501 (January): 105–19.

Torres, Andres. 1995. *Between Melting Pot and Mosaic: African Americans and Puerto Ricans in the New York Political Economy*. Philadelphia: Temple University Press.

U.S. Department of Commerce. *Current Population Survey*. Washington, DC: U.S. Bureau of the Census (various years).

_____. 1980. *U.S. Census of Population and Housing*. Washington, DC: U.S. Bureau of the ensus.

_____. 1990. *U.S. Census of Population and Housing*. Washington, DC: U.S. Bureau of the Census.

_____. 2000a. *U.S. Census of Population and Housing*, Washington, DC: U.S. Bureau of the ensus.

_____. 2000b. *The Hispanic Population of the United States: March 1999, Population Characteristics, Current Population Reports P20-527*. Washington, DC: U.S. Bureau of the Census (February).

_____. 2000c. "Bureau of the Census, Estimates of the Population of Puerto Rico Municipios, July 1, 1999," and "Demographic Components of Population Change: April 1, 1990 to July 1" <www.census.gov/population/estimates/puerto-rico/prmunnet.txt/> (July 21).

Vázquez-Calzada, Jose L. 1979. "Demographic Aspects of Migrations," in *Labor Migration Under Capitalism: The Puerto Rican Experience*, Centro de Estudios Puertorriqueños, History Task Force, ed. Pp. 223–236. New York: Monthly Review Press.

Vega, Bernardo. 1984. *Memoirs of Bernardo Vega: A Contribution to the History of the Puerto Rican Community of New York*. New York: Monthly Review Press.

NOTES

* This chapter was originally presented as a paper at the conference on "Puerto Ricans in New York City" held at the Graduate Center of the City University of New York on September 22, 2000, sponsored by the Center for Puerto Rican Studies at Hunter College. The chapter also draws on some of my research prepared for "The Socioeconomic Status of Hispanic New Yorkers: Current Trends and Future Prospects," a project funded by the Pew Hispanic Center, University of Southern California Annenberg School for Communication, Los Angeles, California. I am thankful to Gabriel Haslip-Viera, B. Lindsay Lowell, and Roberto Suro for useful comments. I also gratefully acknowledge the efficient research assistance of Carola Sandy.

1. Although a population count is available for most ethnic and racial groups in the 2000 population, the figures provided for the Dominican population are estimates based on the analysis of Hernández and Rivera-Batíz (1997). The official Census count of Dominican New Yorkers in the year 2000 was 407,473, but most analysts consider this figure to be a severe undercount. The reason is that, in contrast to the 1990 Census questionnaire, the 2000 questionnaire was changed to exclude "Dominicans" as one of the possible answers that respondents could write in, in response to the question asking for a specific Hispanic/Latino identity (Puerto Rican, Mexican, and Cuban were included). As a result, many Dominicans chose the "other Hispanic/Latino" category. Sociologist John R. Logan has estimated the Dominican population to be 593,777 (Scott 2001). The estimate of 555,000 used in this paper is based on the 1990 Census count (which did include "Dominicans" as one of the write-in categories) plus an estimate of the increased Dominican population between 1990 and 2000 based on natural population growth and Dominican immigration rates in the 1990s. See Hernández, Rivera-Batíz, and Agodini (1995),

and Hernández and Rivera-Batíz (1997).
2. The massive influx of immigrants to New York City is well known. It has led to a population that is close to 40 percent foreign-born. The number of immigrants intending to settle in New York City in the period of 1990 to 1996 was 794,000, according to the data [see New York City Department of City Planning (1996, 1999b)]. Of these, more than 200,000 were Hispanic immigrants originating in Latin America and the Caribbean, with close to 150,000 from the Dominican Republic alone.
3. See, for example, Sullivan (1993).
4. The income shortfall of Puerto Ricans relative to other ethnic and racial groups in New York, including the non-Hispanic Black population has persisted for decades; see Rodríguez (1979, 1989), Powers and Macisco (1982), Tienda (1989), Rivera-Batíz (1994), Rivera-Batíz and Santiago (1994), Torres (1995), and Meléndez (1996, 1998) for documentation of these income gaps going back to 1960.
5 See Tienda (1989), Lemann (1991), Rivera-Batíz (1994), Torres (1995), and Suro (1998).
6 See Rivera-Batíz (1992).
7. A multiple regression analysis of the annual earnings of New Yorkers and those of Americans in general shows that rates of return to education above high school are generally higher in New York than elsewhere. So are the rates of return to years of labor market experience (see Rivera-Batíz 2002b).
8. See Rivera-Batíz (2002a).

Mural painting on the facade of an apartment building in El Barrio (East Harlem), depicting the daily life of Puero Rican New Yorkers, which was restored in the 1990's. *(Photo by Angelo Falcón)*

COMMENTARY

BORICUAS IN 1990S NEW YORK: A DECADE OF ACCOMPLISHMENTS AND DISAPPOINTMENTS

Gabriel Haslip-Viera

In his essay "Puerto Rican New Yorkers in the 1990s: A Demographic and Socioeconomic Profile," Francisco Rivera-Batíz provides a relatively brief but useful outline that broadly focuses on the demographic and socioeconomic status of Puerto Ricans in New York City during the 1990s. Based almost exclusively on data from the United States Department of Commerce and the New York Department of City Planning, he provides much useful information on the continued migration of Puerto Ricans to New York, and the increased dispersal of this community within the city and surrounding suburbs.[1] Rivera-Batíz also imparts valuable data on per capita income, labor participation rates, rates of employment, and unemployment, and also discusses the economic opportunities that Puerto Ricans had in periods when New York City experienced an economic recession (1989–1993), a recovery (1993–1999), and another economic recession (1999–2000 and beyond). His research and the conclusions based on his findings can be a starting point for additional, badly needed, and more specific follow- up research on the Puerto Rican community that should focus on social, economic, and political issues not covered in his essay. Unfortunately, social scientists and even

---

The writer is especially indebted to Angelo Falcón, who provided invaluable advice and assistance in the drafting and editing of these comments.

journalists have been inclined to neglect or ignore these issues—especially in recent years.

Overall, the 1990s were a mixed period of accomplishment and disappointment for Puerto Ricans in New York City. As noted by Rivera-Batíz, the city's Puerto Rican population began to decline for the first time and Puerto Ricans were no longer the majority of its Latino population. Despite this, Puerto Ricans were still able to maintain their position as the largest Latino subgroup in the city. Puerto Ricans in the lower middle class were buying houses and cooperative apartments in rejuvenated parts of the South Bronx and in neighborhoods not traditionally associated with Puerto Ricans and other Latinos. Others were also leaving the city altogether and establishing themselves in Florida or in the surrounding New York City suburbs. There was even a move back to El Barrio and the Lower East Side of Manhattan by a number of Puerto Rican professionals and persons in the arts. These more affluent individuals purchased apartments and row houses, established restaurants, and revived or created cultural institutions, such as the Nuyorican Poet's Café in the Lower East Side and the Julia de Burgos Cultural Center in El Barrio. However, despite this seemingly positive development, the movement back to El Barrio and the Lower East Side also came under increasing criticism because of its connection to an apparent "gentrification" process that also involved the displacement of less affluent Puerto Ricans and other minorities, and the movement of wealthier Anglo Americans into these neighborhoods.[2] Nevertheless, the Lower East Side, and especially El Barrio, seemed poised for a cultural renaissance as the twenty-first century began.

The Puerto Rican presence in the entertainment media and advertising continued to be a controversial issue throughout the 1990s. Marc Anthony, Ricky Martin, Jennifer López, Big Pun, Fat Joe, and other mostly "Nuyorican" singers and rappers became notable success stories or crossover phenomena in hip-hop, salsa, and other forms of popular music. Jennifer López, along with Jimmy Smits, Rosie Pérez, Esai Morales, Michael DeLorenzo, Luis Gúzman, and other "Nuyorican" actors, also created successful careers for themselves in films, such as *My Family* (1995), *Selena* (1997), *It Could Happen to You* (1994), or in television programs such as *L.A. Law*, *NYPD Blue*, and *New York Undercover*.[3] Some of the Hollywood and independent films of the 1990s were also written or based on stories by New York Puerto Ricans. These included the acclaimed independent film *Hanging with the Homeboys* (1991) by the late Joseph B. Vázquez, and the Hollywood films *Q &A* (1990) and *Carlito's Way* (1993), which were based on stories written by New York State Supreme Court Justice Edwin Torres.[4]

These success stories and other phenomena in the entertainment business also generated criticism from several quarters. Too many of the Hollywood films and television programs continued to promote negative stereotypes about Puerto Ricans and other Latinos. For example, *Q & A* and *Carlito's Way* focused on Puerto Rican involvement in the drug trade and other criminal activities.[5] The singer Paul Simon also resurrected the notorious 1950s murder and street gang story of Salvador Agrón in the short-lived and controversial 1996 Broadway musical *Capeman*.[6] There was also the notorious trashing and burning of the Puerto Rican flag in the May 7, 1998, episode of *Seinfeld*, a popular situation comedy that aired on national television throughout the 1990s.

Commercial television, advertising, and print media also came under criticism for their alleged racism in the portrayal of Puerto Ricans and other Latinos. Critics noted that except for well-known sports figures and entertainment personalities, there were hardly any "darker" or "African-looking" Puerto Ricans and other Latinos in both English- and Spanish-language media and advertising.[7] Television programmers, advertisers, and magazine publishers were also accused of consistently promoting a simplistic "off white" or "Mediterranean" image for Puerto Ricans and other Latinos, or "at worst," the stereotype of a mixed, light-skinned *mestizo* (European/Native American or "Indian").[8]

In addition to the accomplishments in popular culture and the arts, the 1990s also witnessed the establishment of the Hispanic Federation of New York City, a new instrument for community organizing and development. The Hispanic Federation was created with support from the United Way of New York City, which had been criticized for years for not being responsive to the needs of the city's Puerto Rican and Latino communities. Utilizing the United Way model, the federation was able to disburse more than $750,000 in annual grants to its organizational members by the end of the decade. Despite this accomplishment, the Hispanic Federation's leadership also came under internal criticism because of its links to the Puerto Rican political network in the Bronx, which defined its agenda from the start. This connection between partisan political interests and the federation's role as a nonpartisan and nonprofit advocacy organization created problems for its mission that easily gave rise to charges of conflict of interest and favoritism in the distribution of grants. Nevertheless, and despite these problems, the federation became yet another model for the organization of Puerto Ricans and Latinos in New York City. It also perpetuated a leadership model replicated among other Latino organizations, where the clients were largely non–Puerto Rican Latinos and the leadership was almost entirely Puerto Rican. However, despite the establishment of new funding and leadership mechanisms, Puerto Rican organizations continued to struggle to keep their doors open throughout the 1990s. The National Puerto Rican Forum went through particularly hard times during this period, but rebounded after the year 2000. Others, like the Puerto Rican Association for Community Affairs (PRACA), one of the oldest and largest Puerto Rican organizations, had to temporarily close its doors by the end of the decade, and is currently struggling to maintain itself along with other organizations, such as the Puerto Rican Legal Defense and Education Fund (PRLDEF).[9]

The leadership of some of the major Puerto Rican organizations underwent important changes. In the early part of the decade, the founding director of the Center for Puerto Rican Studies at Hunter College (El Centro"), Dr. Frank Bonilla, ended his more than twenty-year stewardship of that institution. In a rancorous search process, a replacement was named in 1994, but the Centro remained in turmoil for the rest of the decade.[10] Louis Nuñez, the founding director of the National Puerto Rican Coalition, also retired in 1994 and was replaced by Manuel Mirabal, whose tenure has now lasted for more than ten years. The National Puerto Rican Forum also had major leadership problems throughout the decade, culminating in the selection of a non–Puerto Rican director, an African, who stabilized its finances and continued to head this flagship community organization into the next decade. In 1993, the Puerto Rican Legal Defense and Education Fund, which had had leadership stability problems for some time, selected Juan A. Figueroa, a former Connecticut state legislator, as its president and general counsel, a position that he also held for close to ten years.

Because of major changes in the city's political structure, and despite an increasingly hostile political climate, the number of Puerto Rican elected officials actually increased during the early years of the decade. These changes included the restructuring of city government as a result of a lawsuit that found the city in violation of the Constitution's one-person, one-vote principle. This finding resulted, in part, in the expansion of the city council from thirty-five to fifty-one seats, and this enabled Puerto Ricans to increase their representation on that body from three to nine by the year 2000. Puerto Ricans were also able to consolidate their hold on political power in the Bronx during this period. In addition to the congressional seat held by José E. Serrano, the borough presidency and the leadership position of the Bronx County Democratic organization also came under Puerto Rican control.[11]

The political restructuring and redistricting battles of the early 1990s had other beneficial results. Nydia Velázquez became the second Puerto Rican (and first female Boricua) to be elected to the U.S. Congress, representing parts of Brooklyn, Manhattan, and Queens. In Chicago, a third Puerto Rican, Luis Gutíerrez, was also elected to Congress. Along with José Serrano of the South Bronx, this three-person delegation became a crucial factor in the debates that took place on the political status of Puerto Rico, the U.S. naval presence on the island of Vieques, and the release of the Puerto Rican political prisoners in the late 1990s.

The expansion of the stateside Puerto Rican delegation to the U.S. Congress also coincided with the return of a pro-statehood government in Puerto Rico. The Pedro Rosselló administration dismantled the cabinet-level Department of Puerto Rican Affairs in the United States and downsized it to the Puerto Rican Federal Affairs Administration, transferring its headquarters from New York City to Washington, DC. This began a campaign by Rosselló to circumvent the stateside Puerto Rican political leadership, which was viewed as antagonistic to the statehood movement. As he tried to generate support from conservative Cuban and Mexican American politicians in other parts of the country, his relationship with Velázquez, Gutíerrez, and other stateside politicians remained tense throughout this tenure.[12]

The rise to prominence of Puerto Rican labor leader Dennis Rivera was another important political development of the 1990s. Rivera became a major political force in city and state politics after he was elected president of Local 1199 of the Health and Hospital Workers Union in 1989. He was also pivotal in supporting Puerto Rican political leadership in New York City and Puerto Rico, and he became a major link to the national Democratic Party and national Black leaders such as Jesse Jackson and influential former Congressman Kweisi Mfume, the current head of the NAACP. This role for Puerto Ricans in the labor movement was a new development in the history of this community.

The administration of David Dinkins, the first mayoral administration led by an African American, began with great promise in 1990. Dinkins and his political organizers were able to establish a broad based coalition of African Americans, "white liberals," Puerto Ricans, and other minorities to defeat former federal prosecutor Rudolph Giuliani, in the 1989 election. In actuality, the alliance between Blacks and Puerto Ricans was quite an achievement because Dinkins was part of a group of Black political leaders that had sabotaged former Congressman Herman Badillo's 1984 campaign to become the first Puerto Rican mayor of New York City.[13] Despite this achievement, Dinkins was never able to develop the kind of cohesive political alliance established by Chicago mayor, Harold Washington, in the mid-1980s. Although Puerto Ricans were appointed to positions in city government in significant numbers, with at one point, two deputy mayors, the Dinkins administration turned out to be a major disappointment. The Black and Puerto Rican political coalition that helped elect Dinkins held together when Giuliani defeated Dinkins in 1993, but the enthusiasm that Dinkins generated in 1989 had waned significantly, and this depressed voter turnout, which was a crucial factor in his defeat in the close 1993 election.

During his 1993 campaign, Rudolph Giuliani actively sought the support of Puerto Ricans and other Latinos, but this was rightly seen at the time as a political ploy by most observers.[14] Nevertheless, Giuliani was able to generate support from a loose coalition of "Giulianistas," headed symbolically by the embittered, politically frustrated, and increasingly conservative Herman Badillo. After Giuliani was elected mayor, Badillo remained behind the scenes as a political liaison and advisor. However, Giuliani appointed several Puerto Ricans and other Latinos to his administration, including Ninfa Segarra, who became deputy mayor for health and social services, Ruben Franco, who became chairman of the New York City Housing Authority, and Luís Miranda, who was appointed chair of the city's Health and Hospitals Corporation. As it turned out, many of these individuals resigned or were forced to relinquish their jobs within a relatively brief period of time. However, Ninfa Segarra stayed on for Giuliani's two terms as mayor.[15] Derided as "unqualified" and "widely perceived as the least influential of Giuliani's deputy mayors,"[16] Segarra followed Giuliani like an obedient puppy as he cut or decimated agencies and programs of importance to Puerto Ricans and other minorities.

Early in his administration, Giuliani began to undercut the effectiveness of the Equal Employment Practices Commission, and eliminated the set-aside program for minority vendors who had contracts with the city. He also undermined the effectiveness of the Police Department Civilian Complaint Review Board (CCRB) in an era when complaints of police brutality were increasing. Giuliani's dismissive criticism of the CCRB and his arrogant, confrontational style led to unnecessary and contentious squabbles over the deaths of Anthony Báez and Amadou Diallo and the torture of Abner Louima, among other public controversies involving the police.[17] Guided by the ideology of the right-wing conservative Manhattan Institute for Public Policy and utilizing the periodic shortfall in the city's budget as an excuse, Giuliani also began to cut the budgets of the Board of Education, the Human Resources Administration, the Administration for Children's Services, and the Department of Homeless Services, among other agencies serving predominantly poor and minority constituents. Giuliani even supported reductions in federal and state programs such as Medicaid, while he supported tax cuts for corporations and wealthy individuals proposed in 1993 by the new Republican Party majority in Congress, and by their like-minded ally, George Pataki, who was elected governor of New York in 1994. Using a blunderbuss approach to the problem of social services in general, Giuliani went after real and alleged "freeloaders" and "welfare cheats"—priding himself on having slashed the city's welfare roles and placing the "freeloaders" in a newly instituted workfare program. But as journalist Wayne Barrett put it, Giuliani's welfare cuts also harmed "tens of thousands of the legitimate poor in a feverish hunt for the illegitimate" (Barrett 2000: 11)

The administration of the New York City public schools also became more politicized during Giuliani's tenure. The problem of the revolving chancellorships, which dated back to the 1980s, actually worsened during the 1990s. A total of four chancellors came and went during the course of the decade, each with a new set of ideas for improving the deteriorating system. The decade began with Chancellor Joseph Fernández, a Puerto Rican, who was ousted in 1993 when Ninfa Segarra, a previously "liberal" board member, joined hostile conservatives to vote against his reappointment.[18] Fernández was followed by Mexican American Ramón Cortines, the African American Rudy Crew, and finally by Harold Levy, a corporate businessperson selected by a newly defiant and energized board, over Giuliani's objections. All three of these individuals became involved in confrontational disputes with Giuliani or his surrogate, Segarra, at one point or another during Giuliani's tenure.[19] In the meantime, students in the public school system continued to suffer as political infighting became more contentious and the system deteriorated further.

Giuliani also launched a campaign against the mostly minority students of the City University of New York that lasted for most of his eight years as mayor. Early in his administration, he cut the city's contribution to the university's budget by 17 percent, and in 1995, he supported Pataki's proposed tuition increase by saying that it would be beneficial if it encouraged more students to work, thus "preparing them for the rest of their lives" (Barrett 2000: 310). In taking this position, Giuliani seemed to ignore the reality that most students in the City University were already compelled to work because of their relative poverty, and he also conveniently forgot his own mostly jobless days as an undergraduate at Manhattan College, the conservative Catholic school he attended in the early 1960s. During the final years of his administration, Giuliani also called for an end to most remedial programs in the City University, despite the fact that such programs existed at most colleges and universities, including quite a number of the elite institutions. He also used Herman Badillo, who was appointed chair of the CUNY Board of Trustees, to influence or guide the implementation of these changes.

Overall, Giuliani usually took a hostile and confrontational stance when dealing with issues of concern or importance to Puerto Ricans and other minorities. Unfortunately and with few exceptions, the Puerto Rican/Latino elected officials were not up to the task of challenging Giuliani or Pataki when they attacked government agencies and programs of importance to Puerto Ricans and other minorities. With the exception of Fernando Ferrer,

Nydia Velázquez, and José Serrano, who on occasion protested the actions and policies of the Giuliani administration in public, Puerto Rican legislators such as Efraín González, Olga Méndez, Nellie Santiago, Victor Robles, Rubén Díaz Sr., and others said little or remained silent on important issues such as police brutality, abuses against the homeless, deteriorating schools, and the rise of tuition for Puerto Rican and Latino students at the City University. Overall, there seemed to be no visibility or unity among these individuals when it came to articulating positions or applying pressure on the Giuliani or Pataki administrations. This was in contrast to the generally unified and vocal positions that these same politicians took when they focused on issues of importance to Puerto Rican islanders, such as Vieques, or the island's political status.

In general, Puerto Rican scholars and writers paid little attention to the economic and social issues of critical importance to New York's Puerto Rican community during the 1990s. Employment, housing, homelessness, health care, crime, police brutality, city politics, and the politics surrounding the education of Puerto Ricans and other Latinos did not received the kind of attention they deserved.[20] Instead, many of the writings focused on theoretical issues connected to race, identity, popular culture, and related topics. Frequently adopting the politically safe or fashionable positions and ideas articulated by "postmodernists" and "postcolonialists" (etc.), the most recent (and not so recent) generation of academics published articles in journals and edited volumes with titles such as "Tropicalizations: Transcultural Representation of Latinidad (Re-Encounters with Colonialism)," "Puerto Rican Identity Up in the Air: Air Migration, Its cultural Representations and Me 'Cruzando el Charco,'" and "Ambiguous Identities! The Affirmation of Puertorriqueñidad in the Community Murals of New York City."[21]

Too often these writing were rendered unintelligible to the general reader because of the reliance on ideas and jargon fashionable among postmodernists and other specialists in "cultural studies." The overreliance on and occasional misuse of terms, phrases and concepts such as "discourse," "archaeology,"[22] "narratology," "liminality," "commodification," "subjectivization" and the specialized use of ordinary words, such as "representation," "space," "location," "agency," "meaning," and "memory," generally required a substantial understanding of "postmodernist" ideas and styles of writing.[23] These writers were also inclined to minimize the importance of or failed to engage the relatively few writers who focused on concrete policy issues of migration, employment, health care, city politics and the other issues of economic and social importance to Puerto Ricans and other Latinos. There also was an often abstract and detached quality in much of this writing that failed to illuminate the real day-to-day lives of people in our communities.[24]

With few exceptions, Puerto Ricans and other Latinos in journalism also paid insufficient attention to the issues that affected the daily lives of Puerto Rican New Yorkers and other Latinos during this period, and this was especially true of newspeople in the English-language media. The *New York Times*, the so-called newspaper of record, published only occasional reports on Puerto Ricans and other Latinos in the 1990s, and more often than not, these articles focused on popular culture, or they interpreted social and economic issues from a self-serving elitist or negative perspective. In retrospect, there was probably very little that could have been expected from the Anglo-American media during this period—especially from the conservative New York newspaper and television outlets such as the *Daily News*, the *New York Post*, Fox Television, UPN, and even WCBS, WNBC and WABC, with their inordinate emphasis on reports dealing with violent or sensationalist crimes committed by Blacks, Puerto Ricans and other Latinos.[25] In contrast, the Spanish-language newspapers, as opposed to Spanish-language television, appeared to be more committed to the publication of reports on issues of economic and social importance to our communities. Unfortunately, and with few exceptions, the articles in these newspapers were inclined to be superficial, or they failed to probe the issues in sufficient depth.[26]

Hopefully, in the future, academics, local journalists, and other writers will increase their focus on the bread-and-butter issues that affect Puerto Ricans and other Latinos and approach these issues with greater depth and sophistication. Academics, in particular, have the potential to achieve this goal. However, too few mainland Puerto Ricans are being trained to be professional social scientists and socially committed writers, and too many of these individuals become (or are encouraged to become) interested in the more fashionable and politically safe issues connected to identity, popular culture, and the arts. Quite a number of the professionally trained Puerto Rican islanders have also come to New York and other mainland communities since the 1980s, but too many of these individuals have focused their research on identity and other issues connected to "postmodernism" and "cultural studies." Well-meaning Puerto Ricans and other Latinos, trained as journalists, also face serious obstacles connected to corporate dominance and control over English- and Spanish-language print, radio, and televisions media. Conservative Latino or Anglo-American editors and producers, who are beholden to the corporate owners of major media outlets, are able to exercise control over the content, publication, and broadcasting of reports and stories on Puerto Ricans and other Latinos. At the same time, alternative media have been too few, or have failed to generate a wide enough readership or audience. Between 1994 and 1997, the Institute for Puerto Rican Policy published the short-lived *Crítica: A Journal of Puerto Rican Policy and Politics* with its hard-hitting analyses and exposés. New York listener supported radio also aired *Latino Journal,* and television stations such as NBC and ABC continued to broadcast *Visiones* and *Tiempo.* However, these types of publications and programs were consistently marginalized and were never able to circulate sufficiently, or reach a significant number of listeners and viewers in the Puerto Rican/Latino community.[27] Although the history of the past decade demonstrates that progress in the area of print, radio, and television journalism was slow, limited, or nonexistent, the hope is that a new generation of Puerto Rican and Latino media professionals will be able to make significant inroads in this area with support from Puerto Rican/Latino politicians, community leaders, and the community at large.

REFERENCES

Acosta-Belén, Edna, Margarita Benítez, José E. Cruz, Yvonne González-Rodríguez, Clara E. Rodríguez, Carlos E. Santiago, Azara Santiago-Rivera, and Barbara R. Sjostrom, eds. 2000. *"Adiós, Borinquen querida": The Puerto Rican Diaspora, Its History, and Contributions.* Albany: CELAC, State University of New York at Albany.

Aparicio Frances R. 1998. *Listening to Salsa: Gender, Latin Popular Music, and Puerto Rican Cultures.* Hanover, NH: Wesleyan University Press, 1998.

Aparicio, Frances R. and Susana Chávez-Silverman, eds. 1997. *Tropicalizations: Transcultural Representations of Latinidad* (Re-encounters with Colonialism). Hanover, NH: University Press of New England.

Aparicio, Frances R., and Candida F. Jáquez, eds. 2003. *Musical Migrations, Transnationalism and Cultural Hybridity in Latino/a America.* New York: Palgrave.

Arian, Asher, Arthur S. Goldberg, John H. Mollenkopf, and Edward T. Rogowsky. 1991. *Changing New York City Politics.* New York: Routledge.

Barrett, Wayne. 2000. *Rudy: An Investigative Biography of Rudolph Giuliani.* New York: Basic Books.

Berger, Joseph. 2002. "A Puerto Rican Rebirth in El Barrio." *New York Times,* December 10, B1, 8.

Cardalda Sánchez, Elsa B., and Amílcar Tirado Avilés. 2001. "Ambiguous Identities! The Affirmation of Puertorriqueñidad in the Community Murals of New York City, in *Mambo Montage: The Latinization of New York.* Agustín Laó-Montes and Arlene Dávila, eds. Pp. 263–286. New York: Columbia University Press.

Dávila, Arlene. 2001. *Latinos, Inc.: The Marketing and Making of a People.* Berkeley: University of California Press.

_____. 2003. "Barrio Dreams: Housing and Gentrification in El Barrio." *Centro Journal* 15:1 (2003): 112–137.

Díaz-Stevens, Ana María. 1993. *Oxcart Catholicism on Fifth Avenue: The Impact of the*

Puerto Rican Migration upon the Archdiocese of New York. Notre Dame, IN: University of Notre Dame Press.

Duany, Jorge. 2002. *The Puerto Rican Nation on the Move: Identities on the Island and in the United States.* Chapel Hill: University of North Carolina Press.

Fernández, Joseph A. 1993. *Tales Out of School: Joseph Fernandez's Crusade to Rescue American Education.* Boston: Little, Brown.

Flores, Juan. 1993. *Divided Borders: Essays on Puerto Rican Identity.* Houston: Arte Publico Press.

———. 2000. *From Bomba to Hip-Hop: Puerto Rican Culture and Latino Identity.* New York: Columbia University Press.

García Coll, Cynthia, and Lamberty Gontran. 1994. *Puerto Rican Women and Children: Issues of Health, Growth and Development.* New York: Plenum.

Grosfoguel, Ramón. 2003. *Colonial Subjects: Puerto Ricans in a Global Perspective.* Berkeley: University of California Press.

Haslip Viera, Gabriel. 1994. "El Centro de Estudios Puertorriqueños: An Uncertain Future?" *Critica: A Journal of Puerto Rican Policy and Politics* 5 (October): 1, 6–7.

———, ed. 2001. *Taíno Revival: Critical Perspectives on Puerto Rican Identity and Cultural Politics.* Princeton, NJ: Markus Wiener and Centro de Estudios Puertorriqueños.

Kirtzman, Andrew. 2000. *Rudy Giuliani: Emperor of the City.* New York: William Morrow.

Laó, Agustín. 1995. "Islands at the Crossroads: Puerto Ricanness Traveling between the Translocal Nation and the Global City," in *Puerto Rican Jam: Essays on Culture and Politics.* Frances Negrón-Muntaner and Ramón Grosfoguel, eds. Pp. 169–188. Minneapolis: University of Minnesota Press.

Laó-Montes, Agustín, and Arlene Dávila, eds. 2001. *Mambo Montage: The Latinization of New York.* New York: Columbia University Press.

Morales, Ed. 2002. *Living in Spanglish: The Search for Latino Identity.* New York: St Martin's Press.

Muñiz, Vicky. 1998. *Resisting Gentrification and Displacement: Voices of Puerto Rican Women of the Barrio.* New York: Garland Publishing.

Negrón Muntaner, Frances, and Ramón Grosfoguel, eds. 1995. *Puerto Rican Jam: Essays on Culture and Politics.* Minneapolis: University of Minnesota Press.

Nieto, Sonia, ed. 2000. *Puerto Rican Students in U.S. Schools.* Mahwah, NJ: Lawrence Erlbaum.

Ortíz, Altagracia, ed. 1996. *Puerto Rican Women and Work: Bridges in Transnational Labor.* Philadelphia: Temple University Press.

Rivera, Raquel Z. 2003. *New York Ricans from the Hip Hop Zone.* New York: Palgrave Macmillan.

Rivera-Batíz, Francisco L., and Carlos E. Santiago. 1994. *Puerto Ricans in the United States: A Changing Reality.* Washington, DC: National Puerto Rican Coalition.

———. 1996. *Island Paradox: Puerto Rico in the 1990s.* New York: Russell Sage Foundation.

Rodríguez, Camille, and Ramón Bosque Pérez, eds. 1995. *Puerto Ricans and Higher Education Policies: Issues of Scholarship, Fiscal Policies and Admissions.* New York:

Centro de Estudios Puertorriqueños.
Rodríguez, Clara E. ed. 1997. *Latin Looks: Images of Latinas and Latinos in the U.S. Media.* Boulder, CO: Westview Press.
Rohter, Larry, 1994. "A Puerto Rican Boom in Florida." *New York Times,* January 31, A10.
Sánchez González, Lisa. 2001. *Boricua Literature: A Literary History of the Puerto Rican Diaspora.* New York: New York University Press.
Sandoval-Sánchez, Alberto. 1995. "Puerto Rican Identity Up in the Air: Air Migration, Its cultural Representations and Me 'Cruzando el Charco,'" in *Puerto Rican Jam: Essays on Culture and Politics.* Frances Negrón Muntaner and Ramón Grosfoguel, eds. Pp. 189–208. Minneapolis: University of Minnesota Press.
Schneider, Eric C. 1999. *Vampires, Dragons, and Egyptian Kings: Youth Gangs in Postwar New York.* Princeton, NJ: Princeton University Press.
Torre, Carlos Antonio, Hugo Rodríguez Vecchini, and William Burgos, eds. 1994. *The Commuter Nation: Perspectives on Puerto Rican Migration.* Rio Piedras: Universidad de Puerto Rico.
Torres, Andrés. 1995. *Between Melting Pot and Mosaic: African Americans and Puerto Ricans in the New York Political Economy.* Philadelphia: Temple University Press.
Torres, Andrés, and José Velázquez, eds. 1998. *The Puerto Rican Movement: Voices from the Diaspora.* Philadelphia: Temple University Press.
Zentella, Ana Celia. 1997. *Growing Up Bilingual: Puerto Rican Children in New York.* Malden, MA: Blackwell.

NOTES

1. On the movement of Puerto Ricans from New York City to Florida, the New York suburbs and other areas, see Rohter (1994) and Rivera-Batíz and Santiago (1994). The 1994 report by Rivera-Batíz and Santiago also documented an increased class polarization between Puerto Ricans living in the older, poorer communities of, for example, New York, Chicago, and Philadelphia, and the generally more affluent Puerto Ricans living in the newer communities such as Orlando, Florida, Tampa, Florida, and Los Angeles.
2. On gentrification in El Barrio, see Berger (2002) and Dávila (2003).
3. It also appears that Gregory Nava's film, *My Family*, was the basis for *American Family*, his television mini-series, which was aired on public television in 2002, and also included Puerto Rican actor Esai Morales.
4. Former Young Lords Party member Iris Morales also produced and directed *P'alante, Siempre P'alante*, an important documentary on this group in 1994, and in 1996, Raquel Ortíz and Sharon Simon also produced *Mi Puerto Rico/My Puerto Rico*. Both of these films were shown on public television at the time of their release.
5. Puerto Ricans and other Latinos also continued their protests against the continued preference for Anglo Americans in acting roles that should have been played by Latinos. A major protest erupted in 1994 when Angelica Huston and Marisa Tomei were given the starring roles in *The Pérez Family*, a film about Cuban Americans. A new organization, Latinos for a Positive image, emerged as a result of this protest.

6. On Salvador Agrón and the "Capeman" incident, see Schneider (1999: xviii–xix, 3–26, 262).
7. Another criticism focused on the occasional but consistent use of darker-skinned "Indian-" or "African-looking" actors as criminals, deviants, low-class servants, and other menials in Spanish-language soap operas and other programs.
8. For a much more thorough discussion of this and other related issues, see Dávila (2001: 121, 128, 109–116, 169–170, 201–203, 212, 214, and passim), and various essays in Rodríguez (1997).
9. These and the other observations on institutional change and politics that follow, are largely derived from reports and comments that originally appeared in *Crítica: A Journal of Puerto Rican Policy and Politics*, which was published between June 1994 and April 1997.
10. See Haslip-Viera (1994) and other follow-up comments in the journal *Crítica*.
11. The power of the Puerto Rican politicians in the Bronx party organization was further enhanced when the influential Manhattan assemblyman, Angelo Del Toro, died at the end of 1994, creating a power vacuum in the Puerto Rican politics of East Harlem's El Barrio.
12. The potential power and influence of the stateside Puerto Rican congressional delegation was also eroded when the U.S. House of Representatives came under the control of an energized and more conservative Republican party in 1994. As members of the opposition Democratic Party, the Puerto Rican delegation was placed on the defensive as the Republican majority tried to pass legislation (for example, the "Contract with America") seen as harmful to Puerto Ricans and other minorities. The national Democratic Party also had become more conservative during the 1990s (for example, the "New Democrats"), and as a result, Puerto Ricans and other persons on public assistance were subjected to new and much more severe restrictions when Congress passed the 1996 welfare reform legislation with support from President Bill Clinton and other Democrats.
13. According to Arian et al. (1990: 35), the rejection of Badillo was payback for Badillo's failure to support former Manhattan borough president, Percy Sutton, when he ran for mayor in 1977.
14. In general, Puerto Rican New Yorkers felt neglected and became increasingly alienated from both the Democratic and Republican parties during the 1990's.
15. Antonio Pagán, an increasingly conservative former city councilman, was also appointed commissioner for the New York City Department of Employment at the beginning of Giuliani's second term.
16. See Kirtzman (2000: 67, 187) and Barrett (2000: 322).
17. Organizations such as the Latino Coalition for Racial Justice also emerged during this period to defend Puerto Ricans and other Latinos against police brutality, "racial profiling," and other abuses.
18. The conflict between Fernández, Segarra and the other conservative board members began early in Fernández's tenure, when he and the liberal board members tried to gain approval for two initiatives: a proposal to distribute condoms to high school students because of the spread of HIV, and a proposal to implement a "Children of the Rainbow" curriculum that included a brief segment on children

with gay parents. On the relationship between Segarra and Fernández, see Fernández (1993: 239, 242, 244–245, 248, 271–285, and passim).
19. Segarra remained on Board of Education during her years as deputy mayor, and eventually became chairperson of that body toward the end of Giuliani's second term as mayor.
20. Exception to this include, among others, Torre et al. (1994), García Coll and Gontran (1994), Torres (1995), Rodríguez and Bosque Pérez (1995), Ortíz (1996), Rivera-Batíz and Santiago (1996), Zentella (1997), Muñiz (1998), Torres and Velázquez (1998), Nieto (2000), Acosta-Belén et al. (2000), and Grosfoguel (2003).
21. See Aparicio and Chávez-Silverman (1997), Sandoval Sánchez (1995), and Cardalda Sánchez and Tirado Avilés (2001). Also, see the books and essays by (or in) Flores (1993), Negrón Muntaner and Grosfoguel (1995), Rodríguez (1997), Aparicio (1998), and the more recent publications by Flores (2000), Dávila (2001), Laó and Dávila (2001), Sánchez González (2001), Duany (2002), Morales (2002), Rivera (2003), and Aparicio and Jáquez (2003). It must be said that this writer has also been a contributor to this voguish literature. See Haslip-Viera (2001).
22. As defined by the French cultural philosopher Michel Foucault.
23. An extreme example of this type of writing follows. See Laó (1995: 174):

> The riddles of Puerto Rican colonialism are symptomatic of how much "the pathological" can unveil antinomies and mirages in "the normal." Puerto Rican "colonial exceptionalism" reveals itself still more as truism and seductive fallacy when compared to the notion of the post colonial. The persistence of colonialism with a modernized "local" economy, a "democratized" liberal polity, and a hegemonic cultural politics of ethno-national self-affirmation provides us with perhaps the clearest example of the fact that "the economic, cultural, and political effects of neo-colonialism are structurally colonial," that "we transcended the colonial system but not the ubiquity and primary significance of coloniality," or "that we are not yet postimperial." Spatiotemporal ambiguity, semiotic-theoretical confusion, and too frequent political "lightness" and looseness of commonsensical notions of postcoloniality allow some critics to go to the extreme of classifying the United States as a postcolonial country under the name of critical theory. However, we adopt the notion of post-colonial theory as a form of critique, as an anticolonial project for rearticulating histories, remapping spaces, deconstructing Americo-Eurocentric epistemes, and exploring political agendas.

24. Despite the critique articulated here, some of these essays, books, and collections provided (or currently provide) important or valuable insights into issues of ethnicity, identity, race, gender, sexual orientation, literature, and the arts. For example, the writings of Flores (1993, 2000), Dávila (2001), Dunay (2002), and Rivera (2003) are in my opinion, lucid and particularly useful in this regard. It also needs to be noted

that increasingly, this type of literature has also appeared in journals associated with research on the Puerto Rican community, such as the *Centro Journal* and the *Latino(a) Research Review* (formerly *The Latino Review of Books*).

25. This emphasis on violent crimes by Puerto Ricans and other minorities continued unabated despite a dramatic decrease in such crimes throughout the 1990s. On the decrease in crime in New York City during the 1990s, see Barrett (2000: 349–350, 352–354, and passim) and Kirtzman (2000: x, xiii, 34–38, 58, 71, 90, 93–94, 175, 183, 186, 189, 195).

26. Despite this criticism, it should be noted that *El Diario/La Prensa* appointed its first Puerto Rican and first woman, Rossana Rosado, as managing editor in 1995. In 1999, Rosado was also appointed general manager, publisher, and chief executive officer of the paper. 1995 also witnessed the emergence of New York's first bilingual daily newspaper, called *El Daily News*. However, the commitment to this project from its parent, the *New York Daily News*, was quite limited and the paper closed its doors within a year.

27. Television programs such as *Visiones* and *Tiempo* were consistently consigned to late night or early morning time periods when most people were asleep or otherwise disposed, and this is still the case at the present time.

Mural painting on wall of apartment building in El Barrio (East Harlem), which articulates Puerto Rican nationalism (with ambivalence) at the beginning of the 21st century. Painted by community artist James de la Vega, the mural depicts the 20th century nationalist leader Pedro Albizu Campos with a Puerto Rican flag and "happy symbol" painted on his face. (*Photo by Gabriel Haslip-Viera*)

Chapter 4

De'tras Pa'lante:
Explorations on the Future History of Puerto Ricans in New York City

Angelo Falcón

> "[O]ne of the most difficult things for young people to understand is that life is a struggle. It never ends. And in this regard the struggle for justice and freedom must continue. The work must be linked from one generation to another, and we must see ourselves as links. Everyone has a part to play. No one can afford to sit on the sidelines.
> What affects one of us affects us all."
> —Antonia Pantoja, Interview (1998)

NOTE: This is a significantly expanded version of an essay published in 2001 by the PRLDEF Institute for Puerto Rican Policy, the Policy Division of the Puerto Rican Legal Defense and Education Fund in New York City. The author would like to thank Mia Navarro of the *New York Times* for instigating (although reluctantly) this discussion. For their helpful comments on the draft of this essay, my appreciation goes to Gabriel Haslip-Viera, Maddie Lee, José R. Sánchez, James Jennings, Juan Flores, and my terrific co-workers at the PRLDEF Institute for Puerto Rican Policy: Myra Y. Estepa, José A. García, Mildred Jurado, Raquel Emilia Batista, and Shelley Rappaport. And, oh yeah, my deepest apologies to the Royal Academy of the Spanish Language for the liberties taken here.

> "Men make their own history, but they do not make it just as they please; they do not make it under circumstances chosen by themselves, but under circumstances directly encountered, given and transmitted from the past. The tradition of all the dead generations weighs like a nightmare on the brain of the living.
> —Karl Marx, *The Eighteenth Brumaire of Louis Bonaparte* (1852)

> "I'm gonna light up a beacon on a Puerto Rican
> Strike a matchstick on his head…
> You gonna watch me smile if he drops down dead."
> —Adam and the Ants, from their song, "Puerto Rican" (1978)

The Puerto Rican experience in New York City, spanning more than a century, has always seemed to contain within it the future of others. It is this trait that makes an examination of the future of this community such a daunting task in capturing those essential features of the *de'tras pa'lante* ("backward forward") motion of a past and present that might most usefully point to the unfolding of that which has not yet happened.

At the very start of the new millennium, the world was greeted with the headline, "Puerto Rican Presence Wanes in New York," on the front page of the *New York Times* (Navarro 2000). Now, the word "wanes" can be used in a number of ways. According to the *Random House Unabridged Dictionary* (1999), it could simply mean, "to decrease in strength, intensity, etc.," or to "to decline in power, importance, prosperity, etc." On the other hand, it could have a more ominous meaning: "to draw to a close; approach an end." The picture accompanying this headline on the front page was that of an obviously overjoyed Puerto Rican woman standing on a beach in Puerto Rico, immediately reminiscent of a feminine deodorant commercial. Was she happy to have escaped this "waning" of her community, or did she represent this "waning"? It was an odd coupling of words and images or, one might say, *un de'tras pa'lante*.

The millennium year also saw the production of a new documentary on Puerto Ricans in New York entitled, *Nuyorican Dreams* (Collyer 2000), which premiered at the 2000 Sundance Film Festival. This ninety-seven-minute film follows a Puerto Rican family in Brooklyn over a four-year period and documents what can perhaps better be described as a Puerto Rican nightmare of a family overextended and battered by poverty, drug addiction, criminal behavior, abandoned children and other social problems. Evocative of Oscar Lewis's controversial bestseller, *La Vida* (1965), this viewing of a hyper-dysfunctional Puerto Rican family, while containing faint glimpses of hope, seems more like a viewing at the funeral of the Puerto Rican family (see LeBlanc 2003 for an updated version with a more "zoological" approach).

De'tras Pa'lante: Explorations on the Future History of Puerto Ricans

Beyond all of this negativism, there are other, more positive images that have emerged from the Puerto Rican community in New York City as well. The most prominent have been the spectacular successes of entertainment figures like Jennifer Lopez, Benicio Del Toro, Rosario Dawson, Marc Anthony, Luis Guzman, Miss USA Suzie Castillo, and others. However, while these positive images focus on individual achievements, the negative images are more generalized. Perhaps the most impressive and visible collective Puerto Rican accomplishment in the city, the massive annual National Puerto Rican Parade, was itself marred earlier that year by the negative images of misogynistic assaults by largely Puerto Rican and other Latino men against defenseless women in Central Park during and after the parade, vivid images that were carried by the news media throughout the world (González 2000; Jenkins et al. 2002: 157).

The "Waning" of the Puerto Rican in New York

What do these images, generated at the start of the new century, tell us about the possible future or futures of the Puerto Rican community in New York City? Some hints might come from an examination of the arguments presented in the *New York Times* article on the waning of the Puerto Rican community just mentioned.

Written by a Puerto Rican reporter, the *New York Times* article isolated the following factors as contributing to Puerto Rican decline in New York City:

POPULATION DECLINE. The article reported that for the first time in more than a century the Puerto Rican population in New York City *decreased* in the 1990s. Navarro (2000) referred to Department of City Planning figures that showed a drop in the Puerto Rican population of close to 100,000 between 1990 and 2000. This meant that for the first time in memory, Puerto Ricans were not the majority of the city's Latino population—dropping to around 37 percent of total Latinos in 2000.

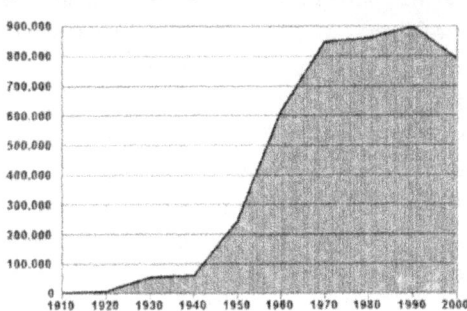

Figure 1. Puerto Rican Population in New York City, 1920-2000

PERSISTENT POVERTY. Adding to the population decline (and probably contributing to it), the article referred to the "puzzling" high poverty rate experienced by Puerto Ricans in New York of about 40 percent. This is seen as puzzling because, unlike other Latinos, Puerto Ricans arrived in the city already as United States citizens since 1917, which *should* have put them at an advantage compared to other newcomers.

HUMAN CAPITAL. The article also focused on the low educational attainment of Puerto Ricans as a factor affecting the poverty status of this community. It was reported that less than 10 percent of adult Puerto Ricans in the city hold a college degree at a time when the economy was demanding highly skilled office labor. Navarro also quoted one educational expert who pointed out the long-term neglect of the schools and the "poor family involvement in education."

MIGRATION PATTERNS. The article made much of the impact of Puerto Rican migration patterns, as it should have, but presented inconsistent scenarios. It pointed to the disruptive effects of the frequent back-and-forth movement between Island and metropolis of many Puerto Ricans, as well as to the dispersal of the Puerto Rican population to other parts of the United States. It also reported on the sizeable return migration to Puerto Rico—38 percent of Puerto Ricans who left the city went to the Island between 1985 and 1990 (and 40 percent of those were born in the States). Despite the evidence of rigorous movement, the article inexplicably pointed out that Puerto Ricans could also be seen as "mostly a static group."

The impact of all this demographic motion is contained in its "bad timing," according to one explanation offered in the article. There is also the negative consequence of Puerto Ricans on the Island already being U.S. citizens, which, according to the article, eliminated the selectivity of the migration that allowed a greater proportion of poor to enter in comparison to other immigrant groups. Puerto Rico, in essence, exports poverty to New York. However, Navarro also noted that Puerto Ricans migrating to other parts of the country (Tampa and Los Angeles are the examples given) were more successful, raising questions about the just mentioned negative impact on Puerto Rican migrants of their U.S. citizenship.

In contrast to these trends, the article went on to explain that Puerto Ricans returning to the Island were poorer and less educated than those remaining in the city. So, New York City exports poverty to Puerto Rico. But, on the other hand, the article points out that retirees and successful young people had also returned to Puerto Rico.

TIMING. As already mentioned, Navarro found that another cause for the problems Puerto Ricans face in this city was related to the migration and its "bad" or "terrible timing." Puerto Ricans migrated to New York in massive numbers just when the economy was changing in ways that would severely disadvantage them as a group. The decline of the manufacturing sector of the city's economy, where Puerto Rican workers were historically concentrated, was seen as the source of the current poverty conditions of this community.

COMPETITION WITH OTHER LATINOS. Perhaps also as a consequence of this timing problem is the broader Latinization of New York City that has been occurring, to the point that Puerto Ricans are today no longer in the majority among Latinos. By 2010, the article points out, city planners project that there will be more Dominicans than Puerto Ricans in the city.

FAILING INSTITUTIONS. Along with citing the failure of the school system, the article also pointed to problems of residential segregation, racial discrimination, the lack of autonomous churches, and the welfare dependency that allowed Puerto Rican single mothers with children to stay out of the labor market. There were also references made to structural poverty, pathology, and indifference by both government and the public.

ATTITUDES. Finally, Navarro refers to the "passionate nationalism" of Puerto Ricans as a problem that has kept their attention on their Island homeland and not on their circumstances or future in New York. This has caused, she observes, many Puerto Ricans to resist acculturation and to blame the United States for the poverty conditions that prompted their migration.

While early on in the article Navarro observes that "there has been no shortage of success stories," she notes that "there is much about the fate of Puerto Ricans that remains puzzling." The myriad and sometimes conflicting developments that she reports on that describe a community that is clearly in decline are perhaps a useful cataloguing of the different ways that Puerto Rican leaders and researchers define the problems besetting Puerto Ricans in New York City. But, upon closer examination, as this essay attempts to show, perhaps it is not.

The *New York Times* article generated a generally negative response in the Puerto Rican community when it was published, probably provoked most viscerally by the "waning" headline more than for the content of the piece (and certainly not helped by the series title of "Falling Back: A Special Report"). Feeling that newspapers like the *New York Times* do not adequately cover Puerto Ricans as the city's largest ethnic group, the appearance of such a pessimistic article on its front page (and above the fold) raised suspicions of bias, despite the fact that the writer is herself Puerto Rican with an excellent record of covering racial and ethnic issues.

The depth of this feeling by Puerto Ricans who see a community besieged by outside forces is reinforced in research by the PRLDEF Institute for Puerto Rican Policy. In preliminary results from a survey on the Census conducted in 2001 among Latino community activists throughout the Northeast and the Caribbean, when asked if they felt there was a policy in Washington, DC to undercount Latinos because of this community's growing numbers, an amazing 65 percent of the Puerto Ricans agreed to this conspiratorial explanation, compared to 44 percent of the other Latinos (PRLDEF Institute for Puerto Rican Policy 2001).

But be that as it may, what does the *Times* article tell us about the future of the Puerto Rican community in New York City? On the surface, of course, the news is not good: Puerto Ricans have had plenty of time to make it in New York City and they have failed, losing whatever footholds they have in politics and other spheres, and dispersing like the wind. It is as if this community was permanently hit and uprooted by a social hurricane. For Puerto Ricans in New York City it is like the end of history. Puerto Rican pride, Navarro observed, is melting into a pool of nostalgia.

The problem with this scenario is that it has been familiar to Puerto Ricans since they began coming to New York City in massive numbers after World War II. The many factors delineated in the *New York Times* article should have killed this community off a long time ago, but as they say in Puerto Rico, *lo que no mata, engorda* ("what doesn't kill you, fortifies you"). Frank Bonilla (1980: 464) put it this way more than thirty years ago in a famous essay, "According to all going theories of history, culture and collective psychology, Puerto Ricans do not exist or are bound to disappear," but, nevertheless, "*seguiremos siendo Puertorriqueños*" ("we will keep on being Puerto Rican").

The *New York Times* piece is perhaps as good a starting point as any for exploring the Puerto Rican future (or futures), but more for what it doesn't say than for what it does say. The many factors shaping the Puerto Rican experience in New York City outlined in the article are certainly real but represent an incomplete accounting and add up to an incoherence that is ultimately unsatisfying and unhelpful. For anyone looking at that analysis for signs of what will and can be, it simultaneously points everywhere and nowhere.

Is the current situation of Puerto Ricans just a function of bad luck ("terrible timing"), a result of a lot of bad decisions, attitudes, and miscalculations, or of forces (many accidental) over which no one has any control? Who or what should be held accountable? Are these factors that affect everyone the same, or are there some things that are unique about the Puerto Rican case? Taking the *New York Times* article as a point of departure, this essay will discuss the factors treated in the article and conclude with observations on where the Puerto Rican community is headed in this city.

Population Decline and the "Disappearance" of the Puerto Rican People?

Navarro's report that city planners estimated that the Puerto Rican population would be declining for the first time in memory by 87,000 (for a drop of 11 percent) between 1990 and 2000 was itself the first time that this development had been reported in the news. This estimate was probably derived from the Census Bureau's Current Population Survey, which was based on a sample of the population; the *New York Times* article, unfortunately, didn't provide this important piece of information. Another sample, drawn for the New York City Housing and Vacancy Survey at the time (Pereira 2000), also conducted by the Census Bureau, put the Puerto Rican population in New York City in 1999 at 750,821, representing a 16 percent drop since 1990.

According to the full Census in 2000, the reality was somewhere in between. The number of Puerto Ricans residing in New York City dropped to 789,172 from 898,753 a decade earlier. This represented a significant decrease of 109,581, or 12.2 percent. As table 1 indicates, this drop in the Puerto Rican population did not occur throughout the city. The drop occurred in those boroughs that have traditionally been home to Puerto Rican neighborhoods (the Bronx, Brooklyn, and Manhattan), while in the remaining boroughs (Queens and Staten Island), the Puerto Rican population grew from 8 to 9 percent. The Puerto Rican population in New York City had, in a sense, become more internally "suburbanized" than before.

Table 1. Puerto Rican Population Change in New York City, 1990-2000

	1990	2000	Percentage Change	Number Change
Bronx	349,115	319,240	-8.6%	(29,875)
Brooklyn	274,530	213,025	-22.4%	(61,505)
Manhattan	154,978	119,718	-22.8%	(35,260)
Queens	100,410	108,661	8.2%	8,251
Staten Island	17,730	28,528	60.9%	10,798
TOTAL	898,753	789,172	-12.2%	(109,581)

Sources: 1990 and 2000 Censuses

What does this population loss mean for the future of the Puerto Rican community? Certainly this would affect this community's voting and economic power, its level of demand for services and so on. But does it have the deeper meaning assigned to it by the *New York Times* article? Is there a necessary connection between population decline and the "waning process"?

A sharp drop in the Puerto Rican population has important symbolic significance. But the reality is that even with this degree of population loss, there remain close to 800,000 Puerto Ricans in New York City today. This means that Puerto Ricans make up 9.9 percent of the city's total population and 36.6 percent of the Latino population; Latinos as a whole make up 27.0 percent of the city's population.

Despite these population changes, Puerto Ricans remain the largest ethnic and Latino group in the city. The 789,172 Puerto Ricans counted by the Census in 2000 was higher than any of the city's other ethnic groups: Italians (692,739), non-Latino West Indians (549,664), Irish (420,810), Germans (255,536), Russians (243,015), Polish (213,447), and even those who identified their ancestry as "United States or American" (213,447). The number of Puerto Ricans in New York City, in addition, is significantly larger than the population of the capitol of Puerto Rico, San Juan, which was put at 421,958 in 2000 by the Census Bureau.

Although the *New York Times* article focused on the sharply declining Puerto Rican population, Navarro's approach gives the impression that what was left was an insignificant number of people when, in fact, the size of the Puerto Rican community in New York City remains quite large by any standard. To look at it another way, if we take this 1990–2000 decrease and project it linearly (and with tongue firmly planted in cheek), it would mean that by the year 3930 the Puerto Rican population in New York City would be reduced to one person, like the old-style boy android in the movie *AI: Artificial Intelligence*.

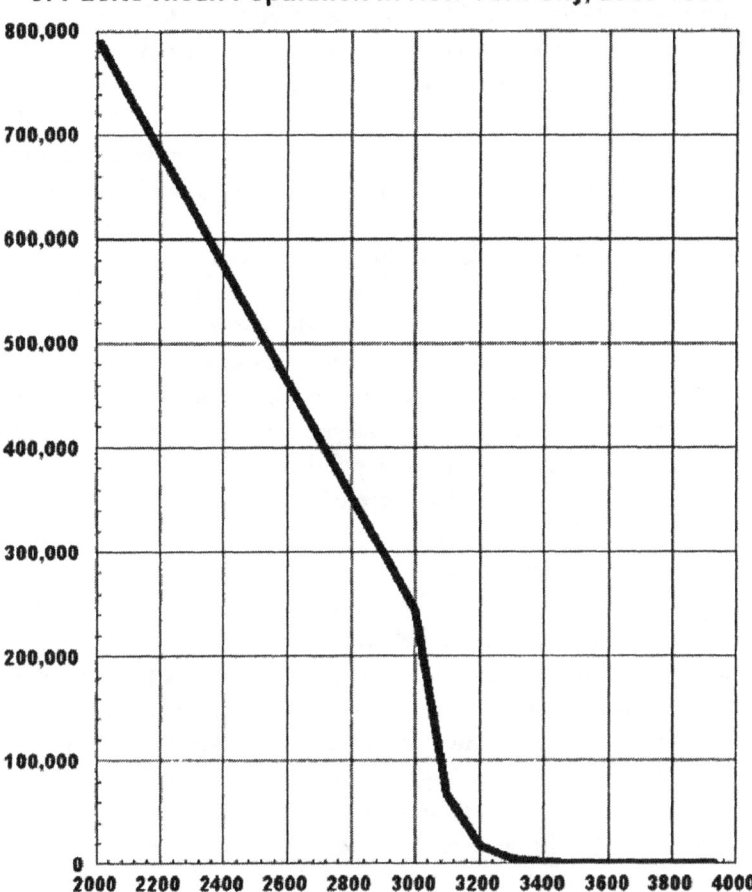

Figure 2. Projected Worst Case Scenario Straight-Line Decline of Puerto Rican Population in New York City, 2000-4000

This is important to note, because as we look at the increased attention by the media and others to smaller and more recently arrived Latino groups, such as Mexicans and Dominicans, largely as part of the growing immigration phenomenon in the city, the sizes of their populations clearly do not diminish their significance for the city. On the other hand, the perception is that Puerto Ricans, despite their larger numbers, have received less news coverage as a community in New York and, as a result, have been rendered nearly invisible in the public mind or seen as a much smaller community than they actually are. It is not uncommon, for example, for people outside New York to inaccurately assume that there are now more Dominicans and Mexicans in the city than Puerto Ricans because of the images projected by the media.

This is interesting, given that more than forty years ago the government of Puerto Rico was trying to allay public fears that there were *too many* Puerto Ricans coming to New York City, at a time when the media referred to the Puerto Rican migration as a "tidal wave" and so forth. Clarence Senior (1961: 20) argued back then that "Compared with either previous or present immigration or with the other internal contemporary migration, [Puerto Rican] numbers are small. But they have been greatly exaggerated by sensationalists and xenophobes." He attributed the problem to what social psychologists and psychiatrists call perceptual accentuation. Today, Puerto Ricans seem to be experiencing the results of a perceptual *de-accentuation*.

How Puerto Rican population numbers are interpreted is of great importance to the future of this community. If there were a perception that the size of the Puerto Rican community is insignificant and decreasing, or that Puerto Ricans are on the verge of extinction, this would have considerable consequences for its development. Policymakers, for example, would not take Puerto Rican interests into account, politicians would not feel the need to respond, the public would not be aware of the contributions and needs of this community and Puerto Ricans themselves, especially young people, may start to internalize a sense that this community, and they, are not significant. However, as the Jewish experience has shown, it is not large population numbers alone that indicate a community's impact on society.

Much of the future of the Puerto Rican in New York City may depend on this community's ability to better project itself on the public consciousness, and back on its own. The Puerto Rican leadership and Puerto Rican institutions, including the Island's government, will need to develop strategies of marketing the role of this community in contributing to the modern history of New York City and raising the public's consciousness of this community's needs. Puerto Rican intellectuals have a major role to play in this regard, as they need to produce, for example, a general history of the Puerto Rican community (a project for which the need remains great).

Much of the Puerto Rican future, therefore, will depend on this community's ability to shape its own image and not remain a victim of others' defining its realities, whether this is the *New York Times* or the mayor of the City of New York. The assumptions that this work has already been accomplished or that someone else will do it for Puerto Ricans have simply not been accurate.

Persistent Puerto Rican Poverty: *La Vida* Revisited

Puerto Ricans have historically been the "poster people" for urban poverty in the United States. With the post–World War II Great Migration, the dramatic growth of the Puerto Rican population in New York City attracted a lot of attention from social scientists and policymakers as the issue of race in urban America grew in salience with the large migration of African Americans to the North during this same period. Oscar Lewis's *La Vida* (and the *Children of Sanchez*) and Glazer and Moynihan's *Beyond the Melting Pot* (1970) are the most well known, but there were others. Popular images of Puerto Ricans as gang members in plays and movies like *West Side Story* and *The Blackboard Jungle* also introduced the exotic Puerto Rican urban dweller to national and international publics. Puerto Ricans became a case study that illustrated Lewis's controversial "culture of poverty" notion, while Glazer and Moynihan used their version of the Puerto Rican experience as an alternative to the racial caste dilemma of African Americans (for a discussion of the linkage between Lewis's and Moynihan's work on the subject, see Briggs 2002: chapter 6).

During the 1980s, William Julius Wilson's urban underclass research brought the Puerto Rican experience back to the attention of social scientists and policymakers who had largely neglected it for a couple of decades. While Wilson's model was based on the African American experience, efforts were made to test it among a wider set of groups, including Latinos and immigrants. The terminology changed from "culture of poverty" to "urban underclass" but it all seemed to amount to the same thing. But, while in the 1950s and 1960s, there was a newness to Puerto Rican poverty, by the 1980s the concern was with its "persistence." While in the earlier period the concern was with values and deviant behaviors, in the 1980s the issue was more with the structural determinants of this poverty.

As the twentieth century was coming to a close, the transmutation of liberalism recast these issues in basic ways. The role of government in shaping effective social policy came increasingly into question as the major liberal reforms of the century had become bureaucratized and increasingly unresponsive to changing circumstances. The Right was effectively challenging the liberal political project of the New Deal and the War on Poverty years, starting with the Reagan administration in the early 1980s. The embrace of punitive welfare reform measures in 1996 by President Clinton and the New Democrats ratified this rightward movement and its renegotiation of the nation's social contact with the poor (the notion of a racially segmented social policy is developed by Williams 2003). Racial questions became more and more complex as immigration and its racial-ethnic diversity grew dramatically in the 1990s. In the midst of all this change, the problems faced by Puerto Ricans and the group's profile had virtually vanished from the public discourse.

With Census 2000, the Latino population was "rediscovered" with a vengeance by marketers and politicians alike, particularly the new immigrants. In New York City, however, Puerto Ricans represented a countertrend, as already discussed in this essay, with their numbers diminishing. The poverty problem for Puerto Ricans was being addressed, some probably assumed, by their leaving New York City. The Puerto Rican poor, anecdotal evidence suggested, were leaving along with the better off, back to Puerto Rico, out into the New York suburbs, and into small to medium-size cities like Reading, Pennsylvania. For Puerto Ricans, suburbanization and return migration were not just the purview of a growing middle class, but also of those at the bottom of the socioeconomic ladder. In a fundamental way, the Puerto Rican experience has redefined the nature of the American mythic move to the suburbs as no longer a sign of affluence and generational upward mobility.

At the same time, the level of Puerto Rican poverty in New York City has remained unacceptably high and relatively constant at over 30 percent, double the rate for non-Latinos (see table 2). The evidence indicates that this poverty persists into second and third generations, as the generational upward mobility hasn't occurred at the scale that past social science projected for all groups. The only positive development, if it can be called that, is that in the 1990s new Census data revealed that among the city's population and among Latino groups in particular, Dominicans had displaced Puerto Ricans as the community with the highest poverty level.

Table 2. Household Poverty Level, Latinos and Non-Latinos, New York City, 1999

Households:	Puerto Ricans	Dominicans	Mexicans	Cubans	Central/South Americans	Other Latinos	Non-Latinos
below 100% of poverty level	32.8%	37.7%	26.5%	24.9%	16.6%	23.3%	15.2%
between 100%-124% of poverty level	7.2%	9.1%	11.7%	5.2%	9.2%	7.4%	4.5%

Source: Housing & Vacancy Survey (Local Census) (1999). Bureau of the Census, US Department of Commerce

However, the policy discourse in the city and nationally had changed to the point where this poverty is seen as intractable and beyond the capacity of society and the state to seriously address. Its persistence among Puerto Ricans for more than half a century, rather than being cause for alarm and a major mobilization of resources and interventions, has become a sign that not much can be done about it. It is either a condition that Puerto Ricans will just have to learn to live with or, at worst, a non-problem hyped up by Puerto Rican leaders to promote their personal careers, as some argued was the case with welfare.

As we look to the future, the prospects for addressing the persistent poverty of New York City's Puerto Rican population appear dim unless the way we look at this problem changes in fundamental ways. It has become clear that this poverty situation is the result of a confluence of structural forces that include the exportation of poverty by Puerto Rico as a result of the inadequacy of the Island's economic development, the increasingly racialized class polarization of the New York economy, the increasingly punitive and short-term social policies being pursued by a conservative U.S. national state, and the destructive values, behaviors, and structures they generate for too many Puerto Ricans and other poor and working-class people (see, for example, Conway et al. 2001). The solutions, therefore, lie in developing frameworks that take in the global, national, and local dynamics of social change and policy that include the resolution of the political and economic status of Puerto Rico, as well as the adoption of a national urban policy at the scale warranted to address the problem of a persistent urban poverty. Puerto Ricans would need to be an important part of the mobilization of American society to achieve this type of reorientation in thinking, policy, and politics.

The Continuing Puerto Rican Problem in the Schools: Beyond Bilingual Education?

In 1972, Puerto Ricans sued the New York City Board of Education because of the public schools' failure to provide their children with an adequate education, resulting in the landmark Aspira Consent Decree two years later. The persistence of Puerto Rican educational problems has been a long term one, the subject, for example, of official reports by the New York public school system in the late forties and fifties (Guerra 1948 and Board of Education 1958; see *Handbook on Puerto Rican Work* 1954: 37–44 for a more critical view of this period). With such a long history in the New York City public schools and despite expectations that Puerto Ricans would be making educational progress, Nieto recently published a book noting that Puerto Rican students' "achievement levels tend to hover around the lowest in the country, and the drop-out rate from high school tends to be among the highest of any other group. Longevity does not seem to make a difference" (Nieto 2000: xi).

Education is an important area of concern for Puerto Ricans, a younger population. According to year 2000 Census statistics, more than a third (34.1 percent) of Puerto Ricans in the United States (outside of Puerto Rico) were under eighteen years or age, compared to less than a quarter (23.5 percent) of non-Latino Whites. However, more than a third (35.7 percent) of Puerto Ricans twenty-five years of age and older had less than a high school diploma, compared to only 11.6 percent of non-Latino Whites (U.S. Census Bureau 2001). That Census also found that only 13.0 percent of Puerto Ricans had a bachelor's degree or higher, compared to 28.1 percent of non-Latino Whites.

In New York City, a survey taken in 1999 found that 42.0 percent of Puerto Ricans twenty-five years and older had less than a high school diploma, compared to 11.8 percent of non-Latino Whites (see table 3). Only

11.1 percent had a bachelor's degree or higher, compared to 45.0 percent of non-Latino Whites. These same data show that Puerto Ricans have an educational attainment profile very similar to the more recently arrived Dominican population. Only the most recently arrived Mexican population has a significantly lower educational attainment profile than both of these groups. Other Latinos (such as Cubans and Central and South Americans) had the highest educational attainment among Latinos, but still lower than that of non-Latino Whites.

TABLE 3 - Educational Attainment of Latinos and Non-Latinos 25 Years and Older New York City, 1999

	Puerto Ricans	Dominicans	Mexicans	Cubans	Central / South Americans	Other Hispanics	Non-Latino		
							Whites	Blacks	Asians / Others
Less than H S	42.0	47.6	64.4	30.9	35.1	25.6	11.8	21.3	24.3
At least H S	58.0	52.4	35.6	69.1	64.9	74.4	88.2	78.7	75.7
B.A. or more	11.1	10.5	8.8	27.9	18.1	25.7	45.0	18.9	38.0

Source: Calculated by author from Housing & Vacancy Survey (Local Census), Bureau of the Census, U.S. Department of Commerce

One problem consistently encountered in trying to assess the educational status of Puerto Ricans in New York City public schools is the lack of data specific to this community. As the Latino population in New York City has grown dramatically, making Latinos the largest group of students in the public schools (39 percent of the total), and as it has become increasingly diverse along national-origin lines, the data collected by the school system have, paradoxically, become less specific and useful. While up until the 1960s the school system collected data that differentiated between Puerto Ricans and other Spanish-speaking students, in the last thirty years or so, those same data have been collapsed into one category, Hispanic. The result is that it becomes impossible to make sense of the educational experience of Puerto Ricans who are second and third generation compared to those of other Latino groups, who are largely recent immigrants.

The issue of bilingual education, for example, highlights this problem. The popular perception is that most Latino students are enrolled in bilingual programs. The reality in the New York City public schools is that only 26 percent of Latinos are even classified as being eligible for such programs and only 16 percent are actually enrolled in what are loosely called bilingual programs (Rappaport 2002). Because of the Aspira Consent Decree, these programs have been identified as Puerto Rican–driven, although they have expanded to include other Latino and non-Latino groups. It is not clear because of the lack of data how many Puerto Rican students are actually enrolled in these programs. Much of the advocacy for these programs comes from the Puerto Rican leadership, but it appears that the vast majority of Latino students in these programs are not Puerto Rican. Therefore, although the issue of bilingual education is not one that engages the majority of Latino students as a whole, it appears to be even less so for Puerto Ricans. And yet, we have no real sense to what degree this is the case and how these programs and the issue of language affect Puerto Ricans specifically today.

It is clear that for Puerto Ricans, an educational agenda that goes well beyond bilingual education needs to become a priority. We urgently need to ascertain the status of Puerto Rican students within the vast New York City public school system. As the New York City public schools system changes its governance structure from a Board of Education to a mayoral-run Department of Education, will Puerto Rican representation in the dramatically downsized bureaucracy and watered-down local school governance bodies virtually disappear? In one of the most racially and ethnically segregated school systems in the country, will the continued overconcentration of Puerto Ricans in poor neighborhoods and the effects of that overconcentration on educational underperformance be addressed in any way? Is there a process of resegregation occurring in New York City, as affluent Whites are returning in greater numbers to a city they once abandoned, gentrifying not only neighborhoods but public schools as well? Given the current hostility toward diversity in some quarters, will any progress be made in the underrepresentation of Puerto Ricans among schoolteachers and administrators? Will the transition issues of the articulation of Puerto Rican students between Puerto Rico and New York ever be seriously addressed?

The relationship between educational attainment and economic and political progress is one of the most direct and important in American society today. For Puerto Ricans it is seen as critical to the future of this community, but the issue needs to be put in context. Educational progress for Puerto Ricans cannot be divorced from other social processes, such as the need for immediate poverty-reduction policies, desegregating our neighborhoods and schools along racial-ethnic and class lines, and assuring the good health and nutrition of our young people. The current situation is one in which education is disconnected from these things, with the result being the reinforcement of social conditions that depress the educational attainment for the vast majority of Puerto Rican youth. With the ending of policies such as open admissions at the City University of New York, the disproportionate number of failing schools and high proportion of uncertified teachers in predominantly Puerto Rican community school districts, the continuing resistance to the adoption of a fully multicultural curriculum and staff, and so on, the educational prospects for Puerto Ricans as a community appear bleak, with all the negative consequences associated with low educational attainment.

While there has been a long history of struggle and advocacy by Puerto Ricans to make the city's educational system more accountable and effective, this advocacy has declined in recent years. Coalitions like the Puerto Rican/ Latino Education Roundtable and others have disappeared (Nieto 2000: chapter 8). Much of the Puerto Rican educational leadership has either become part of the bureaucracy (with, for example, bilingual teachers and administrators being the only advocates for bilingual education) or extensions of government (as more and more Puerto Rican community organizations become public school system contractors, even those organizing parents). Unless the existing Puerto Rican leadership is more creative and determined to develop a new and more relevant educational agenda for their community, we can't expect this to come from outside of our community.

Puerto Rican Migration: From Push-Pull to Mambo?
Migration has always been central to the Puerto Rican experience. The fact that today there are almost as many Puerto Ricans living Stateside as there are in Puerto Rico is the clearest testament to this reality (in 2000 there were 3.4 million Puerto Ricans in the United States and 3.8 million residents on the Island). Before the American Civil War, Puerto Rican immigration was primarily to New Orleans; after that city was devastated by the war, the focus of immigration became New York City. The earlier movement of Puerto Ricans to the city was overwhelmed by what has come to be known as the Great Migration of the 1940s and 1950s. In the 1970s a substantial return migration to the Island began and after that New York City ceased to be the main hub through which Puerto Ricans migrated, as increasing numbers of Puerto Ricans moved directly from Puerto Rico to a number of other cities, mostly in the Northeast and Midwest (Foulkes and Newbold 2000; for the first study of return migration, see Hernández Álvarez 1976). In the 1990s, this direct migration from the Island, combined with that from New York and other Northeast cities to the South, made Florida the state with the second largest number of Puerto Ricans. A migration that was once firmly anchored in New York City has become more complex and fluid as it has become a larger and larger part of the total contemporary Puerto Rican reality (Rivera-Batíz and Santiago 1996).

In 1940, New York City was home to 88 percent of all Puerto Ricans living Stateside, a percentage that has declined to 23 percent today (see figure3). Despite this, New York City remains central to the Puerto Rican experience both Stateside and in Puerto Rico, as, for example, the use of the term "Nuyorican" to describe all Stateside Puerto Ricans signifies, given the millions and millions of Puerto Ricans who have lived in New York over the last century (Pérez 2002). But while New York remains the center for Puerto Ricans Stateside in many areas, its place in the total Puerto Rican experience is and will continue to change and become less important following current population trends.

It is also important to note that the decline in the number of Puerto Ricans in New York City in the 1990s was not unique nationally. While the Stateside Puerto Rican population grew from 1990 to 2000 by 25 percent, it declined during this decade in four other major cities besides New York. These were Chicago, with a decline of 6,811 Puerto Ricans, for a 6 percent decrease; and three cities in New Jersey: Jersey City (-13,567 for a 4 percent drop), Newark (-11,895 for a 5 percent drop), and Paterson (-3,567 for a 13 percent drop). Given the scale of the decrease in Puerto Rican population in New York City, the effect it had was that New York State was the only state to register a decline of its Puerto Rican population, having decreased by 36,308 for a 3 percent decline.

To put the population decline question in an even broader context, it is important to note that beyond these major cities, the Stateside Puerto Rican population dropped in 1990-2000 in 164 other smaller cities and other places throughout the United States. These represent altogether about 10.8 percent of all 1,503 cities and other places reported on in the 2000 Census (CDPs or Census Designated Places). Of the 10 places in the country with the highest percentage drop in their Puerto Rican population, half (5) were in California, 2 each were in Florida and New Jersey, and 1 was in Massachusetts. The 5 places with the biggest 1990-2000 drops in Puerto Rican population were: Olympia Heights, FL (-72.4 percent), Marina, CA (-59.0 percent), Seaside, CA (-55.1 percent), Baldwin Park, CA (-48.4 percent), and Pompano Beach Highlands, CA (-43.8 percent); none, interestingly enough, were in the Northeast or Midwest.

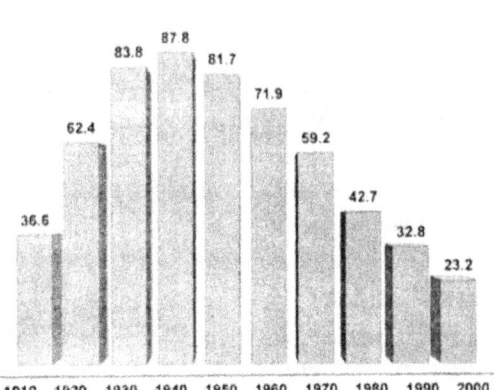

Figure 3. Puerto Ricans in New York City as Percentage of Total Stateside Puerto Ricans, 1910-2000

While much of the discussion of the impact of migration focuses on the movement of human capital, this continual and massive Puerto Rican population movement has made the Puerto Rican reality unique in some ways and prescient in others. Technically, this is a migration internal to the United States, but in reality it is international, given the ambiguous and contested political status of Puerto Rico. One result is that this is largely a transnational experience that predates that of other Latinos to New York in its scale. While the role and motivations of the government of Puerto Rico in shaping the size and directions of this migration are still being debated, it clearly was an active player in this process to the point of claiming to be the spokesperson for this diaspora until the late 1960s. The current vigorously active involvement in Stateside Puerto Rican communities by the Sila Calderon administration of Puerto Rico through its Puerto Rico Federal Affairs Administration offices throughout the U.S., which includes launching a voter registration campaign, continues this tradition, although a change in the island's political leadership could easily change this.

In this context, the New York City experience has itself been unique. But what does it say about the future of Stateside Puerto Ricans? What does it mean when people leave in such numbers from such a historically central place given the advantages of a longer history and population size. What does it mean to say that this reflects the reality of discouraged Puerto Rican entrepreneurs (surrendering, almost wholesale, bodegas to Dominicans, who in turn seem to be surrendering them to Middle Easterners) (Baker 2000: 171–172), as well as what appear to be the discouraged poor? After years of struggle, just when Puerto Ricans in New York City appeared poised to become a major force in what everyone agrees is a revitalized city…they start leaving.

"Commuter" and "circular" are adjectives usually applied to characterize Puerto Rican migration to New York. Cheap air fares, encouragement from the Puerto Rican government, and being U.S. citizens since 1917 made it easier for Puerto Ricans to come to the city compared to other immigrant groups, and, at least on the surface, these were advantages. However, these factors were also seen as negative. The circular migration kept Puerto Ricans from growing roots in New York; the Puerto Rican government's role retarded the group's political development; citizenship made Puerto Ricans think they were Americans making American demands for rights. With such massive migration since World War II, elites in Puerto Rico began to worry that these "Nuyoricans" might want to have a voice in Island affairs, such as determining its political status (Wagenheim and Jiménez de Wagenheim 1996: 322; also see Lorenzo-Hernández 1999). Debates among Puerto Ricans about whether these Statesiders were part of the Puerto Rican nation or a new racial-ethnic minority in the United States started in earnest in the late 1960s. Could you not speak much Spanish and still consider yourself Puerto Rican? (For a position that looks positively at the term "Nuyorican", see Pantoja 2002: 197; for a critical view, see Torres Santiago 2002).

Then in the 1970s there was the start of a significant "return" migration to Puerto Rico. The social anomie of the salsa music they brought with them, the crime, the brashness, and the poor Spanish all started to come back to haunt the islanders, kind of like when you almost throw up but wind up swallowing your own vomit—you feel awful at the moment, but eventually it wears off. So years later, the Nuyorican goes from threat to a major bridge to U.S. culture and commercialization in Puerto Rico. Stateside Puerto Rican politicians now go to Puerto Rico to fund-raise, and they see the Island as part of their constituency. The government of Puerto Rico now puts resources into mobilizing Puerto Rican voters Stateside and the Island's governor backs candidates for major political office in the United States. As Duany (2000: 219) nicely put it, "the constant displacement of people—both to and from the Island—blurs the territorial, linguistic, and juridical boundaries of the Puerto Rican nation."

But is there another side to this shift from push-pull to mambo, with all its fluidity, movement, reciprocity, simultaneity, and so forth? There is a growing 1.5-plus generation Puerto Rican that is not as transnational and about which we know all too little. As already mentioned, data collected by the New York City public schools make this group invisible in terms of educational policy discussions and planning. This is not a group of much interest to those studying transnationalism and the rediscovered field of immigration studies, although many are involved in these processes. This slower-moving 1.5-plus generation would be more the object of that unfashionable topic, "assimilation"; as Father Fitzpatrick (1996: 88) put it, "assimilation is not a politically correct term among Puerto Rican scholars." (Also see Alba and Nee 1997). In 1968 the 1.5-plus generation was the subject of a *New York Times* article that found that they were "entering New York's scene in force, and that their dramatic growth in number is accompanied by significant social advances" (Hoffman 1968). As of this writing, the finishing touches are being made on a major study of the city's second generation that will present a systematic and scholarly assessment of the status of these later generation Puerto Ricans in comparison to other racial-ethnic groups (Waters et al. 1999), which should also shed some new light on this community's population decline in the 1990s.

Most of the current research and analysis on Puerto Rican migration is that it is much too general or theoretical, either trying to provide an overall characterization (like circular migration) or generating a duality (like a poor working-class mass and a growing middle class), or focusing in a romantic way on overly abstract concepts such as "crossing borders," "negotiating spaces," or even on the "mambo" as a open-ended tergiversation (Laó Montes and Dávila 2002: 2) As the increasingly complex migration patterns of the 1990s point out, this experience is much more variegated. The trick will be to capture the primary Puerto Rican migration experiences at the global and very local levels to go beyond the empirically sophisticated but increasingly abstract research we have today (Sites's 2003 notion of "primitive globalization" is helpful in this regard). Beyond inventorying population movements, weighing the relative importance of demographic variables for this or that, and narrowing the questions to make them more palatable to academic journals, the relation of migration to social structures, historical and political developments, culture and language, and so on will need to be better established and elaborated before we can get a more useful sense of the meaning of migration for Puerto Ricans.

Puerto Rican Arrival: Being at the Wrong Place at the Wrong Time?
The idea that Puerto Ricans arrived in New York City in their greatest number at the wrong time is one of the recurring explanations for this community's persistent economic disadvantage. Most recently, for example, Baker (2002: 161) opens her chapter on New York by observing that, "Puerto Ricans entered the New York labor market at the worst possible time—the onset of deindustrialization." While she goes on to nicely describe the structural factors that shaped this timing, this way of phrasing the problem tends toward an anthropomorphic approach to the Puerto Rican community. Somehow Puerto Ricans should have collectively known better, kind of as if they were a person.

The problem is that for a collectivity to be at the "wrong place at the wrong time" requires a whole series of forces and structures in which "wrong" for one set of players is "right" for another. While Baker and others have done a good job of describing how the forces of deindustrialization have marginalized so many Puerto Ricans, they, for example, never adequately discuss why it was not, instead, an opportunity for Puerto Ricans to incorporate themselves better into the New York economy as it was for other racial-ethnic groups.

It turns out that it was this "bad" timing that brought Puerto Ricans to New York in massive numbers precisely when it did. The economic and social restructuring that was occurring both in the United States and Puerto Rico conspired to bring Puerto Ricans to the city in the way it did at the time. Corporations, government, technology, and culture all came together with policies, structures, and resources to do this. The mediating role of the government of Puerto Rico in this process is being better understood (Duany 2002: chapters 7 and 8; and Maldonado 1997: chapter 13), as is the role of other players and forces in shaping that migration and the options from which individuals had to choose. How to fundamentally reshape that role in ways that generate more positive outcomes for Puerto Ricans, instead of simply working around its edges, does not appear to attract as much attention today from analysts and community leaders.

The basic problem with the "bad timing" notion is that it fails to make the necessary connections, acting as if Puerto Rican migration is totally accidental. This mode of thinking promotes the determining role of fate and takes the force of agency away. The upshots are a fatalistic resignation to forces greater than us and, as a result, an inability to assign blame and hold institutions and society accountable. Puerto Rican migration, as the evidence increasingly illustrates, is not accidental and was shaped by very identifiable forces. It could have been and still could, therefore, be reshaped.

Puerto Ricans and the Latinization Process: Sinking in a (Sea of) Rising Panethnicity?

Along with the recent declining number of Puerto Ricans in New York City, there is the issue of the long-term declining Puerto Rican percentage of the city's total Latino population (see figure 4). Since 1960, the Puerto Rican percentage of total Latinos in the city went from a high of 81 percent to a post-1930 low of 37 percent in 2000. This coincides with the subsiding of the mass Puerto Rican migration of the 1940s and 1950s and mid-1960s changes in U.S. immigration laws that facilitated the entry of greater numbers of others from the Caribbean and Latin America. Puerto Ricans ceased to constitute the majority of Latinos in New York City in the late 1980s for the first time since the 1940s, although they remained the largest group.

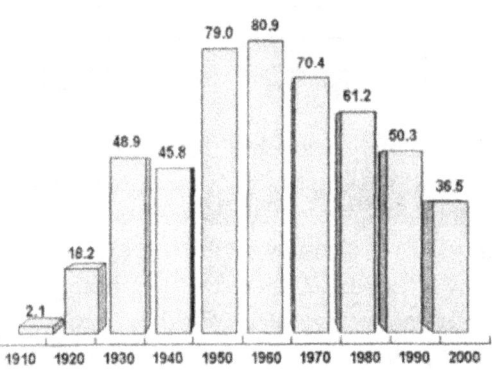

Figure 4. Puerto Ricans as Percentage of all Latinos in New York City, 1910–2000

By 2000, the Latino population of New York City had gotten larger and more diverse than ever (see table 4). Puerto Ricans remained the largest Latino group and, combined with Dominicans, constituted the majority. Populations followed them from eighteen other countries and four other Census-generated categories ("Spanish American," "Spanish," "Other South American," and "Other Central American").

Table 4. Latino Subgroups in New York City, 2000

	Number	Percent
Hispanic or Latino (of any race)	2,160,554	100.0
Puerto Rican	789,172	36.5
Dominican (Dominican Republic)	406,806	18.8
Mexican	186,872	8.6
Ecuadorian	101,005	4.7
Colombian	77,154	3.6
Cuban	41,123	1.9
Spanish	32,105	1.5
Honduran	25,600	1.2
Salvadoran	24,516	1.1
Peruvian	23,567	1.1
Panamanian	16,847	0.8
Guatemalan	15,212	0.7
Argentinean	9,578	0.4
Spaniard	8,233	0.4
Other South American	6,836	0.3
Venezuelan	6,713	0.3
Nicaraguan	6,451	0.3
Other Central American	5,534	0.3
Chilean	5,014	0.2
Costa Rican	4,939	0.2
Spanish American	4,027	0.2
Bolivian	2,942	0.1
Uruguayan	1,907	0.1
Paraguayan	1,658	0.1
Not elsewhere classified	356,743	16.5

Source: Census 2000 Summary File 1 (SF 1) 100-Percent Data

Care needs to be taken in interpreting these figures since this Census accounting of Latino subgroups is misleading. Because of an unfortunate unpretested rewording of the "Hispanic question" in the Census in 2000, the part of the question where individuals wrote in their Hispanic identification led a disproportionate number of respondents to choose broad categories like "Latino" or "Hispanic" for those not otherwise specified as Mexicans, Puerto Ricans, and Cubans. The result, which I call the "Other Hispanic Problem," was that while they were counted as Hispanics, groups like Dominicans and Colombians were miscounted in terms of their specific national origin. According to one estimate, Dominicans in New York City could have been underspecified by as much as 30 percent, meaning that their population was probably closer to 528,800 than to the 406,806 officially reported by the Census (Logan 2001).

This "Latinization" of New York has raised a whole host of issues as the population's Puerto Rican component continues to shrink, most dramatically at the very end of the twentieth century. What does this say about the historical role Puerto Ricans, no longer the majority Latino group, although still the largest, have played in New York? Is this yet another indication of the waning of this community as Dominicans are poised to become the largest Latino group in the city within this decade?

There is, for example, an ethnic succession problem within the Latino community. In the political sphere, of the twenty-seven Latinos elected to posts in the Congress, Borough President, New York State Senate, New York State Assembly, and the New York City Council from the city, twenty-three (or 85 percent) are Puerto Rican. Since 2001, however, the number of Dominican elected officials has doubled from two to four, but there are no elected officials from the other Latino groups. This Puerto Rican overrepresentation among Latino elected officials is largely explained by the longer history of this community in New York and by the effects of not having to overcome the obstacles that other Latinos have because of their lack of automatic U.S. citizenship, which has resulted in Puerto Ricans representing perhaps as much as 60 percent or more of the total Latino electorate.

Does this create a situation where Puerto Rican elected officials see themselves as gatekeepers for the other Latinos, or are they following more pan-Latino strategies? Are there major conflicts between these groups as upcoming communities like Dominicans are openly challenging what many see as a Puerto Rican hegemony? Or are Puerto Ricans increasingly seeing their agenda changing to accommodate this growing Latinization? The composition of the cadre of Latino elected officials is already beginning to change as Dominicans join their ranks at a greater rate than before and from outside their traditional Washington Heights base. Even in the Bronx, the center of Puerto Rican political influence, there is a growing Dominican population in the western part of the borough that is beginning to field candidates for political office. Puerto Rican political leaders will have no choice but to adjust to this changing reality, making the essentialist Puerto Rican nationalism of some increasingly unviable.

Under these new circumstances, Puerto Rican institutions are coming under increasing pressure to change their missions to accommodate these demographic changes. There is the current debate over the future of the Museo del

Barrio, which in late 2002 appointed a non–Puerto Rican (an upper-class Mexican) as its director for the first time in its history and has broadened its exhibits to wider Latin American themes and subjects (see Dávila 2001 for the genesis of this issue). Puerto Rican studies programs in the City University of New York and elsewhere are groping with the same issue, already expressed in a shift to "Latino," "Caribbean," "Hispanic," or "Latin American" studies in the naming of these programs and departments, and having further implications for the content of their course offerings and staffing (see discussions of this by Aparicio and Flores in Poblete 2003: chapters 1 and 9, respectively). Hybrid terms like "Puerto Rican/Latino" or "Puerto Rican/Hispanic" are increasingly being used to mixed reviews. Puerto Ricans see it as a way of broadening their constituency (Laó Montes 2001: 127 and passim), while other Latinos tend to see it in a more cynical light as a strategy "to leverage more power and inflate their numbers without being willing to share power" (Jones-Correa 1998: 116).

The role of race and gender in this process also becomes more important and complex. Grosfoguel and Georas (2001) discuss the effects of a racialized Puerto Rican identity on inter-Latino relations in New York City, while Flores (2001: 203; also see Martin Alcott 2003) presents the dilemma that this Latinization poses for Puerto Rican writers. There is the tension between adopting an ethnic immigrant or a racial-ethnic minority framework for adaptation, something that is largely defined from outside of these communities. In terms of gender, based on their observations of the diverse Latino neighborhood of Corona in Queens, Ricourt and Danta (2003: 149) provocatively find, "Women play different roles from men in the creation of Latino panethnicity."

At the more personal level, there is evidence of greater inter-Latino marriages that are creating "Domirican," "Mexirican," and "Ecuadorican" children whose impact on the nature of pan-ethnicity is unclear (see Gilbertson et al, 1996). Puerto Ricans, especially second-plus generations, are also marrying Blacks and Whites at greater rates, resulting in some instances in Puerto Rican identity giving way to African American and ethnic White identities. The role of Puerto Ricans, for example, in the original production of rap and hip-hop music is an important indicator of this community's relationship to the African American community and the mutual cultural influences that have resulted (Flores 2000; Rivera 2001 and 2003).

The relationship between these various groups is also mediated by their legal status in this country, and in unexpected ways. By comparing Puerto Ricans with African Americans and Dominicans, Baker (2002) does a nice and provocative job of discussing how having U.S. citizenship has been, ironically, a bad thing for Puerto Ricans coming to New York City. In terms of

African Americans, Baker concludes that Puerto Ricans' "foreignness," especially in terms of language, meant their citizenship could not be counted on even in competition with the highly discriminated against African American community (Baker 2002: 169). In terms of Dominicans, she finds that "their lack of citizenship has opened up some doors that have been closed to Puerto Ricans specifically because of their citizenship and because they have been politicized to recognize and demand their rights" (Baker 2002: 171; for another view of how these groups are adapting differently, see Rey-Hernandez 1999-2000).

The simplistic notion that with the greater Latinization of New York, Puerto Rican influence will decline appears to miss the point. The Puerto Rican experience in this city has been "Latinized" from its beginnings, as Cuban, Dominican, and Puerto Rican freedom fighters organized together in anti-imperialist crusades; as Spaniards, Cubans, and other Latinos represented Puerto Ricans in political, judicial, and other offices; as Cubans and Dominicans became "Puerto Rican" by migrating to Puerto Rico and then to New York; as Puerto Ricans are treated as illegal immigrants by New Yorkers who know no better. In this history there have always been adjustments, transformations, accommodations, and even conflicts that have shaped the Puerto Rican community that we have today. Ahistorical accounts of Puerto Rican–other Latino relations, such as those of Jones-Correa (1998: 114–116) on Queens and Solis (2001: 346–347) on undocumented Mexicans, present a highly inaccurate picture of that relationship and are unhelpful in their apparently antagonistic view of the role that they interpret Puerto Ricans playing. Others, mostly non-Latino writers, have a tendency to focus on and overblow the conflicts between Latinos based on the thinnest of information (see, for example, Mollenkopf et al. 2001: 44). Then there are those hopelessly romantic and fuzzy pan-ethnic musings by writers like Richard Rodríguez (2002). There are examples of Puerto Ricans being confused with recent immigrants, despite their relatively long history in the United States, such as the book on Puerto Ricans published under the series theme of "The New Americans" (Pérez y González 2000). By carefully historicizing this Latinization process, we avoid these types of simplified and ultimately unhelpful formulations that are so common today.

Because of Puerto Rico's political status as an unincorporated territory of the United States since 1898, Puerto Ricans are technically migrants to New York City while Latinos coming from foreign countries are considered immigrants. This is increasingly seen as an artificial distinction, but it has its effects in limiting the inclusion of Puerto Ricans in immigration studies. However, there is much to be learned from the much longer and larger-scale migration experience of Puerto Ricans that is applicable to Latino and non-

Latino immigrant groups. The role of the government of Puerto Rico, for example, parallels that of the new role that Latin American consulates are playing in New York and other places in the United States with their diasporas. As we begin to see elected officials emerge from the Dominican and other Latino immigrant communities, there is much to learn from the Puerto Ricans community's experience in this regard, having had Puerto Ricans running for elective office in New York City since the 1920s. (see, for example *Centro Journal* 2003). There is the deeper process of transnationalism and its political simultaneity that the Puerto Rican migration experience has been a precursor to, which more and more social scientists are attempting to understand today. The "Puerto Ricanization" of the broader Latino immigrant experience becomes a critical piece that ties a Puerto Rican past to a Latino immigrant future.

The Infrastructure(s) of Puerto Rican Reality: Playing Dominoes Alone?

The structural determinants of the Puerto Rican condition have always been presented as being in tension with the cultural. Failing schools and labor markets join with the colonial status of Puerto Rico on the outside, while failing community-based organizations, churches, and businesses are cited from the inside. Civil society was failing Puerto Ricans, it seems, before it became fashionable social science in the 1990s. Mediating institutions promoted by the right stopped mediating good outcomes with Puerto Ricans (and Blacks) before everybody else. Puerto Ricans went from being one of the major guinea pigs of the "culture of poverty" experiments of the 1960s to becoming the anomaly of the urban underclass fad of the 1980s. Going further back in history, to the 1920s, for instance, newspaper and other accounts reveal a much richer organizational life among the much smaller Puerto Rican community, providing another example of Putnam's (2000) general "bowling alone" thesis. With no more than 50,000 Puerto Ricans in New York in the 1920s, Vega counted 15 Puerto Rican civic organizations and 200 bodegas and 125 restaurants owned by Puerto Ricans in that period; given the small size of the community at the time, that indicates a higher level of organization than we have today (Falcón 1984: 25). With close to 800,000 Puerto Ricans in New York City today, a recurring complaint is the paucity of Puerto Rican restaurants (not to mention good ones).

Today, the problems that beset so many Puerto Ricans are piled on a particular policy area, usually education, or a top ten list of them. A once confident and deadly serious Marxism has given way to often flaky and fun-filled postmodern meditations for that small group intent on theorizing about the Puerto Rican condition, while the majority either generate laundry lists of symptoms or wait around for solutions from someone else.

A basic dilemma for the Puerto Rican community is the grossly uneven development of its infrastructure as a kind of deformed sub-civil society. An assumption is made by far too many people that all racial-ethnic communities enjoy the same array of institutions within them, with the focus usually being the question of access to mainstream institutions. The reality is much different. Any cursory assessment would reveal that the Puerto Rican community's institutional infrastructure disadvantages it. A comparison with the Black community in this regard is instructive (see table 5).

TABLE 5. A Comparison of Institutional and Related Resources Between African-Americans and Puerto Ricans in New York City

	African Americans	Puerto Ricans
Identity	Racial	Ethnic/Cultural
Nature of problems	American	Foreign
Leadership structure	National	Local/Regional
Civil rights organizations	Large, Old Line, Major White Support	No Equivalent
Educational infrastructure	Historically Black Colleges	Much Younger, Less Developed Equivalent
Religious infrastructure	Historically Black Churches	No Equivalent
Business sector	Weak	Weak
Public sector representation	Overrepresented at lower levels	Municipal parity achieved much more recently; Underrepresented at state and federal levels

While Blacks and Puerto Ricans occupy similar places as the so-called native minorities in New Yorkers' minds, a comparison of the resources they have to draw upon as collectivities reveals significant differences (see Falcón 1988; also see Torres 1995). In table 5 a number of areas are compared to illustrate the point and will not be fully elaborated on here.

The general point is that the legacy of slavery experienced by African Americans has, ironically, produced a number of institutions, such as Black churches and historically Black colleges, which have become important resources for them. It also defines their condition as an American problem (as opposed to being "foreign" in nature) that provides the African American community with additional resources absent from the Puerto Rican community. In terms of the church, the Puerto Rican population is overwhelmingly Catholic, with a smaller and growing percentage being Protestant. The Catholic Church can be characterized as a "colonial church" that has not, especially in New York, significantly included Puerto Ricans in its leadership, while the faster-growing Pentecostal and other Protestant churches have been too small and decentralized to play the leadership role that the Baptist Church has played in the African American community (see Díaz-Stevens 1996).

These differences are also having an impact on public sector employment. In New York City, Puerto Ricans entered public sector jobs in significant numbers at a later date than African Americans, largely due to the effects of the Black civil rights movement. The longer-term public sector employment overrepresentation of African Americans has resulted in the development of a lower middle class of civil servants at a level not seen in the Puerto Rican community, forming the basis of middle-class Black areas of the city such as St. Albans, Queens. In addition, this has resulted in the loss of an important source of pension income in the Puerto Rican community. Taking those sixty-five years of age and older, an analysis of the 1999 New York City Housing and Vacancy Survey indicates that in 1998, only 20 percent of Puerto Ricans reported having any pension income, compared to 30 percent each of non-Latino Whites and Blacks. Of those receiving pension incomes in this age group, Puerto Ricans only received 69 percent of what non-Latino Blacks received and 62 percent of what non-Latino Whites received. This, of course, contributes to the poverty rate of the Puerto Rican elderly in the city.

The result is a "hierarchy of powerlessness" among racial-ethnic minority groups that is not fully appreciated by analysts and policymakers (some attempts to begin to address this issue include Rios and Mohamed 2003; Mindiola et al. 2002; Piatt 1997; and Torres 1995). This also reveals the existence of an unevenly developed sub-civil society within the Puerto Rican community that, for example, creates a leadership vacuum filled by the relatively new political class of Puerto Rican elected officials (Falcón 2002). This class now plays a disproportionate role in the agenda setting and leadership on Puerto Rican issues. As this group of Puerto Rican elected officials grows, it also begins to develop more of a class-oriented self-interest that serves to displace its priorities from a community empowerment agenda to a more self-serving set of interests. The absence of comparable countervailing forces, like business, religious, and labor leaders, is civically unhealthy.

The one sector that appeared at one point to be able to play this countervailing role within the Puerto Rican community was the nonprofit sector. At one point during the late 1960s and early 1970s, the federal War on Poverty, with its "maximum feasibility participation" approach, created conditions that gave the nonprofit organizations resources and an independence in New York City that allowed them to play a major leadership role in representing Puerto Rican community interests (Pantoja 2002: 109 and passim). However, since that period, these organizations have increasingly become extensions of government, and government has learned how to constrain their independence with greater effectiveness over these years. Puerto Rican civic organizations are, as a result, experiencing greater difficulties in playing a progressive role within their community (for some of this history, see Fitzpatrick 1971: 53–76; and Rodriguez-Fraticelli et al. 1991). In demonstrating the role that the broader political context and structures play in shaping the content of that social capital, it stands as a good example of the limitations of the social capital notion popular today. As Berman (1997: 428–429) has effectively argued in her analysis of the role of civil society, using the case of the collapse of the Weimar Republic, "if a population increasingly perceives its government, politicians, and parties to be inefficient and unresponsive, diverting public energies and interest into secondary associations may only exacerbate the problem, fragment society, and weaken political cohesion further." This is a process that is affecting not only Puerto Ricans but also most other racial-ethnic communities. It affects Puerto Ricans disproportionately, however, since its nonprofit sector plays a much larger role within this community because of its unevenly developed infrastructure.

There appear to be few structures reinforcing Puerto Rican identity beyond the political (see Centrie and Valentín-Juarbe 1998), and even here it plays a weak role. What then makes the Puerto Rican a still-identifiable collectivity? An important part of the answer is the residential segregation Puerto Ricans experience Stateside (in a sense, Puerto Rico itself is segregated, which is why it is Puerto Rican). As studies have demonstrated, Puerto Ricans are among the most segregated Latino groups in the country (Massey and Bitterman 1985). Except for Blacks, Puerto Ricans are the most segregated community in New York City. This is a condition popularly represented in Woody Allen movies and televisions series like *Friends* and *Sex and the City*, where Black and Latinos virtually have no interaction with Whites.

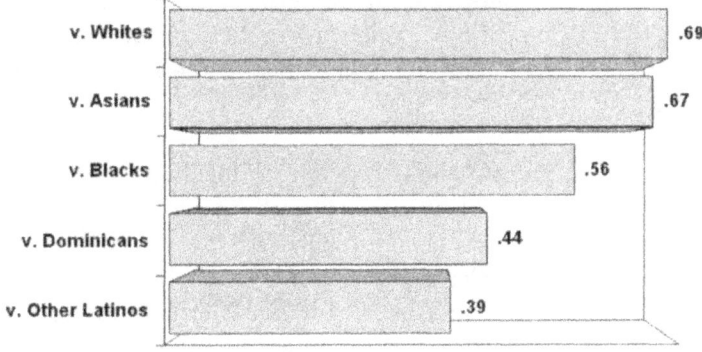

Figure 5. Puerto Rican Segregation from Different Racial-Ethnic Groups New York City, 2000 (Index of Dissimilarity)

Source: Author's calculations based on data from Census 2000 Summary File 1 (issued September 2001)

Based on Census 2000, an index of dissimilarity can be calculated that reveals the level of segregation between racial-ethnic groups (see figure5). These figures indicate that Puerto Ricans are most segregated from Whites and Asians, moderately segregated from Blacks, and least segregated from other Latinos. The fact that these figures reveal very little integration between these groups is troubling (for a fuller discussion of the implications of this, see Baker 2002: chapter 7, and Iceland et al. 2002).

Puerto Ricans are less residentially segregated from Whites than are Blacks (whose index of dissimilarity in terms of Whites is .84), but more than Asians (index=.50). However, because the unit of analysis utilized in calculating this index is the census tract, it is possible that at a lower level of geography, like the block, Puerto Rican segregation may be higher. Puerto Rican residential patterns have been more dispersed at higher levels of geography but appear to subject to a more detailed residential segregation at a lower level given the specific experience of this community with housing markets, government policy toward them, and so on. This is speculative and based mostly on anecdotal evidence, but a line of inquiry that should be pursued.

It is this residential segregation, which becomes school segregation, that makes it necessary to factor in race and ethnicity in decision making about, for example, redistricting and that complicates what otherwise would be more class-based solutions to social problems. While there is some debate about whether this is a voluntary or forced condition, it is clear that in the Puerto Rican case the argument no longer holds that these are newcomers self-segregating themselves. There is also the reality that whatever the cause, the strong relationship between this level of racial-ethnic segregation and a whole array of negative social conditions (such as a high incidence of poverty and poor health) is indefensible. While in New York City this relationship has been broken in the African American community in areas such as southern Queens, no equivalent development exists in the Puerto Rican community, a concrete expression of the outcomes of the "hierarchy of powerlessness" briefly discussed earlier.

Puerto Rican Nationalism and Assimilation: The Unmeltable *Boricua*?
The other side of the structural is the cultural. As the theorizing about the Puerto Rican condition became increasingly narrow and loose, blaming the victim became more popular until being a "victim" became an object of ridicule from the right and then the neo-liberals. Puerto Ricans' nationalism, possession of U.S. citizenship, and experience as a subordinate racial-ethnic minority group are seen as creating attitudes that retard their incorporation into American society. Puerto Ricans won't take the same jobs some newly arrived immigrants would. Puerto Ricans won't allow themselves to be dis-

criminated against in their jobs, in the voting booth, or in their communities. Puerto Ricans don't want to learn English and assimilate. Puerto Ricans, basically, have no one to blame but themselves for their condition.

The notion that it is the nationalism of Puerto Ricans that keeps them from acculturating into American society seems plausible but simply doesn't hold up upon closer examination of the available evidence. At one point in the early 1960s, Glazer and Moynihan argued the reverse in their classic, *Beyond the Melting Pot*: Puerto Ricans were acting more like the immigrants of old who wanted to become part of the American mainstream and interpreted their experience in the U.S. in individualistic terms, unlike American Blacks, who saw themselves as an oppressed racial minority group and blamed American society. They predicted that, as a result, Puerto Ricans would "leapfrog" Blacks in New York in their social status, a prediction they had to retract in the 1971 edition of the book. By the late 1970s, Moynihan (1979) was talking about the progress both of these groups had made and Glazer (1988) was referring to them as "native minorities" in contrast to the more industrious "new minorities" (for a fuller discussion of Glazer and Moynihan's changing views on Puerto Ricans, see Falcón 1995).

It is interesting that with the systematic knowledge we now possess about how groups incorporate themselves in the mainstream of any society that the discussion on the subject of Puerto Ricans remains so dominated by "either-or" generalizations. The debate over whether Puerto Ricans are, or are not willing to be assimilated or acculturated into American society, assumes some monotonic response from what is a very diverse group that will respond to these processes in different ways. Puerto Ricans have always been assimilating and acculturating in different degrees into American society, just as the people and institutions of Puerto Rico have. How could they not?

The big issues are on what terms this assimilation is occurring and to what extent different sectors of the Puerto Rican people are doing so. There is no one Puerto Rican response to these processes so how do factors such as generation, gender, race, class, nativity and so on affect them and what would a mapping of this look like within the Puerto Rican community? How does this affect such things as political trust and mobilization, labor market incorporation, and neighborhood development? We really do not have a good sense of these things because too many analyses have taken the Puerto Rican experience either as being homogeneous or bi-polar. So that when we find that Puerto Rican poverty rates are 30 percent and higher than for most other groups, we need to also discuss the 70 percent who are above the poverty line, but this is rarely done. The need for a more nuanced approach to understanding the Puerto Rican reality or, rather, realities is urgent given the much more complex challenges we face today.

At the same time, this acculturation process does not occur in one direction. Puerto Ricans have impacted culturally and in other ways on New York and American society. The notion of some pure American cultural state into which groups and individuals assimilate simply doesn't exist. American society itself is constantly changing and being influenced by groups like Puerto Ricans all the time. This is a process that needs to be assessed continually, because it is not an innocent one. The way authentic lifestyles that emerge out of migration, everyday life, and other sources are appropriated by a predatory corporate culture and commodified also needs to be viewed with a critical lens, and resistance to this process needs itself to be constantly assessed and encouraged.

The problem most analysts of the Puerto Rican reality seem to have is that they have become good critics of the effects of corporatization but tend to romanticize community resistance to it. Recent examples of this problem can be found in Laó Montes's discussion (2001) of Latino social movements in New York City, which fails to address the disappearance of most of the "resisting" organizations he profiles, Camarillo and Bonilla's (2001: 128–130) broad review of anemic Latino policy responses, and Aparicio's insightful discussion (2001) of racialized media images of Puerto Ricans but that addresses community resistance to them in an overly cursory manner. In the 1990s, the Young Lords, whose existence in New York lasted perhaps three to four years, had increasingly become an object of political nostalgia, as exemplified by Nelson (2001), Gandy (2002), Briggs (2002: 190), and Melendez's (2003) memoir, the latter being one of the more balanced accounts available. In these examples and additional ones in Torres and Velásquez (1998), this community resistance is romanticized in a way that provides no guide for more effective movements—it is just celebratory despite whatever marginal gains (and even setbacks) have been experienced.

The notion that Puerto Rican nationalism is a significant force in determining the lack of acculturation of this community in New York is interesting in light of many studies that have argued that Puerto Rican nationalism is either nonexistent or weak. Anthony Smith has called it a "primitive nationalism" compared to others; at another point (1983: 123) he includes Puerto Ricans with other groups who "failed to develop any kind of nationalism," while the stateless nature of Puerto Rico as a nation has defined it by others, such as statehooders, as a non-nation. At the same time, while it would seem that an important aspect of Puerto Rican nationalism's ability to retard this group's acculturation into American society would be feelings of anti-Americanism, elections in Puerto Rico have consistently indicated that over 90 percent of the Puerto Rican electorate favors being connected to the United States as either a commonwealth or state. In the United States, except for a small intellectual and political elite, the majority of Puerto Ricans support these U.S.-connected political statuses for the Island (Falcón 1993). The underlying anti-American sentiment simply does not appear to be a major component of Puerto Rican nationalism, as witnessed by Puerto Rico's embrace of American commercial culture, albeit largely in Spanish. This could change, and has been different in the past, but this does seem to be the current state of affairs.

If anything can be said to retard the acculturation or assimilation of Puerto Ricans, it would be their racial-ethnic identity, what some might call their "ethno-nationalism," which has been formed within the American experience. Largely shaped by experiences of discrimination as an identifiable racial-ethnic group, it is this hostile American environment that ultimately defines whether Puerto Ricans see themselves as only the latest of a long line of immigrants joyfully melting away in some mythic American pot, or a racial-ethnic minority group hampered by and fighting against American racism. Because of the wide range of Puerto Rican racial types, some Puerto Ricans have acculturated as have European immigrants of the past, including those who changed their names to sound more American; there are darker-skinned Puerto Ricans who have acculturated into Black identities; there are those who have redefined their Puerto Rican identity, or in the case of Nuyoricans, have had their Puerto Ricanness redefined by those on the Island in negative terms. There are also those, usually a younger generation, who now see themselves as "Hispanics" or "Latinos." There are those, as well, who see their primary identification as "Taino," referring to Puerto Rico's indigenous population (Haslip-Viera 2001). Because we have tended to see this process in bipolar terms, this variegated Puerto Rican response to American acculturation and assimilation processes is lost, as is our understanding of what is going on in this regard; for an interesting analysis of the complexity of identity formation among Puerto Ricans in the case of Arturo Schomburg, see Hoffnung-Garskf (2001).

Especially since the 1950s, there has been an important division within New York's Puerto Rican community between the Spanish- and the English-dominant. The government of Puerto Rico's migration office had always been a natural center for Spanish, largely Island-centered Puerto Ricans to cluster around, while the relatively new social agencies became the base of a largely 1.5-plus generation that was English-dominant (see, for example, Pantoja 2002: 77–78 and passim). Language has always been critical in structuring relationships within the Puerto Rican community and between Puerto Ricans and other Latino groups, as a current study of spoken Spanish in New York City is exploring (Scott 2002; also see Zentella 2002 and DePalma 2003). While issues like the freeing of the Puerto Rican nationalists or the campaign to remove the U.S. Navy from the Puerto Rican island of Vieques have helped blur the generational distinction between the Stateside- and Island-centered Puerto Rican—a blurring that the current Popular Democratic Party (PPD) administration on the Island is promoting in their staffing of the Stateside operations of their Puerto Rico Federal Affairs Administration (PRFAA)—this is a relationship that has had its historical ebbs and flows (Duany 2002: chapter 7; and Camarillo and Bonilla 2001: 127).

Much of the way that Puerto Ricans identify themselves revolves around race. While Puerto Ricans in New York City are technically an ethnic group, their experience has been racialized and defined in racial terms. A recent survey of Puerto Rican women Stateside and in Puerto Rico (Landale and Oropesa 2002) found that in response to an open-ended question about their race, majorities of both groups indicated that their race was "Puerto Rican," concluding that "Puerto Ricans think of race much more in terms of their national origins or ties with other Hispanic groups than they do in terms of the color of their skin," a finding made some time ago in de la Garza et al. (1992). Clara Rodriguez (2000: chapter 3) provides individual examples of this, while Falcón (1995) demonstrates the relatively small impact of race on Puerto Rican policy preferences, and Espino and Franz (2002) show how race plays differently on Puerto Ricans in the labor market than with other Latinos.

This constitutes a continuing challenge by Puerto Ricans and other Latinos to the dominant dichotomous Black-White American conception of race, leading more and more analysts to use the hybrid term "racial-ethnic" when referring to groups like Puerto Ricans. There are some who view the assertion of Puerto Rican identity in racial terms to represent a denial of this community's African or darker roots, a part of an even more complex phenomenon (Sánchez González 2000 ; also see Hernández 2002). At the same time, because so much of the classification of Puerto Ricans is based on the Census's self-identification question, we also do not really know how many second-generation-plus Puerto Ricans have been "lost" or "converted" to an African American, White ethnic, or Hispanic/Latino racial-ethnic identification.

Conclusion

What can we finally say about the future of Puerto Ricans in New York City? As the foregoing discussion indicates, there is no easy answer to this question. The issue that we started with, Puerto Rican population decline, for example, can be seen in both negative and positive terms. While we referred to it as reflecting discouragement among Puerto Ricans of different social classes, we also see the energy and resources that this out-migration from the city is creating in Puerto Rican communities in other parts of the country and in

Puerto Rico. The persistent problems of poverty, educational attainment, poor housing, residential segregation, and so on will no doubt continue to plague Puerto Ricans in New York City for some time to come. However, these problems will probably locate the Puerto Rican community and its experience in a place that may make it indispensable to the solutions of this society's most intractable problems. At the same time that we see so many Puerto Ricans enmeshed in these social problems and focus on this, we also see many overcoming them individually and collectively with creative and imaginative solutions, a point made by Bryant Serrano (2002) in her study of the treatment Puerto Rican in introductory sociology texts.

As we survey the Puerto Rican experience over time, its relevance to others, especially Latino immigrants, becomes more and more obvious. If we do not allow artificial constructs like immigration or citizenship status to get in the way, the applicability of lessons from the Puerto Rican past and present widens greatly (for the social construction of Puerto Rican citizenship, see Rivera Ramos 2001; for an illustration of how an overly formal application of citizenship invisibilizes the Puerto Rican, see Murphy et al. 2001). The Puerto Rican future, rather than that of a special interest group or an exotic racial-ethnic community, can be seen as tied to a broader New York City future. How we deal with the adaptation of newer communities to the city, how transnationalism has been transformed and operates today, how U.S. relations with Latin American countries affect it domestically in terms of immigration, and how language influences identity formation and the institutional process are all areas where experiences like that of Puerto Ricans in New York City can be critical to better understanding.

When we look at instances where the Puerto Rican experience and struggle for being in the city resulted in solutions, or even hints at solutions, to its many social problems, the list is impressive. In the field of education, for example, there was the landmark Aspira Consent Decree of 1974, which mandated bilingual education programs for Puerto Ricans and eventually all English-language learners in the New York public schools. The decree was the result of a lawsuit brought by Puerto Ricans against what was then called the Board of Education. Another example is the important role Puerto Ricans played in the fight to decentralize the school system, especially in the Lower East Side, and to institute open admissions in the City University of New York.

In the political arena, examples include the specific citing of the Puerto Rican case by the United States Supreme Court in the elimination of English literacy tests for voting (Weaver 1966); the Puerto Rican success in reaching parity in electoral representation at the local, state, and congressional levels of government and demonstrating a propensity toward public service; the Puerto Rican introduction of ethnically focused publicly funded citywide programs, such as Aspira of New York and the Puerto Rican Community Development Project (PRCDP); and the elimination of the height requirement for the hiring of New York City police officers, specifically done in response to Puerto Rican legal pressure.

The creation of a unique literary, musical, theatrical, and poetic presence in the city through salsa, Latin rap and hip hop, Nuyorican poetry, and so on that are distinctly New York and Rican at the same time (Sandoval-Sánchez 1999: chapters 2 and 3; Negrón-Muntaner 2000; Rivera 2001; Morales 2002: chapter 5; and Rivera 2003). Puerto Rican contributions to the history of New York City have been many and will continue to be made well into the future. Some of these contributions have fallen on hard times of late, but all have been important in the evolution of the city's public life.

There are a number of aspects of the Puerto Rican experience in New York that require further research that could yield useful answers to durable social questions. We already mentioned the impact of migrating to the U.S. as a U.S. citizen and its implications for other immigrants. There is the paradox of the high electoral participation among all social classes of Puerto Ricans in Puerto Rico, and the sharp drop in such participation once they arrive in New York, a relationship that could hold the key to ways to increase the voting rates of poor and working-class New Yorkers (Falcón 1983).

There is also the role of the government of Puerto Rico since at least 1948 in representing the interests of Puerto Ricans in New York, a role that is becoming increasingly analogous to that of Latin American consulates today. At a very basic level, the current experience of Mexicans in the United States with the issuance of identification cards by consulate offices (*matrícula consular*), for example, is analogous to the government of Puerto Rico issuing "green" identification cards (once known as *Saldañas*) to Stateside Puerto Ricans (see Matos-Rodríguez and Hernández 2001: 32–35). The Puerto Rican experience with this mechanism of representation, containing both positive and negative aspects, conveys important lessons for contemporary Latino immigrants.

The almost wholesale and relatively rapid abandonment of the bodega by Puerto Ricans is a phenomenon much discussed within this community, but not seriously studied for its lessons about Puerto Rican migration as well as the future of Dominican and other Latino entrepreneurship (Baker 2002: 152–156; also see early study comparing Korean and Latino greengrocers discussed in Curtis 1985).

There are many more areas where the Puerto Rican experience has much to teach this city, as well as much that this city has to teach Puerto Ricans. But within the Puerto Rican community there is a need to recognize this and to develop ways to impart these lessons to newer generations and create mechanisms to assure that this transmission is ongoing.

However, if there is a problem in the Puerto Rican present with this community's very ability to control something as basic as the images of its presence in New York City, then the Puerto Rican future is in jeopardy. As this essay has attempted to demonstrate, Puerto Ricans, even in worst-case scenarios, will be in New York for a long, long time to come. But *as a community* that is recognized, and as actors in determining their own fate, Puerto Ricans may then have, to quote an almost-three-decade-old report, "an uncertain future" (U.S. Commission on Civil Rights 1976). It is quite telling in this regard that the entry "Puerto Ricans" in *The Encyclopedia of New York City* concludes by stating that by the mid-1990s, they "continued to identify themselves as Puerto Rican and retained ties with Puerto Rico." (Sanchez Korrol 1995: 961) It is both revealing and chilling that a statement as obvious as this should have to be made at all.

What does the Puerto Rican community need to do to take greater control of its future history in New York City? A number of fairly obvious areas need to be focused on. A basic but certainly not exhaustive list of challenges facing Puerto Ricans in the city today includes the following (in no particular order):

- The leadership of the Puerto Rican community—in politics, business, culture, the nonprofit world, labor, and religion—needs to come together to acknowledge the critical challenges facing their community in this new century. The failure of many of our leaders and institutions to seriously address the deep social problems facing the community needs not only to be acknowledged but also to documented and analyzed with an eye toward shaping solutions.
- The growing issue of the identity of Puerto Rican institutions needs to be confronted in a more serious manner. The uncritical accommodation to the pressures from funding sources and demographic changes is creating a crisis among Puerto Rican institutions as they embrace pan-Latino agendas without regard to its impact on the Puerto Rican population. This is especially the case given the fiscal fragility of many of these institutions.
- The increasing disconnect between the Puerto Rican community and its elected officials needs to be addressed. Can the priorities of this Puerto Rican political class be altered in ways that are more relevant to their community, is there a need for the creation of a new political leadership with a fundamentally different set of values, or both?
- How can the Puerto Rican community effectively challenge its depen-

dence on the Democratic Party and that party's long-term position of taking the Puerto Rican vote for granted?
- Can the Puerto Rican nonprofit sector be reinvigorated and refocused on Puerto Rican community needs? Can its ambitiousness and vision of the past (for example, the Puerto Rican Community Development Project plan of the sixties, the long-term planning of the early Puerto Rican Forum and Aspira, the brashness of the Young Lords and other progressive movements) be restored and made relevant to a new century?
- Can the considerable resources already present in the Puerto Rican community be marshaled in new and more effective ways? These resources include our youth in the schools and universities, our intellectuals based in Puerto Rican studies programs and research centers like the CUNY Center for Puerto Rican studies, the growing Puerto Rican leadership in the labor movement, and so on.
- Are there ways that the high-profile Puerto Rican presence (and financial resources) in the entertainment field, such as Jennifer Lopez, Marc Anthony, and Benicio del Toro, can be brought back into the Puerto Rican community in more effective and coordinated roles?
- Can the ties between New York and Island Puerto Ricans be the basis of a relationship that brings resources more effectively to help Stateside Puerto Rican communities develop economically, culturally, and in other ways? Is it possible to break the habit of Island Puerto Rican political leaders to view Stateside Puerto Ricans as simply pawns in their political strategies?
- How can the progressive and oppositional aspects of the Puerto Rican movement (and even the sense of a movement) be revisited, revised for a new century, and nurtured in ways that tie the Puerto Rican problematic to a broader agenda for social change?
- How can the Puerto Rican community make effective use of its growing consumer power to hold the corporate sector (including both the English- and Spanish-language media) from the Goya Foods to the Citigroups accountable, as well, and more importantly, develop its own economic base?

With all these challenges before it, the fact is that the Puerto Rican community in the city is alive and kicking. The Puerto Rican experience in New York is, as this essay mentioned in its opening, in many ways critical to an understanding not only of this community's future, but that of New York City as a whole. Discussing Latinos in general in this regard, Suro (1999: 157) usefully observes:

> The Puerto Rican story helps establish a perspective that makes it

easier to understand the Latino experience at the end of the century. It shows how dangerous it can be to rely on the kind of social science that paints group identities on the basis of census data and then predicts outcomes. There is no way of knowing how today's Latino immigrants will end up simply on the basis of the human capital they bring with them. They arrive as Spanish-speaking peasants. They become citizens of postindustrial America.

To stress the uniqueness of the Puerto Rican experience (Cordasco and Bucchioni 1973: xviii) or to see it as an "exception" (Chavez 1991) is to overlook just how more and more communities are becoming "Puerto Rican" in this age of economic restructuring and globalization (for example, on the role of Puerto Rican women as pioneering transnational labor, see Ortiz 1996). Whether it was the underclass debate with its roots in the controversy over the culture of poverty thesis, or the current debates over multiculturalism, or the claims made in the past that Puerto Ricans would bring a multiracial sensibility to New York as "rainbow people," or the impact of neoliberal policies on Latin America and Puerto Rico via "Operation Bootstrap" and its offspring, or white American youth's adoption of hip-hop culture and the early Puerto Rican role in its creation, it should be recognized that there is much in the Puerto Rican past that we are finding in other people's futures. As Davis (2000: 103) recently concluded, "Puerto Rican poverty, which rebuts the facile claim that citizenship provides a magic carpet for immigrant success, is the spectre that ineluctably haunts all debates about the future of the Latino metropolis."

As we debate the Puerto Rican future in New York City, we will come to understand that it will not simply be a linear projection of recent trends or that it can merely be reduced to streams of data and their statistical manipulation. It will be a debate about the future of New York City and the United States in whose destinies Puerto Ricans have been incorporated...and *not*, by the way, of their own will. The late Father Fitzpatrick (1971: 184) concluded his now classic study of the Puerto Rican in New York City with the following observation:

> Toynbee says that the city without a challenge is a city which is dying. If that is true, New York and the Puerto Ricans are very much alive. If the history of New York City tells us anything, it tells us this: At the dark moments when people were convinced that the city was being destroyed, it was actually breaking through into a new and richer life. This may not be the basis for contentment and peace, but it is the basis for confidence and hope.

While the tasks before the Puerto Rican community of New York City are formidable in terms of forging its own future, they must be tackled with such confidence and hope. The *de'tras pa'lante* of Puerto Rican future history can only be made by Puerto Ricans themselves *metiendole de'tras pa'lante* at it. As the great Puerto Rican institution builder, Antonia Pantoja, observed about herself in her memoirs:

> Many people have called me a visionary. I never liked this characterization because I considered my ideas and projects practical answers to the resolution of problems. Now, I accept that I am a visionary, if being a visionary means that I have tried to transform reality (2002: 197).

This is a basic lesson upon which the Puerto Rican community needs to build in the making of its future history.

REFERENCES

Alba, Richard, and Victor Nee. 1997. "Rethinking Assimilation Theory for a New Era of Immigration." *International Migration Review* 31: 4 (winter): 826–974.

Aparicio, Frances R. 2001. "Racializing the Puerto Rican Day Parade: Recent Media Representations of U.S. Puerto Ricans in the Public Space." Unpublished paper, University of Chicago.

Baker, Susan S. 2002. *Understanding Mainland Puerto Rican Poverty*. Philadelphia: Temple University Press.

Berman, Sheri. 1997. "Civil Society and the Collapse of the Weimar Republic." *World Politics* 49: 3 (April): 401–429.

Board of Education, City of New York. 1958. *The Puerto Rican Study 1953–1957: A Report on the Education and Adjustment of Puerto Rican Pupils in the Public Schools of the City of New York*. New York: New York City Board of Education.

Bonilla, Frank. 1980. "Beyond Survival: Por que Seguiremos Siendo Puertorriqueños," in *The Puerto Ricans: Their History, Culture and Society*, Adalberto López, ed. Pp. 453–466. Cambridge, MA: Schenkman.

Briggs, Laura. 2002. *Reproducing Empire: Race, Sex, Science, and U.S. Imperialism in Puerto Rico*. Berkeley: University of California Press.

Bryant Serrano, María I. 2002. "The Social Construction of Puerto Ricans in Introductory Sociology Textbooks." Ph.D. dissertation, George Mason University.

Camarillo, Albert M. and Frank Bonilla. 2001. "Hispanics in a Multicultural Society: A New American Dilemma?" in *America Becoming: Racial Trends and Their Consequences, Vol. 1*, Neil J. Smelser, William Julius Wilson and Faith Mitchell, eds. Pp. 103–134. Washington, DC: National Research Council.

Centrie, Craig, and Juan Valentín-Juarbe. 1998. "'It's a Small Frog That Will Never Leave Puerto Rico:' Puerto Rican Men and the Struggle for Place in the United States," in *The Unknown City: The Lives of Poor and Working-Class Young Adults*. Michelle Fine and Lois Weis, eds. Pp. 84–107. Boston: Beacon Press.

Centro Journal. 2003. Special Issue: "Puerto Rican Politics in the United States," José E. Cruz, ed. 15: 1 (spring). New York: CUNY Center for Puerto Rican Studies.

Chavez, Linda. 1991. *Out of the Barrio: Toward a New Politics of Hispanic Assimilation.* New York: Basic Books.

Collyer, Laurie. 2000. *Nuyorican Dream* (documentary film). Co-produced by John Leguizamo and Jelly Bean Benitez. New York: Big Mouth Productions.

Conway, Dennis, Adrian J. Bailey, and Mark Ellis. 2001. "Gendered and Racialized Circulation-Migration: Implications for the Poverty and Work Experience of New York's Puerto Rican Women," in *Migration, Transnationalization, & Race in a Changing New York*, Hector R. Cordero-Guzmán, Robert C. Smith and Ramón Grosfoguel, eds. Pp. 146–163. Philadelphia: Temple University Press.

Cordasco, Francesco and Eugene Bucchioni. eds. 1973. *The Puerto Rican Experience: A Sociological Sourcebook.* Totowa, NJ: Littlefield, Adams and Co.

Curtis, Charlotte. 1985. "Hard Work vs. Success." *New York Times*, March 19, p. C12.

Dávila, Arlene. 2001. "Culture in the Battlefront: From Nationalist to Pan-Latino Projects," in *Mambo Montage: The Latinization of New York*, Agustín Laó Montes and Arlene Dávila, eds. Pp. 159–180. New York: Columbia University Press.

Davis, Mike. 2000. *Magical Urbanism: Latinos Reinvent the US City.* New York: Verso.

de la Garza, Rodolfo O., Louis DeSipio, F. Chris García, John García, and Angelo Falcón. 1992. *Latino Voices: Mexican, Puerto Rican & Cuban Perspectives on American Politics.* Boulder, CO: Westview Press.

DePalma, Anthony. 2003. "God's Word, Echoing in English; Hispanic Pentecostal Churches Face Bilingual Problem." *New York Times*, July 2, p. B1.

Díaz-Stevens, Ana María. 1996. "Aspects of Puerto Rican Religious Experience: A Sociohistorical Overview," in *Latinos in New York: Communities in Transition*, Gabriel Haslip-Viera and Sherrie L. Baver, eds. Pp. 147–186. Notre Dame, IN: University of Notre Dame Press.

Duany, Jorge. 2002. *The Puerto Rican Nation on the Move: Identities on the Island and in the United States.* Chapel Hill: University of North Carolina Press.

Espino, Rodolfo, and Michael M. Franz. 2002. "Latino Phenotype Discrimination Revisited: The Impact of Skin Color on Occupational Status." *Social Science Quarterly* 83: 2 (June): 612–623.

Falcón, Angelo. 1983. "Puerto Rican Political Participation: New York City and Puerto Rico," in *Time for Decision: The United States and Puerto Rico*, Jorge Heine. ed. Pp. 27–54. Lanham, MD: The North-South Publishing Company.

_____. 1984. "A History of Puerto Rican Politics in New York City: 1860s to 1945," in *Puerto Rican Politics in Urban America*, James Jennings and Monte Rivera, eds. Pp. 75–98. Westport, CT: Greenwood Press.

_____. 1988. "Black and Latino Politics in New York: Race and Ethnicity in a Changing Urban Context." *New Community* (London) 14: 3 (spring): 370–384.

_____. 1993. "A Divided Nation: The Puerto Rican Diaspora in the United States and the Proposed Referendum," in *Colonial Dilemma: Critical Perspectives on Contemporary Puerto Rico*, Edwin Meléndez and Edgardo Meléndez, eds. Pp. 173–180. Boston: South End Press.

_____. 1995. "Puerto Ricans and the Politics of Racial Identity," in *Racial and Ethnic*

Identity: Psychological Development and Creative Expression, Herbert W. Harris, Howard C. Blue and E.H. Griffith, eds. Pp. 193–208. New York: Routledge.

———. 2002. "El fracaso de la clase política latina." *El Diario-La Prensa*, December 25, p. 11.

Fitzpatrick, Joseph P. 1971. *Puerto Rican Americans: The Meaning of Migration to the Mainland*. Englewood Cliffs, NJ: Prentice Hall.

———. 1996. *The Stranger is Our Own: Reflections on the Journey of Puerto Rican Migrants*. Kansas City, MO: Sheed & Ward.

Flores, Juan. 2000. *From Bomba to Hip Hop: Puerto Rican Culture and Latino Identity*. New York: Columbia University Press.

———. 2001. "Life Off the Hyphen: Latino Literature and Nuyorican Traditions," in *Mambo Montage: The Latinization of New York*, Agustín Laó Montes and Arlene Dávila, eds. Pp. 185–206. New York: Columbia University Press.

Foulkes, Matt, and K. Bruce Newbold. 2000. "Migration Propensities, Patterns, and the Role of Human Capital: Comparing Mexican, Cuban, and Puerto Rican Interstate Migration, 1985–1990." *Professional Geographer* 52: 1: 133–145.

Gandy, Matthew. 2002. "Between Borinquen and the *Barrio:* Environmental Justice and New York City's Puerto Rican Community, 1969–1972." *Antipode: A Radical Journal of Geography* 34: 4 (September): 730–761.

Gilbertson, Greta A., Joseph P. Fitzpatrick, and Lijun Yang. 1996. "Hispanic Intermarriage in New York City: New Evidence from 1991." *International Migration Review* 30: 2 (summer): 445–459.

Glazer, Nathan. 1988. "The New New Yorkers," in *New York Unbound: The City and the Politics of the Future*, Peter D. Salins, ed. Pp. 54–72. New York: Basil Blackwell.

Glazer, Nathan, and Daniel Patrick Moynihan. 1970 (1963). *Beyond the Melting Pot: The Negroes, Puerto Ricans, Jews, Italians, and Irish of New York City*. Cambridge: MIT Press.

González, Juan. 2000. "New Steps Needed to Police Parade," *Daily News*, June 16.

Grosfoguel, Ramón, and Chloé S. Georas. 2001. "Latino Caribbean Diaspora in New York," in *Mambo Montage: The Latinization of New York*, Agustín Laó Montes and Arlene Dávila, eds. Pp. 97–118. New York: Columbia University Press.

Guerra, Emilio L. 1948. "The Orientation of Puerto Rican Students in New York City." *Modern Language Journal* 32: 6 (October): 415–420.

Handbook on Puerto Rican Work. 1954. Puerto Rican Affairs Committee, Communist Party, USA (January).

Haslip-Viera, Gabriel, ed. 2001. *Taíno Revival: Critical Perspectives on Puerto Rican Identity and Cultural Politics*. Princeton, NJ: Marcus Wiener Publishers.

Hernández, Tanya Katerí. 2002. "Multiracial Matrix: The Role of Race Ideology in the Enforcement of Antidiscrimination Laws, A United States-Latin America Comparison." *Cornell Law Review* 87: 5 (July): 1093–1176.

Hernández Álvarez, José. 1976 [1967]. *Return Migration to Puerto Rico*. Westport, CT: Greenwood Press.

Hoffnung-Garskof, Jess. 2001. "The Migrations of Arturo Schomburg: On Being Antillano, Negro, and Puerto Rican in New York 1891–1938." *Journal of American Ethnic History* 21: 1 (fall): 3–46.

Hofmann, Paul. 1968. "City's 2d-Generation Puerto Ricans Rising from Poverty," *The New York Times*, April 23, p. 49.

Iceland, John, Daniel H. Weinberg, and Erika Steinmetz. 2002. *Racial and Ethnic Residential Segregation in the United States: 1980–2000—Census 2000 Special Reports*, CENSR-3 (August). Washington, DC: U.S. Census Bureau.

Jenkins, Sacha, Elliott Wilson, Chairman Jefferson Mao, Gabriel Alvarez, and Brent Rollins. 2002. *Egotrips's Big Book of Racism!* New York: Regan Books.

Jones-Correa, Michael. 1998. *Between Two Nations: The Political Predicament of Latinos in New York City*. Ithaca, NY: Cornell University Press.

Landale, Nancy S., and R.S. Oropesa. 2002. "White, Black or Puerto Rican? Racial Self-Identification Among Mainland and Island Puerto Ricans." *Social Forces*, 81: 1 (September): 231–254.

Laó Montes, Agustín. 2001. "Niuyol: Urban Regime, Latino Social Movements, Ideologies of Latinidad," in *Mambo Montage: The Latinization of New York* Agustín Laó Montes and Arlene Dávila, eds. Pp. 119–157. New York: Columbia University Press.

Laó Montes, Agustín, and Arlene Dávila, eds. 2001. *Mambo Montage: The Latinization of New York*. New York: Columbia University Press.

LeBlanc, Adrian Nicole. 2003. *Random Family: Love, Drugs, Trouble, and Coming of Age in the Bronx*. New York: Scribner.

Lewis, Oscar. 1965. *La Vida: A Puerto Rican Family in the Culture of Poverty – San Juan and New York*. New York: Random House.

Logan, John. 2001. "Population Counts for Hispanic National Origin Groups, New York City, 2000." <http://www.albany.edu/mumford/census> (printout in author's possession).

Lorenzo-Hernández, José. 1999. "The Nuyorican's Dilemma: Categorization of Returning Migrants in Puerto Rico." *International Migration Review* 33: 4 (winter): 988–1013.

Maldonado, Alex W. 1997. *Teodoro Moscoso and Puerto Rico's Operation Bootstrap*. Gainesville: University Press of Florida.

Martin Alcott, Linda. 2003. "Puerto Rican Studies in a German Philosophical Context: An Interview with Juan Flores." *Nepantla: Views from the South* 4: 1 (spring): 139–146.

Massey, Douglas S., and Brooks Bitterman. 1985. "Explaining the Paradox of Puerto Rican Segregation." *Social Forces* 64: 2 (December): 306–331.

Matos-Rodríguez, Félix, and Pedro Juan Hernández, eds. 2001. *Pioneros: Puerto Ricans in New York City, 1896–1948*. Charleston, SC: Arcadia Publishing.

Melendez, Miguel. 2003. *We Took the Streets: Fighting for Latino Rights with the Young Lords*. New York: St. Martin's Press.

Mindiola Jr., Tatcho, Yolanda Fores Niemann, and Nestor Rodríguez. 2002. *Black-Brown Relations and Stereotypes*. Austin: University of Texas Press.

Mollenkopf, John, David Olson, and Timothy Ross. 2001. "Immigrant Political Participation in New York and Los Angeles," in *Governing American Cities: Inter-Ethnic Coalitions, Competition, and Conflict*, Michael Jones-Correa, ed. Pp. 17–70. New York: Russell Sage Foundation.

Morales, Ed. 2002. *Living in Spanglish: The Search for a Latino Identity in America.* New York: St. Martin's Press.

Moynihan, Daniel Patrick. 1979. "Patterns of Ethnic Succession: Blacks and Hispanics in New York City." *Political Science Quarterly* 94: 1 (spring): 1–14.

Murphy, Arthur D., Colleen Blanchard and Jennifer A. Hill, eds. 2001. *Latino Workers in the Contemporary South.* Athens: University of Georgia Press.

Navarro, Mireya. 2000. "Puerto Rican Presence Wanes in New York (Falling Back: A Special Report)," *New York Times*, February 28, pp. A1, B7.

Negrón-Muntaner, Francis. 2000. "'Feeling Pretty': *West Side Story* and Puerto Rican Identity Discourse." *Social Text* 18: 2 (June 1): 83–106.

Nelson, Jennifer A. 2001. "'Abortions under Community Control': Feminism, Nationalism, and the Politics of Reproduction among New York City's Young Lords." *Journal of Women's History* 13: 1 (Spring): 157–80.

Nieto, Sonia, ed. 2000. *Puerto Rican Students in U.S. Schools.* Mahwah, NJ: Lawrence Erlbaum Associates.

Ortíz, Altagracia, ed. 1996. *Puerto Rican Women and Work: Bridges in Transnational Labor.* Philadelphia: Temple University Press.

Pantoja, Antonia. 1998. "*Memorias de una Vida de Obra* (Memories of a Life of Work): An Interview with Antonia Pantoja" (interviewed by Wilhemina Perry). *Harvard Educational Review* 68: 2 (Summer): 244–258.

_____. 2002. *Memoir of a Visionary.* Houston: Arte Público Press.

Pereira, Joseph. 2000. "Table 1: Frequency and Percent Distribution of Selected Racial/Ethnic Groups in New York City: 1996 and 1999." Unpublished data: City University of New York Center for Urban Research—prepared for presentation before a meeting of the Board of Advisors of the Latino Economic and Welfare Policy Project of the PRLDEF Institute for Puerto Rican Policy, New York City, June 24, 2000.

Pérez, Marvette. 2002. "The Political 'Flying Bus': Nationalism, Identity, Status, Citizenship and Puerto Ricans." *Critique of Anthropology* 22: 3 (September): 305–322.

Pérez y González, María. 2000. *Puerto Ricans in the United States.* Westport, CT: Greenwood Press.

Piatt, Bill. 1997. *Black and Brown in America: The Case for Cooperation.* New York: New York University Press.

Poblete, Juan, ed. 2003. *Critical Latin American and Latino Studies.* Minneapolis: University of Minnesota Press.

PRLDEF Institute for Puerto Rican Policy. 2001. *The Latinos & Census 2000 Community Survey.* Unpublished data, Puerto Rican Legal Defense and Education Fund.

Putnam, Robert. 2000. *Bowling Alone: The Collapse and Revival of American Community.* New York: Simon and Schuster.

Rappaport, Shelley. 2002. *Beyond Bilingual Education: Meeting the Needs of English Language Learners in the NYC Public Schools.* New York: Puerto Rican Legal Defense and Education Fund.

Rey-Hernandez, Cesar A. 1999–2000. "Puertorriqueños y dominicanos: migrantes ante el reto de la identidad nacional." *Homines: Revista de Ciencias Socialies* 20–22 (January–December): 389–398.

Ricourt, Milagros, and Ruby Danta. 2003. *Hispanas de Queens: Latino Panethnicity in a New York City Neighborhood*. Ithaca, NY: Cornell University Press.

Rios, Diana I., and Ali N. Mohamed. 2003. *Black and Brown Communication: Latino and African American Conflict and Convergence in Mass Media*. New York: Praeger.

Rivera, Raquel Z. 2001. "Hip-Hop, Puerto Ricans, and Ethnoracial Identities in New York" in *Mambo Montage: The Latinization of New York*, Agustín Laó Montes and Arlene Dávila, eds. Pp. 235–261. New York: Columbia University Press.

———. 2003. *New York Ricans from the Hip Hop Zone*. New York: Palgrave Macmillan.

Rivera Ramos, Efrén. 2001. *The Legal Construction of Identity: The Judicial and Social Legacy of American Colonialism in Puerto Rico*. Washington, DC: American Psychological Association.

Rivera-Batiz, Francisco L., and Carlos E. Santiago. 1996. *Island Paradox: Puerto Rico in the 1990s*. New York: Russell Sage Foundation.

Rodríguez, Clara E. 2000. *Changing Race: Latinos, the Census, and the History of Ethnicity in the United States*. New York: New York University Press.

Rodríguez, Richard. 2002. *Brown: The Last Discovery of America*. New York: Viking.

Rodríguez-Fraticelli, Carlos, Carlos Sanabria, and Amílcar Tirado. 1991. "Puerto Rican Nonprofit Organizations in New York City." in *Hispanics and the Nonprofit Sector*, Herman E. Gallegos and Michael O'Neill, eds. Pp. 38–48. New York: The Foundation Center.

Sánchez González, Lisa. 2000. *Boricua Literature: A Literary History of the Puerto Rican Diaspora*. New York: New York University Press.

Sánchez Korrol, Virgina. 1995. "Puerto Ricans." in Kenneth T. Jackson, ed. *The Encyclopedia of New York City*. New Haven, CT: Yale University Press.

Sandoval-Sánchez, Alberto. 1999. *José, Can You See? Latinos On and Off Broadway*. Madison: University of Wisconsin Press.

Scott, Janny. 2002. "In Simple Pronouns, Clues to Shifting Latino Identity." *The New York Times*, December 5.

Senior, Clarence. 1961. *Strangers Then Neighbors: From Pilgrims to Puerto Ricans*. New York: Anti-Defamation League of B'nai B'rith.

Sites, William. 2003. *Remaking New York: Primitive Globalization and the Politics of Urban Community*. Minneapolis: University of Minnesota Press.

Smith, Anthony D. 1983. *Theories of Nationalism*, 2nd ed. New York: Holmes & Meier.

Solís, Jocelyn. 2001. "Immigration Status and Identity: Undocumented Mexicans in New York," in *Mambo Montage: The Latinization of New York*, Agustín Laó Montes, and Arlene Dávila, eds. Pp. 336–361. New York: Columbia University Press.

Suro, Roberto. 1999. *Strangers Among Us: Latino Lives in a Changing America*. New York: Vintage Books.

Torres, Andrés. 1995. *Between Melting Pot and Mosaic: African Americans and Puerto Ricans in the New York Political Economy*. Philadelphia: Temple University Press.

Torres, Andrés, and José E. Velázquez, eds. 1998. *The Puerto Rican Movement: Voices from the Diaspora*. Philadelphia, PA: Temple University Press.

Torres Santiago, José Manuel. 2002. "Pido la Palabra: ¿'Nuyoricans' o puertorriqueños?" *El Diario-La Prensa*, August 27, p. 11.

Umana-Taylor, Adriana J., and Mark A. Fine. 2001. "Methodologist Implications of Grouping Latino Adolescents into One Collective Ethnic Group." *Hispanic Journal of Behavioral Sciences* 23: 4 (November): 347–362.

U.S. Census Bureau. 2001. *Current Population Survey, March 2000*. Washington, DC: Ethnic and Hispanic Statistics Branch, Population Division (Internet Release Date: March 6).

U.S. Commission on Civil Rights. 1976. *Puerto Ricans in the Continental United States: An Uncertain Future*. Washington, DC: U.S. Commission on Civil Rights.

Wagenheim, Kal, and Olga Jiménez de Wagenheim, eds. 1996. *The Puerto Ricans: A Documentary History*. Princeton, NJ: Marcus Wiener Publishers.

Waters, Mary. C., John Mollenkopf, and Philip Kasinitz. 1999. "The Second Generation in New York City: A Demographic Overview." Paper presented at the Annual Meeting of the Population Association of America, March 25, New York City.

Weaver, Jr., Warren. 1966. "Law on Puerto Rican Vote Upheld by Supreme Court: 7–2 Ruling Declares Literacy in Spanish Meets State Test—Dissenters Fear Widening of Congressional Power." *The New York Times*, June 14, p. 1.

Williams, Linda Faye. 2003. *The Constraint of Race: Legacies of White Skin Privilege in America*. University Park: Pennsylvania State University Press.

Zentella, Ana Celia. 2002. "Spanish in New York," in *The Multilingual Apple: Languages in New York City*, 2nd ed, Ofelia García and Joshua A. Fishman, eds. Pp. 167–202. Berlin: Mouton de Gruyter.

CHAPTER FOUR
Commentary

A large Puerto Rican flag carried by marchers at the Puerto Rican Day parade, June 2004. (*Photo by Angelo Falcón*)

COMMENTARY

FORGING A NEW, NEW YORK: THE PUERTO RICAN COMMUNITY, POST-1945

Clara E. Rodríguez

Early on in my career a Mohawk friend who had been raised on the reservation in New York shared with me an early school experience. She sat in class as a young child and heard the teacher speak about Indians in ways that made her feel sick and embarrassed. She ran home crying and asked her mother if all of these things were true about Indians. Her mother looked at her straight on and then asked her, is your mother that way? Your older sister? Your uncle? The people you know here? She knew they were not. No more needed to be said.

I also think about the many students that I have known over the years and the variety of their experiences and reactions to the negative literature that they had read about Puerto Ricans. They range from stories like those above (few) to the more common, "I'm third-generation poor. I guess we are an underclass. I want to be different." to the occasional "That's what I come from, but that's not what I am...that's not all we are!" And, sometimes, "We are much more than that."

When I originally sat down to organize my thoughts for this chapter, I

An earlier version of these comments on Angelo Falcón's "De'tras Pa'lante: Explorations on the Future History of Puerto Rican in New York City" was delivered at the symposium entitled, "Contra Viento y Marea"—Historical Reflections on Puerto Ricans in New York City, 1945 to the Present...and the Future," held on September 22, 2000, at the CUNY Graduate Center, 365 Fifth Avenue, New York City.

had been engaged in researching the history and contributions of Puerto Ricans in the States to the world of media. In reviewing historical materials for this project (some of which I will cite below), I was struck by a sharp contrast. This was between the depictions of Puerto Ricans in mainstream media as generally problematic, for example, in films, television, and the press, and the rich, full, lived experience of Puerto Ricans as conveyed by writers, commentators, and in memoirs from the Puerto Rican community. Over the years I saw a similar contrast between the social science and policy works I continually read and my own experience as a Puerto Rican woman living in Bronx communities with large numbers of Puerto Ricans. In his chapter of this book, Angelo Falcón also refers to these social science works, that is, the culture of poverty and underclass literature. I was again reminded of this contrast when I read the *New York Times* article that forms the basis of Falcón's chapter.

The *New York Times* Article and the History of Media Coverage
The Article Appears at an Extraordinary Moment

As Falcón notes, the story on the waning of the Puerto Rican presence appeared at an extraordinary moment. The article appeared as the country was experiencing a "Latin music boom." The "spectacular successes of [Puerto Rican] entertainment figures" like Ricky Martin, Jennifer Lopez, Marc Antony, Son by Four, and others were being continuously covered by major news outlets (cited in Falcón, author's parenthesis). At the time, the public was almost bombarded by the music of these Puerto Rican artists, as their songs figured prominently at the top of numerous music charts. The Puerto Rican community was vicariously enjoying the success of these entertainers, proud that some of its own had achieved such popular recognition. So as the New York Puerto Rican community was celebrating the mega success of its offspring, the *New York Times* article was describing the community (from which almost all of them had come) as deteriorating with regard to population, poverty, human capital, institutions, and attitude. Not that you can't have major luminaries and a depressed community at the same time—it's just that this did not seem to be the mood of the community as I saw it. Rather, as one young woman from Intervale Avenue in the Bronx said at a meeting, the sense I had was that we were "moving on."

The article also appeared after the National Puerto Rican Day Parade had finally been acknowledged by the press as the major event it had always been. Beginning in 1958, it had been mounted year after year, at great cost in terms of time, energy, and funds, and often with major conflicts. Despite the problems, the parade had succeeded in garnering huge crowds for decades. Yet, it had consistently received minimal coverage in English-language news outlets.

In the midst of the highly political issues always enveloping it, for example, issues of the island's political status and conflicts over more local issues and groups, it had managed to get thousands of people to march down Fifth Avenue in an orderly way. It had also managed to attract sufficient numbers to the parade so that by 1991 it was dubbed by its organizers, "the largest outdoor cultural event in the whole United States." It had also spawned similar parades in many other cities throughout the United States. By the time the *New York Times* article was written, the parade had managed to get major network coverage that lasted for hours and hours (amazing for any event!). Moreover, I speculated that audience ratings must have been high for this, given the commercial sponsorship of this televised time.

By the year 2000, the numbers attending had also finally been acknowledged by most in the city to exceed a million and a half. In fact, *New York* magazine (1999) cited a figure of two million spectators. Moreover, most of the stories being written about the parade portrayed the event as one that both Puerto Ricans and non–Puerto Ricans attended and enjoyed. *New York* magazine, for example, referred to the parade as "both a dazzling display of ethnic pride and a joyous, salsa-driven party." However, as Falcón notes, this Puerto Rican success story was marred when later that year the media gave extensive coverage to the negative images of misogynistic assaults by men against defenseless women in Central Park during and after the parade. These men were assumed to be largely Puerto Rican and Latino. As reporter Juan González (2000) noted, these vivid images were carried around the world. Not covered in the media was the long history of the parade, which had managed to proceed without such incidents for decades. Nor was the violence erupting at other parades, such as that over gays marching in the St. Patrick's Day parade, raised as a point of comparison to describe the crowd dynamics and mob behavior that often takes place in settings where emotionalism is high. Also generally uncovered in the media were the numerous Puerto Rican and other Latino men and women who came out and decried these attacks.

More importantly, the *New York Times* article appeared about a month before the decennial census took place. Despite the flaws of the census, it still provides the most accurate, comprehensive data on Puerto Ricans and would have given us a better idea about whether the Puerto Rican population was indeed declining and by how much. Yet, the story was done before these figures were available. I was reminded of a discussion that I had had with a *New York Times* reporter just prior to the release of the 1990 census. At that time the reporter was insisting that Puerto Ricans had become a minority within the New York City Latino population. As it turned out, the subsequent 1990 figures showed Puerto Ricans were still a majority. As Falcón (graph 4) notes in his chapter, they constituted 50.3 percent of all Latinos at the time. But it was difficult to get this reporter to consider the possibility that there might be a bias in the assumption that Puerto Ricans were a Latino minority then. I could not understand why so much energy was going into this argument, particularly when the data had yet to be released. I recall the same argument had surfaced even earlier with another reporter, and I had wondered then why the media believed (or wanted to believe) that Puerto Ricans were "diminishing." Why was this the story they wrote, when there were so many other more important stories? What difference did it make whether the number of Puerto Ricans was increasing or decreasing? Was it, as Falcón suggests, that by diminishing the size, they could diminish the significance of the problems, issues, and concerns of this community?

The emphasis on declining numbers and declining significance in the *New York Times* article also reminded me of the numerous discussions that took place in government and policy arenas during the white flight era. The South Bronx (the area with the largest number of Puerto Ricans) was often described as vacant, depopulated, devastated, and like the bombed-out areas of Berlin after World War II. The analogies were not far from the truth, and people were leaving. But rather than addressing the needs of those still living there, the South Bronx was essentially written off during the mid-1970s and an unofficial policy of benign neglect was followed (Sánchez 1990, Bronx Museum of the Arts 1979). Although many people were leaving the Bronx, there were still over one million people living in the borough. Moreover, rather than being neglected, many of them now required greater attention. Many had greater needs for services because landlords had abandoned so many buildings, businesses had closed, and arson initiated by landlords was rampant.

Deficit Models

Falcón notes that the article states that there is "no shortage of success stories," but he also observes that it describes "a community that is clearly in decline." He reviews the arguments in the article that are used to describe this community in decline and he expands on the arguments presented in the article. In so doing, he provides a greater depth of analysis, as well as post-census figures. He leads us to a more complex understanding of the Puerto Rican past and present, and its implications for the future of New York City. His analysis also leads us to further questions, particularly about the use of deficit models. For example, do declining numbers mean a waning presence? How accurate are claims that there is "poor family involvement in education," a lack of autonomous churches, and a problematic attitude toward assimilation, which is hampered by their "passionate nationalism" and makes them unwilling to acculturate. Also, what kinds of analyses and data do we need to do to have a better sense of the extent of, as well as the causes of, welfare dependency, persistent poverty, and low educational attainment among Puerto Ricans in New York City? Are those returning to Puerto Rico primarily the poor or the professional success stories? Are they both? To what extent does the series title, "Falling Back: A Special Report," reinforce a deficit-model approach?

Data Problems

In his review, Falcón discusses a number of difficulties with the arguments. I would add a few more. With regard to the data, if we are going to make generalizations about persistent poverty in the New York Puerto Rican community, we need longitudinal studies that examine specific families over time. Only a few researchers have done this; for example, Lloyd Rogler's earlier descriptive study of 100 Puerto Rican families did not find much support for this thesis. We also need to examine "who" is in the data. As I noted in a much earlier volume, given the shifts in population,(that is, new [im]migrants arriving from Puerto Rico, Puerto Ricans leaving New York to go elsewhere or to go back to Puerto Rico), we need to know to what extent we are measuring the same population over time (Rodríguez 1991). In addition, we need to determine to what extent those who reported they were Puerto Rican were indeed Puerto Rican and not undocumented immigrants from other countries wanting to obscure their undocumented status.

A Continuing History

To me, it seemed that the problem was not so much the article itself as it was the history of such articles in relation to the Puerto Rican community. For example, have other groups gotten similar front-page coverage when their numbers decline? Had I just missed the stories on how the numbers of Greeks or Italians had declined in New York City? Or have I just tended to become embroiled with reporters on the "Puerto Rican stories"? Why have the stories about the Puerto Rican community that I've been interviewed for over the years generally been approached from a deficit perspective? Why has most of the time I've spent with these reporters been spent on attempting to correct superficial deficit approaches, only to be thankful that I was not quoted in what ended up as another negative story about Puerto Ricans. I first began thinking more seriously about this problem many years ago when a reporter approached me about wanting to do a story on a typical Puerto Rican family. I introduced him to a Puerto Rican student who happened to work in my office. She later told me he wasn't interested in her family because there were no major social problems in the family. Her mother had managed to raise and educate thirteen children by herself in New York City. I don't recall any success stories in the article that he wrote.

The difficulties with past writings on Puerto Ricans have been noted often (see, for example, Rodríguez 1995, Rodríguez et al. forthcoming 2004, and Torres and Rodríguez, 1991). Some of the difficulties include: using deficit models, conveying a strong sense of "otherness," using inappropriate contexts for analysis, generalizing from singular or extreme cases to the whole group, deprecating indigenous views, obscuring the colonial relationship, and overemphasizing an assimilationist perspective. This literature has stressed that we should beware of repeating the mistakes of the past. Despite this literature, however, I am repeatedly surprised at how often journalistic literature focuses on the problems that Puerto Ricans have or present, or on what Puerto Ricans gain from their relationship with the United States, such as food stamps and student aid. This is as opposed to stories that might have discussed what Puerto Ricans have given, or presently contribute, to the United States. Or how the United States benefits from the relationship between Puerto Rico and the United States—or even how both benefit.

Recently, both Jorge Duany (2003) and Raúl Duany (2003), in their responses to a *National Geographic* (May 2003) piece on Puerto Rico, take note of this particular, but unfortunate, lens that has been and still continues to be used when covering Puerto Rico and Puerto Ricans. Raúl Duany (2003) notes that, as the U.S. Navy prepared to withdraw from Vieques island in May, 2003, *National Geographic*'s May issue "generated great consternation within the Puerto Rican community." Puerto Rico's Resident Commissioner felt compelled to point out other dimensions not covered in the article. For example, he noted that:

- Puerto Rico was the United States' eighth largest trading partner and
- the world's fourth largest purchaser of U.S. products per capita. (Indeed, Puerto Rico bought more products than many larger countries, such as Italy, Russia or China.)
- in 2001 alone, Puerto Rico purchased 16 billion dollars' worth of U.S. goods, which, in turn fueled the creation and maintenance of more than 270,000 U.S. jobs in the States;
- more than 100 of the U.S. *Fortune* 500 multinationals operated out of the island and generated more than 47 billion in exports in the year 2002;
- 25 percent of all the pharmaceutical products in the United States were made in Puerto Rico;
- 80 percent of the twenty largest-selling prescription drugs (that is, sixteen of the top twenty) were also made in Puerto Rico;
- when we consider the hemisphere as a whole, Puerto Rico is the fifth

largest exporter, after the U.S., Canada, Mexico, and Brazil;
- despite the protests against navy bombing on the island of Vieques (wouldn't the residents of Martha's Vineyard similarly protest? Would the navy ever consider such maneuvers there?), close to 40,000 Puerto Ricans are on active duty or reserve status in the U.S. armed forces;
- the U.S. Army's two recruiting companies on the island are consistently tops in recruiting worldwide;
- more basically, this island, which in the past was often referred to as "our small island in the West Indies" (Jorge Duany 2003), has a population larger than half of the states in the U.S., and a buying power of $25 billion a year; and finally,
- the workforce in Puerto Rico is composed of skilled, bilingual U.S. citizens, who do not have voting representation in Congress; nor do they have the right to vote for president.

There are certainly lots of ways to view the above "facts." For example, they can be seen as evidence of either strengths or dependence. But the point here is that these are important "facts" that paint a picture of economic power and some important contributions, and they tend not to be included in the pictures often painted by some news reporters.

The Larger Contexts

Facts like those above determine the parameters and contexts within which Puerto Ricans live and function. But, as noted, in some works, coverage is superficial and Puerto Ricans' problems often become the focus, to the exclusion or obfuscation of other dimensions, or even a fuller, more in-depth picture. Puerto Ricans end up being seen as an anomaly, a problem, or uniquely hindered. Therefore, it is important to understand the situation of Puerto Ricans within larger contexts and within a deeper historical framework. For example, the article focused on Puerto Ricans in New York City and informed the world that the number and proportion of Puerto Ricans in New York City had declined 12.5 percent. There were now 107,600 fewer Puerto Ricans in the five boroughs of New York City than there had been in 1990. This was, indeed, the first time that the Puerto Rican population had dropped in 60 years (Junco 2001). However, to quote Mark Twain, who informed the press when told that his death had already been announced that reports of his demise had been greatly exaggerated, talk of the demise of the Puerto Rican population was similarly overstated. At the same time that the numbers of Puerto Ricans had declined in New York City, the numbers of Puerto Ricans in the state and in the country as a whole had increased. In fact, the numbers of Puerto Ricans outside the city but in New York State increased substantially (i.e., 38 percent) during this period (Buettner 2001). Also, as Falcón notes, while the Puerto Rican population declined in the Bronx, Brooklyn, and Manhattan, it grew in the more suburban boroughs of New York, that is, Staten Island and Queens.

Moreover, the population of Puerto Ricans in all states had increased by a considerable amount, from 2.7 million in 1990 to 3.4 million in 2000—an increase of 24.9 percent (U.S. Census Bureau 2000: 2). In addition, the Puerto Rican population in Puerto Rico continued to grow and increased 8 percent over the decade for a total of 3.8 million in 2000. So, although the numbers of Puerto Ricans had declined in New York City, their numbers were robust elsewhere. The population of Puerto Ricans in Florida, for example, almost doubled to 482,000 (Junco 2001). There were now more Puerto Ricans in Florida than in New Jersey or San Juan, making Puerto Ricans the second largest Latino group in Florida, after Cubans (Duany 2002). Consequently, what was going on was not the "demise" or "the waning" of the Puerto Rican population, but a shift in the distribution of a population that has continued to grow substantially in the United States. These shifts (both the declines and increases of Puerto Ricans in various parts of the country) are to be expected as a population ages and moves to retirement areas, or as people move in search of, or in response to, greater economic opportunities.

Also, if we examine the larger picture, we see that in the same way that the Puerto Rican population was shifting, so were other populations. At the same time that the Puerto Rican presence was ostensibly waning in New York City, the main demographic or census story for the country as a whole was the huge growth of the Latino population. Officially, the U.S. Latino population encompassed 37 million people and constituted almost 13 percent of the total U.S. population in the year 2001 (U. S. Bureau of the Census 2001: 1). This was greater than the population of Spain or Canada. Moreover, these figures did not include the 3.8 million Latinos in Puerto Rico (Rodríguez 1991: chapter 1). If they had been added, the count would have been 39.1 million. Nor did these figures include, or estimate, the undercount, that is, those Latinos who were living in the United States but were not counted for one reason or another (U. S. Bureau of the Census 2001: 4; Rodríguez 1994). The big story should have been what most people were already observing in their particular cities, suburbs, and towns: that Latinos were rapidly increasing and accounted for one of every eight Americans as the twenty-first century began (National Council of La Raza 2001).

On the local New York City level, the same trends were apparent. At the same time that Puerto Ricans were decreasing in numbers, the numbers of other Latinos had increased. Consequently, New York City was just as, or more, Latino than ever. Indeed, Latinos constituted 27 percent of New York

City's population, surpassing in numbers the African American population, which accounted for 26.6 percent of the total. Whites were a minority, accounting for 44.6 percent of the total population. Asians made up another 9.8 percent of the total and "Other Race" equaled 14 percent, with the majority of this group being Latinos (Buettner 2001) (The data on Latinos are derived from a different question than the data on race; consequently the race figures are different from the Hispanic figures.)

Moreover, the "face of America" was changing more generally; as *Time* magazine had declared earlier, a "browning of America" was taking place. By 1980, one of every four Americans was of non-European background. This was a dramatic change from where the U.S. was at the start of the twentieth century, when one of every eight U.S. residents had non-European ancestors. Immigration to the country was also starkly different. In 1900, almost 85 percent of the immigrant population was from Europe and 2 percent were from Latin America and Asia combined. At the end of the century, the picture was reversed: only 15 percent were from Europe and 77 percent were from Latin America and Asia combined. (U. S. Bureau of the Census 2000, 2002a, 2002b, 2002c). This was the bigger context.

An Alternative Story

In light of this shift to a country with a more acknowledged Latina/o presence, I think a more interesting story would have been how the Latino past is different from the present, and what this can it tell us about the future. As Falcón notes, the size of the Puerto Rican population in New York City remains "quite large by any standard." Given that in 2000 Puerto Ricans were still the City's largest ethnic group, that they constituted 9.9 percent of the total New York City population and 36.6 percent of the city's Latino population, a number of alternative stories could have been written. For example:

- Puerto Ricans Still Dominate Five Decades After the Peak Migration
- Moving On: A Special Report, Fewer but Stronger
- Puerto Ricans' Influence Endures in New York City

In telling these stories, we would have to look at what has been accomplished in the Puerto Rican community and how the history of Puerto Ricans in New York has influenced the world we live in today. On the simplest level, it seems that such a story would show that (1) there was a history and (2) much was accomplished that changed New York for the better. It is especially important to do stories of this kind, given the kind of problematic media coverage the Puerto Rican community has had in the past.

A Short Review of the History of Puerto Ricans in New York, Post-1945

The "bad timing" that Falcón explores very well still needs a bit more fleshing out. First of all, although the largest migration waves occurred after World War II and through the 1950s, there are much earlier roots in New York City. According to research conducted thus far, by the latter half of the nineteenth century there was a small community of Puerto Ricans in New York, composed mainly of merchants, political exiles, and some skilled workers. By 1874, the first Puerto Rican newspaper had already been published in New York City; it was entitled *La Voz de Puerto Rico*. In addition, the independence party of Cuba and Puerto Rico had already established offices in Philadelphia and New York, and the first Puerto Rican civic organization had been established by 1892 (see, for example, Kullen 1992, Rodríguez-Fraticelli et al. 1991, Sánchez Korrol 1994, Haslip-Viera and Baver 1996, and Olmo 1991).

However, Puerto Ricans began to arrive in largest numbers during what has been called the U.S. "immigration hiatus" period, that is, after the United States had closed its borders to immigrants from elsewhere. In the 1920s, the United States passed immigration laws that severely restricted immigration for more than forty years—until 1965, when a new Immigration Act was passed. The1965 act overturned the immigration quotas established in earlier acts and opened up immigration again, ushering in the current high rates of immigration from Latin America and Asia to the United States. The two world wars that occurred in the first part of the twentieth century also contributed to the immigration hiatus. Countries in Europe restricted emigration from their countries during wartime. After the wars, as these countries rebuilt their economies, few of their citizens were interested in leaving or had the means to do so (Massey 1995). Puerto Ricans were the first (non-refugees) to arrive in large numbers after this immigration hiatus.

The fact that the large majority of Puerto Ricans arrived during this period is significant. Although the city had considerable diversity, the reigning ideology of the time sought to disavow or downplay this diversity. For example, there was a substantial African American population, and the city had been host to wave after wave of immigrants, many of whom had also experienced a "racialization" of sorts soon after arrival. However, Puerto Ricans entered settings where many of the children and grandchildren of immigrants had unequivocally embraced the entrenched, assimilationist ideology of the era—and perhaps of even earlier eras. By the 1950s, the city had become habitually disinclined to accept, and disapproving of, ethnic and cultural differences. The celebrated diversity, cosmopolitanism, and international flavor that is so much an acknowledged part of New York City today were sadly lacking when Puerto Ricans came in large numbers.

Forging a New, New York: The Puero Rican Community, Post 1945

Puerto Ricans who came during the Great Migration, between 1946 and 1964 (Stevens-Arroyo and Díaz Stevens 1982), also arrived during a period of heightened political conservatism, that is, the McCarthy era (Massey 1995). This political climate influenced both the reception of Puerto Ricans and their portrayal in the media. The acts of the Nationalist Party against the House of Representatives further inflamed media perception. The now-classic film *West Side Story* (1961), and its earlier 1958 live version further solidified the view of Puerto Ricans as urban, immigrant, gang-related invaders. As Falcón and others have pointed out, other films would underscore and harden these menacing images and bring them to the attention of national and international publics (Pérez 1997).

Also, the social science literature of the day would focus on the problematic aspects of Puerto Ricans. Between 1947 and 1971, a period of relatively low book production, well-known or distinguished presses published more than twenty major social science works focusing on Puerto Ricans. Many of these works were written by scholars who were, or would become, nationally celebrated; these included C. Wright Mills, for whom there is today a prestigious award given by the American Sociological Association; well-known immigration and labor historian Oscar Handlin; the famous and infamous Oscar Lewis, who received as much monetary support for his studies as he did disapproval from the countries he studied (he was pressured to leave both Cuba and Mexico, and he created a storm of controversy over his book on Puerto Ricans, *La Vida*). Last but not least, was our now distinguished late senator from New York, Daniel Patrick Moynihan, along with the much-cited Harvard sociologist Nathan Glazer. There were, in addition, other well-known and respected social scientists, such as Sidney Mintz, Rev. J. P. Fitzpatrick, Melvin Tumin, Arnold Feldman, Eric Wolf, J. H. Steward, and Clarence Senior, who would also focus on Puerto Ricans. Few of those who wrote on Puerto Ricans deviated from the prevailing paradigms of the time, which emphasized assimilation, obfuscated the colonial relationship, neglected political sovereignty issues, had an exclusive, noncomparative focus on Puerto Rico, tended to overgeneralize from small numbers or extreme cases to all Puerto Ricans, and applied categories and contexts developed in the United States but not necessarily relevant to Puerto Ricans. As a result, of the predominance and influence of this academic literature, Puerto Ricans tended to be problematized and seen within implicit deficit frameworks, which highlighted negative as opposed to positive dimensions. Important aspects of Puerto Rican history tended either to be excluded or presented from a Eurocentric perspective, and revisionist or critical work tended to be marginalized. In the 1970s, a new literature began to surface that questioned many of these earlier works and opened new avenues of inquiry (For more on this see, Rodríguez 1995 and Rodríguez et al. forthcoming 2004). Puerto Ricans were not the first to be viewed through these lenses, but, as Falcón notes, they were "one of the major guinea pigs." They were also the major Latino game in town, constituting, as Falcón's graph 4 indicates, the overwhelming majority of all Latinos in New York between 1950 and 1970.

Puerto Ricans were, however, one of the first groups to experience (and analyze) the impact of major economic restructuring, which would later come to affect scores of other workers throughout the country and to create major rustbelt areas, downsizing, and blue-collar structural unemployment (Rodríguez 1974: 113–119ff, Rodríguez 1979, and Bonilla and Campos 1985). As both the *New York Times* article and Falcón point out, major structural shifts in political-economic structures would lead to a decrease in the manufacturing jobs held by many Puerto Ricans. Although structural analyses of the Puerto Rican situation are today often noted, it was not mainstream scholars who developed these structural analyses. Indeed, these structural analyses tended to be ignored by mainstream academics and policymakers, until it was apparent that the very structural factors that were affecting Puerto Ricans during the 1960s and 1970s were now also affecting larger groups of workers in the United States.

Other forces, for example, rigid binary racial contexts and linguistic and educational barriers and battles, would also affect Puerto Ricans in a variety of ways (Rodríguez 1991). We have forgotten that, "once upon a time," Puerto Ricans with a noticeable accent were not allowed to teach. A stark example of this occurred in the late 1960s. A top-level Puerto Rican director of a city agency was curious to find out if discrimination toward Puerto Ricans by the Board of Examiners did exist. He had been educated in New York City's public schools and had gone on to graduate from Columbia University and then Yale Law School. He took the teacher's exam and passed with almost perfect scores, but was turned down by the Board because they thought he had an accent. (To this day, I have never heard anyone say he had an accent.) Puerto Ricans were not the first to experience this type of discrimination, for a "noticeable accent" has often been in the ear of the beholder. Consequently, and for example, a "noticeable accent" was undoubtedly also heard by Irish examiners from Jewish applicants. However, the changes instituted because of Puerto Rican experiences and battles have altered this situation significantly for newcomers.

Puerto Ricans also came at a time when there was rampant suburbanization of industries and people, federally supported policies of highway construction, and urban renewal that depleted available low-cost housing in the central cities. Later, the mass construction of federally subsidized public housing would destroy integrated working-class communities through eminent domain, disrupt local businesses, and concentrate low-income populations into high-rise towers with minimal services. At that time, even public housing was segregated, with Blacks and Puerto Ricans generally concentrated in some areas of the city and the White poor placed in other projects away from inner-city neighborhoods. Puerto Ricans were not the first or the only ones to be affected by these changes, but this was an important part of the context that receives short shrift in discussions of Puerto Ricans. It is also a part of the context that has changed. Today, there is actual, enforceable legislation to penalize housing segregation. This is not to say that it doesn't still occur. But, at the time, such practices were more the norm, generally undisclosed, seldom challenged, or seriously penalized. The effects of these phenomena on the early Puerto Rican migrants have yet to be fully analyzed.

Being "the first" during this period is difficult to explain to others who have not been the first. It is a bit like the first-born in a family explaining what it is like to the second, third, or tenth-born in a family. But perhaps analogies are useful here. Being the first Black woman to refuse to sit at the back of the bus, is quite different from being the hundredth, thousandth, and so on. Being "the first" to integrate a club, housing area, school, beach, barber shop, or any other place that is homogeneously different from you and opposed to your presence is different from being the ten thousandth person to do so. Puerto Ricans were the first wave of Latinos to come after 1945, and they changed the world of New York City for those who came later. Without the numerous battles fought by Puerto Ricans (sometimes via organized activity and sometimes via the day-to-day less formal resistance to injustice), few institutions would be as open as they are today. Puerto Ricans opened the doors through which others would follow.

A Changed New York
Drawing from my earlier work in Acosta-Belén et al. (2000), I will note, in passing, just a few of the changes that influenced subsequent generations of immigrant and nonimmigrant New Yorkers. As Falcón noted, Puerto Ricans fought for and secured the Aspira Consent decree, which required that the Board of Education more formally address the needs of non-English speakers in school. This led to the development of English as a Second Language programs and bilingual programs, serving not only Puerto Ricans but also other Latinos, Asians, Europeans, and Africans. These programs came to employ large numbers of teachers from Latin America, the U.S., and abroad who had knowledge of another language. Puerto Ricans established Puerto Ricans Studies programs and departments, many of which have evolved into Latino and Latin American Studies or Ethnic Studies programs. To give a sense of this growth, during 1969, 5 Puerto Rican Studies programs were

established within the senior colleges of the City University system. By 1973, the programs had grown to 17 with more than 155 course offerings and enrollments of more than 6,240 students. Programs were also established within the State University colleges (for example, Albany and Buffalo), within the Rutgers University system in New Jersey; and in several midwestern institutions, such as Northeastern Illinois University, Wayne State, and Indiana University by the early 1970s (Acosta-Bélen 1993: 190). Such programs of study had been unprecedented in the States, in Puerto Rico, and in most Latin American countries. They would alter the climate on campuses and come to serve not just Puerto Rican students, but all students. They would also expand to incorporate new populations and interests.

Puerto Ricans also established many of the bilingual colleges and programs at the postsecondary level that today serve non–Puerto Rican newcomers to the United States. For example, in 1968, the Eugenio Maria de Hostos Community College was founded, making it the first bilingual college in the country. In 1974, Boricua College was established as a private, four-year bilingual college. Puerto Ricans also had always been actively involved in trying to improve the educational institutions that had been failing its children. Prominent among those trying to implement these improvements was Dr. Antonia Pantoja, who established Aspira in 1961 as a bilingual counseling agency to help youth in high schools pursue careers in professional, technical, and liberal arts fields. It is strange to reflect from today's vantage point, where bilingual (Spanish-English) counselors and agencies are fairly common in New York City, that—at that time—this was a courageous first. That it had never been done before and that many opposed its efforts and some high schools refused to allow chapters to form. Nevertheless, within three years, there were fifty-two Aspira clubs functioning throughout New York City high schools. Students, families and a few professionals now had a place to go. Aspira has since become a national organization with chapters in different states and in Puerto Rico; and it continues to serve those—no longer just Spanish-speaking—who need a place to go for guidance.

Similarly, Puerto Rican social entrepreneurs achieved other firsts. The still-existent Puerto Rican Family Institute was created in 1963 to assist recent migrant families. In 1964, the PRCDP (Puerto Rican Community Development Project) published its comprehensive study and plan, which would result in a number of self-help community-based programs to assist Puerto Ricans in the States. In 1966, the very first theater company in the United States to bring Shakespearean as well as English- and Spanish-language plays written by Latinos to the barrios was begun by Miriam Colon. This was the Puerto Rican Traveling Theatre, which continues to develop talented writers, actors, and directors in its workshops and provides an important venue for dramatists from other countries, as well as the United States, to have their works performed. It also continues to showcase works that have received much critical acclaim and many awards. Again, we take somewhat for granted the multitude of excellent Spanish-language repertory companies that we are lucky to have in New York. They produce plays that often speak to a uniquely Latino experience in Spanish and in English, and they hire Latino talent. Most of these plays would not otherwise be performed, yet they contribute immensely to the development of the dramatic arts in New York City. This was not always the case. Puerto Ricans pioneered in this regard and altered the state of New York City dramatic production.

Similarly, prior to the establishment of the Museo del Barrio (the Community's Museum) in 1969, museums had little space for works by Puerto Rican and Latina/o artists. Today, the Museo del Barrio is a full-fledged museum, nationally recognized for its excellent art programs. Since its inception, it has served as a doorway for artists from Latin America to exhibit their works in the United States. Other organizations were also begun that were dedicated to developing the artistic talents of community youth, including Taller Boricua and the Nuyorican Poet's Cafe. These and others continue to serve the Puerto Rican and other communities. Although much of this pioneering organizational activity took place in New York, similar major changes in the way things were done also took place in Puerto Rican communities across the nation. For example, the Taller Puertorriqueño in Philadelphia, the Latino Institute in Chicago, the Alianza Hispana in Boston, La Casa de Don Pedro and F.O.C.U.S. in Newark, and a variety of civic clubs and organizations throughout the Northeast and Midwest are examples of how Puerto Ricans were establishing similar institutional and organizational vehicles elsewhere. Falcón notes some of the pressures many of these institutions are under to expand their missions. From my vantage point, most of these institutions have always expanded and been open to others. The questions today concern whether the history and initial community-based missions of these organizations will be preserved, and, the extent to which the institutions will be able to continue to offer Puerto Rican–themed programs and to publicly acknowledge their Puerto Rican roots.

Puerto Ricans also established the Puerto Rican Legal Defense Fund in 1972 to challenge systemic discrimination. In the years that followed, it brought forth many class-action suits, including the landmark case against the New York City Board of Education that resulted in the establishment of bilingual programs throughout the city and elsewhere. As Falcón notes, PRLDEF was also responsible for eliminating the height requirement for New York City police officers. This had kept out hundreds of Latinos and others from entering the NYPD. Today, thanks in large part to PRLDF, we are able to legally demand that Spanish and other language interpreters be present in voting areas. "Once upon a time," for a very long time, many Puerto Rican citizens were discouraged from voting because such bilingual resources were not available, frowned upon when requested, or summarily rejected. In contrast to today, when politicians and others encourage new immigrants to become citizens and to vote, many Puerto Ricans were not encouraged to register to vote. Consequently, many who were cognizant of political issues from reading Spanish-language newspapers and hearing Spanish-language news on radio and television were disenfranchised. Political analysts at the time blamed Puerto Rican passivity and a colonized mentality for the community's nonparticipation in the electoral process. They ignored the fact that more than 80 percent (double the U.S. rate) of Puerto Ricans voted in Puerto Rico.

Puerto Ricans fought for reforms in the voting area and demanded (as citizens) translators in other areas, such as the courts, hospitals, and schools. Puerto Ricans did not win all these struggles, but many changes did come about, and their struggles contributed to a rethinking of immigrant rights. I recently read the comments of a Mexican immigrant woman that brought these struggles to mind. She had become involved with a community-based organization called Mothers on the Move, or MOM. In the MOM newsletter she was asked how her involvement with the organization had helped her "experience as an immigrant living in the South Bronx." She said, "Now, I know that I and my family have rights and that we can do things to defend them. For example, I know that I have the right to speak Spanish and that I have a right to demand translation in Court, in my daughter's schools or in the hospitals. I have also learned that, as an immigrant and as a mother, I can be more involved in other problems in my community" ("News from MOM," December 2002, p. 2) Such thinking was inconceivable when Puerto Ricans first arrived. It was radical when Puerto Ricans first began to demand, as Spanish-speaking citizens, such rights. The very demands/requests were often disparaged.

In the same way that many of us take for granted programs like English as a second language, we also take for granted the work that has been accomplished by many of our educators, historians, and others in the trenches of academia. There have always been members of the Puerto Rican community who have said that we have a history and that it is important to preserve, understand, and communicate this history. This is a tradition that has been in place for centuries in Puerto Rico. It has been continued through both written and oral communication. In New York, this tradition has continued and perhaps become more crucial for a variety of reasons. Originally it was not taught, and it is still not taught in many places. In some cases, U.S. history books suggested the history was unimportant. Without attention to this history, it may seem to many to be nonexistent. Developing a gradual awareness that few if any research and archival centers were collecting archival materials on the history of the Puerto Rican community, the Center for Puerto Rican Studies was established in 1973 within the City University of New York. Today it houses the largest repository of materials on Puerto Ricans in the states and serves as an important research center not just for Puerto Rican students and scholars but for others interested in comparative work.

A focus by this Center and others on Puerto Rican history has yielded an interesting, generally neglected sense of the history of Latinos in New York (see Haslip-Viera and Baver 1996 for more on the history of Latinos in New York). A very abbreviated history of these efforts shows that the history of Puerto Ricans and Latinos goes back much further than *West Side Story* would lead us to believe. For example, we see that early on, Puerto Ricans established a variety of mutual aid, political, civic, social, and union organizations in the United States. Between 1900 and 1919, these included Union International de Tabaqueros, La Resistencia, Asociación Latino Americana, Union Benefica Español, La Aurora, La Razon, El Ejemplo, El Tropical, and Club Ibero-Americano. According to Rodríguez-Fraticelli et al. (1991), prior to World War I, clubs were organized in the United States by the better-educated and most radical sector of the Cuban and Puerto Rican working class. They served as information and fund-raising centers for the revolutionary cause in Puerto Rico. By 1925, the Casa de Puerto Rico (the Puerto Rican House) had been established by Puerto Rican professionals and intellectuals in New York City to promote Hispanic culture, customs, and traditions. In the following year, the Ateneo Obrero was established by Puerto Rican workers for cultural and educational purposes and to address the needs of the already existent second generation in New York. Soon after, in 1927, the Puerto Rican and Hispanic League was established in New York to unite, educate, and represent all Spanish-speaking organizations to the authorities. This organization also urged electoral participation and the improvement of conditions in New York.

After this early start, organizations continued to proliferate in New York. Casita Maria, an important agency still serving Latinos in New York, was founded in 1934. Unknown to most is the fact that the first Puerto Rican, Oscar García Rivera, was elected to the New York State Assembly in 1937. He represented an East Harlem district in Manhattan. As Falcón notes, after the war, in 1948, the Puerto Rico Department of Labor set up the Migration Division in New York, which provided services and assistance to both agricultural laborers and urban residents. The Festival of St. John the Baptist (Fiesta de San Juan Bautista) was an annual event that was first held at St. Patrick's Cathedral in New York. It went on to become an annual, hugely attended religious and cultural event in the New York Puerto Rican community. In 1956, the Council of Hometown Clubs (El Congreso del Pueblo) was founded. This was a self-supported, voluntary organization composed of eighty clubs of working-class migrants, who saw Puerto Rican cultural traditions as an important force in the struggle for civil rights. The Council assisted newcomers in finding shelter, housing, and jobs. In 1957, the Puerto Rican Forum (today the National Puerto Rican Forum) was incorporated to develop Puerto Rican leadership and to address issues of housing, economic development, education, and juvenile delinquency. Since, as Falcón notes, the bulk of the Puerto Rican community was concentrated in New York City for a long time much of the history thus far uncovered took place in New York. However, by the fifties, Puerto Rican communities had also been established in other states, such as Connecticut, New Jersey, Massachusetts, Illinois, and Pennsylvania (see Cardona 1995: 440–448, 407). In due course, other researchers emerged by the mid-1980s to record their histories (see, for example, Padilla 1985, 1987, Cruz 1998, Whalen 2001).

What impressed me as I began to review this history was that throughout this long period, and despite what has been a generally harsh reception of Puerto Ricans in the States, Puerto Ricans have always managed to meet the challenges and build institutions that would meet the needs of the community and that would come to serve other communities as well. A final example of this was the performance of the first "Latin opera," *Hommy*, at Carnegie Hall in 1973. The opera was about a Puerto Rican child who was born deaf, blind, and mute but had the gift of communicating as no one else could through his ability to feel and play "salsa" music. After this, Latino performances at Carnegie Hall were less unusual. In hindsight, what is so remarkable about the significant accomplishments of this period is that they symbolized what were then major departures from the way things had always been done. So much that we take for granted today was never done then, in some cases not even conceived of, for example, living, eating, or simply going to the park or beach in certain neighborhoods, or aspiring to attend college. Even speaking Spanish in a downtown corporate elevator was akin to a political act. How much life has changed; how much these early migrants contributed to these changes.

In the public sphere, the past is quickly forgotten if it is not publicly and routinely acknowledged. Recently, *New York* magazine, a very influential and generally not very Latino-oriented magazine titled one of its issues "Nueva York" and dedicated the issue to Latinos (see *New York Magazine* 1999). Few remember that twenty-seven years ago the same magazine (August 7, 1972) had a special issue dedicated to "The City's Latin Soul" that focused on the "Latin impact on New York Style." It provided a review of the best Latin restaurants, music, and nightclubs, and on its cover it had re-christened New

York "The Big Mango" (as opposed to "The Big Apple"). Most have forgotten that, as New York Puerto Rican writer Nicholasa Mohr noted, Puerto Ricans had "created a [Spanish-speaking] benchmark in New York City culture." This was echoed throughout the nation as Puerto Ricans re-created communities in new cities (Mohr 1987: 160).

This diaspora of Puerto Ricans across the country was already evident by 1977. Puerto Ricans, always responding to shifts and change, began to create national organizations. Consequently, a number of national Puerto Rican organizations surfaced, for example, the National Puerto Rican Coalition (1977), the National Congress for Puerto Rican Rights (1981), the Association of Puerto Rican Executive Directors (1981), the Committee for Hispanic Children and Families (1982), the Puerto Rican/Latino Education Roundtable (1983), the Latino Coalition for Racial Justice (1986), the Hispanic AIDS Forum (1988), and, the first community foundation, the Hispanic Federation (1990). As the names of many of these organizations indicate, their "official" missions had expanded beyond Puerto Ricans to include other Latinos. For example, when the Committee for Hispanic Children and Families and the Puerto Rican/Latino Education Roundtable were established in 1982 and 1983 respectively, the former specifically wanted to address the needs of Latino children and the latter wished to organize around educational issues. Similarly, when the Latino Coalition for Racial Justice was established in 1986, it was to deal with racial attacks against minorities. Finally, the Hispanic AIDS Forum was established in 1988 to combat the spread of AIDS within the community. Unofficially, Puerto Rican organizations had always served, employed, and been directed by Puerto Ricans and non-Puerto Ricans.

Finally, the custom of having a specially designated period to celebrate Puerto Ricans in New York was apparently begun in 1953 when Vincent Impellitteri, then mayor of New York City, proclaimed the first week in November as Puerto Rican Week to celebrate Puerto Ricans' contributions to New York City (Cardona 1995: 391, according to a report in the *New York Times*, November 1, 1953, p. 46). In 1987, when New York City's Comité Noviembre (the November Committee) launched the first of its annual, month-long series of performances, lectures, seminars, and other events celebrating Puerto Rican heritage in the States, few realized then that they were following a long tradition and revitalizing or refurbishing a model for other states and other groups to follow. This addition of new immigrants to New York and elsewhere continues to add "to the ever-widening bands of Spanish threads in the fabric of many cities" (Rodríguez 1991: 18, 159).

What stands out for me in this thumbnail review of the history of Puerto Ricans in New York are several features: the resilience, the unquestioned call to stand up for Puerto Rican rights and principles, and an unnameable but supremely admirable ability to change, adapt, withstand all onslaughts, and get stronger in the process. This history suggests not a passive community, as some of the past literature (see Rodríguez 1995) and the media have often suggested, but a community that has constantly reacted to changes in its situation and has always attempted to defend and improve—as best it could—its situation.

A Personal Post-Note
As I look back on this history, I feel very proud to have been a small part of it all. I also feel proud to see how much Puerto Ricans have changed New York City. However, after so many years of researching Puerto Ricans and Latinos, it seems that despite all the work that has been done, we are still struggling with having our histories told in a way in which we recognize ourselves. This is not to say that we should not admit or address our problems as a community, but rather that the predominant paradigms that are often used to study Puerto Ricans seem to be so alien to us. In the past, they have seldom been balanced or historically informed. As Falcón notes, Puerto Ricans passed from being the guinea pigs of social science researchers pursuing culture-of-poverty research in the 1960s and 1970s to becoming the anomaly of the urban underclass fad of the 1980s. In both of these perspectives, Puerto Ricans were problematic. Throughout these periods there were researchers, historians, commentators, and just plain folk who were instrumental in calling attention to the deficits of both these approaches. Their criticisms and the resulting disparate and sometimes inconsistent or incoherent findings of many of the studies conducted using each of these paradigms helped to shift the paradigms and the frameworks through which Puerto Ricans were viewed. Interestingly, these new paradigms were often begun or fueled by relatively unresearched articles, books, or commentaries, such as Ken Auletta's *The Underclass* or Linda Chavez's chapter in *Out of the Barrio* on Puerto Ricans as an exception. Others, such as Oscar Lewis's *La Vida* were highly funded, yet subsequently discredited. As the Falcón chapter points out, however, we continue to see new (and old) versions of these and other perspectives that focus on social problems and give only token attention to other accomplishments. We also continue to see hugely funded projects that minimally involve Puerto Ricans in the study of Puerto Ricans.

I have often been invited, along with other Puerto Rican colleagues, to attend foundation meetings as initial, generally uncompensated "advisors" to what then became million-dollar projects that never called on us again. I say "advisors" in quotes, for it did not seem that many of the recommendations we made were understood or implemented. When the works were published, we were again forced to counter or question some of the conclusions.

For example, we were asked by policy makers, Puerto Rican organizations, or students to explain some of these erroneous or ill-conceived findings that were being taken as gospel. We were asked why Puerto Rican women preferred to have another child so they could continue to depend on welfare, or to explain what the Puerto Rican community was going to do now that the Puerto Rican family had ceased to exist because of the rise in female heads of households. We were also asked to explain why Puerto Ricans were an underclass, or why Puerto Ricans *were all* an underclass, not why Puerto Ricans *had* an underclass. These were conclusions and generalizations that even some Puerto Rican policymakers came to believe. It is not that we can ignore social problems, but that we need to understand that, as Falcón points out, the Puerto Rican community is highly diverse, multilayered, constantly changing, and with its own histories, traditions, and researchers.

A Bodega Story

Another example comes to mind that illustrates how paradigms have influenced the way in which the Puerto Rican community has been viewed by influential parts of the research community and others. Falcón mentions the wholesale selling of Puerto Rican bodegas to Dominicans. I recall one heated conversation with a well-known demography scholar who was convinced that the reason that Puerto Ricans had not made it in the United States was because they, unlike the Dominicans, had no entrepreneurial skills. No amount of arguing would convince him otherwise. This thesis was generally accepted in many policy and think tanks. My own experience of growing up in areas where Puerto Rican–owned bodegas were a dime a dozen mattered little. Nor could I point to accessible history books in English that had bothered to focus much on what had been (in the pre-Reagan era) an unimportant (because of its commonality) dimension of Puerto Rican life in New York. I recall subsequently attending a Museo del Barrio exhibit in which a Puerto Rican bodega had actually been reconstructed. I remember thinking then how important it was to tell and preserve our history. I had half begun to believe that Puerto Rican bodegas were a figment of my imagination.

It seems that I, like many of my Puerto Rican colleagues, have spent too much of my time responding in one way or another to articles such as the one Falcón focuses on. You wonder after a while if it is worth your time. For you sometimes spend a lot of time deconstructing, researching, writing, and discussing such works, only to see their ideas return in another guise, in student papers, or, unfortunately, in policy and funding guidelines or influential newspapers and magazines. Despite the fact that you get tired, what I have seen is that unless these articles, books, and so forth are examined closely, they come to have an even larger impact on how policymakers view the situation.

They come to influence the research agenda for funding agencies and for scores of faculty and graduate students who will continue to publish similar pieces until it is finally evident that the models and analyses don't quite fit the problem or people. After more than tens of millions of dollars had been given to researchers who agreed to include the concept of the underclass in their proposals, it was concluded that the idea was not a very useful concept—and difficult to measure besides. As we told them in the first place.

In this newest round, the pundits seem to say that Puerto Ricans have waned and so we need no longer look at them or their experience. There is a danger to this thinking, for it may convince others that we must look at Latino immigrants as if nothing had come before. This encourages the view of all Latinos as recently arrived immigrants. As long as we continue to view Latinos as the newcomers, we will not have a clear view of the past or the future. We have to see what has happened to the Puerto Rican community in the past and see its various outcomes and portrayals. To ignore such an inspiring history is to leave out important parts of U.S. history and to shortchange both old and newer immigrants, who will be less able to see and apply the lessons of the Puerto Rican experience.

REFERENCES

Acosta-Bélen, Edna. 1993. "The Building of a Community: Puerto Rican Writers and Activists in New York, 1890s-1960s," in *Recovering the U.S. Hispanic Literary Heritage*, Ramón Gutiérrez and Genaro Padilla, eds. Pp. 179-195. Houston: Arte Público Press.

Acosta-Belén, Edna, Margarita Benítez, José E.Cruz, Yvonne González-Rodríguez, Clara E. Rodríguez, Carlos E. Santiago, Azara Santiago-Rivera, and Barbara R. Sjostrom. 2000. *"Adiós, Borinquen querida": The Puerto Rican Diaspora, Its History and Contributions*. Albany: CELAC, State University of New York at Albany.

Auletta, Ken. 1982. *The Underclass*. New York: Random House.

Bonilla, Frank, and Ricardo Campos. 1985. "Ethnic Orbits: The Circulation of Capitals and Peoples." *Contemporary Marxism* 10: 10 (spring): 148–167.

Bronx Museum of the Arts. 1979. *Devastation/Resurrection: The South Bronx*. New York: Bronx Museum of the Arts.

Buettner, Ross. 2001. "Puerto Rican Count Falling: No Longer City's Hispanic Majority." *New York Daily News*, May 22, pp. 5–6.

Cardona, Luis Antonio. 1995. *A History of the Puerto Ricans in the United States of America*. Vol. 1. Bethesda, MD: Carreta Press.

Pérez, Gina M. ed. 2001. *Centro Journal* (Special Issue: Puerto Ricans in Chicago) 13: 2 (fall). New York: Center for Puerto Rican Studies.

Chávez, Linda. 1992. *Out of the Barrio: Towards a New Politics of Hispanic Assimilation*. New York: Basic Books.

Cruz, José E. 1998. *Identity and Power: Puerto Rican Politics and the Challenge of Ethnicity*. Philadelphia: Temple University Press.

Duany, Jorge. 2002. "La 'Puertorriqueñización' de la Florida." *El Nuevo Día*, June 16.
———. 2003. "Representaciones Coloniales." *El Nuevo Día*, May 14.
Duany, Raúl. 2003. "Puerto Rico's Undivided Loyalty." *The Miami Herald*, April 18.
González, Juan. 2000. *Harvest of Empire: A History of Latinos in America*. New York: Viking.
Haslip-Viera, Gabriel, and Sherrie L. Baver, eds. 1996. *Latinos in New York: Communities in Transition*. Notre Dame, IN: University of Notre Dame Press.
Junco, Maite. 2001. "Hispanic Diversity and Decline of Puerto Ricans in NYC." *Bloomberg News Reports*, May 22.
Kullen, Allan S. 1992. *The Peopling of America: A Timeline of Events That Helped Shape Our Nation*. Washington, DC: Americans All and the Portfolio Project.
Massey, Douglas S. 1995. "The New Immigration and the Meaning of Ethnicity in the United States." *Population and Development Review* 21 (3): 631–652.
Mohr, Nicholasa. 1987. "Puerto Ricans in New York: Cultural Evolution and Identity," in *Images and Identities: The Puerto Rican in Two World Contexts*, Asela Rodríguez de Laguna, ed. Pp. 157–160. New Brunswick, NJ: Transaction Publishers.
National Geographic. 2003. "True Colors: Divided Loyalties in Puerto Rico" 203: 3 (March): 34–55.
National Council of La Raza (NCLR). 2001. "Beyond the Census: Hispanics and an American Agenda," Press Release. Washington, DC: NCLR (August).
New York Magazine. 1999. Special Issue: "Nueva York: The Latin Explosion" 32: 34 (September 9): 22–49.
Olmo, José. 1991. "Puerto Rican History: 500 Years in Brief," Special Supplement: "Puerto Rican Heritage Month Cultural Guide." *Daily News*, November 3.
Padilla, Félix M. 1985. *Latino Ethnic Consciousness: The Case of Mexican-Americans and Puerto Ricans in Chicago*. Notre Dame, IN: University of Notre Dame Press.
———. 1987. *Puerto Rican Chicago*. Notre Dame, IN: University of Notre Dame Press.
Perez, Richie. 1997. "From Assimilation to Annihilation: Puerto Rican Images in U. S. Films," in *Latin Looks: Images of Latinas and Latinos in the U.S. Media*, Clara E. Rodríguez, ed. Pp. 142–163. Boulder, CO: Westview Press.
Rodríguez, Clara E. 1974. *The Ethnic Queue in the United States: The Case of Puerto Ricans*. San Francisco: R&E Research Associates.
———. 1979 "Economic Factors Affecting Puerto Ricans in New York," in *Labor Migration Under Capitalism: The Puerto Rican Experience* Centro de Estudios Puertorriqueños, History Task Force, ed. Pp. 197–221. New York: Monthly Review Press.
———. 1991. *Puerto Ricans: Born in the USA*. Boulder, CO: Westview Press.
———. 1994. "A Summary of Puerto Rican Migration to the United States," in *The Puerto Rican Women and Children: Issues in Health, Growth and Development*. Garcia Coll, C. and Lamberty, G, eds. Pp. 11–28. New York: Plenum Press, 1994.
———. 1995. "Puerto Ricans in Historical and Social Science Research," in *Handbook of Research on Multicultural Education*, James A. Banks and Cherry A. McGee Banks, eds. Pp. 223–244. New York: Macmillan.
Rodríguez, Clara E., Irma M. Olmedo, and Mariolga Reyes-Cruz. 2004 forthcoming. "Deconstructing and Contextualizing the Historical and Social Science Literature

on Puerto Ricans," in *Handbook of Research on Multicultural Education*. 2nd ed. James A. Banks and Cherry A. McGee Banks, eds. San Francisco: Jossey-Bass.

Rodríguez-Fraticelli, Carlos, Carlos Sanabria, and Amilcar Tirado. 1991. "Puerto Rican Nonprofit Organizations in New York City," in *Hispanics and the Nonprofit Sector*. Herman E. Gallegos and Michael O'Neill, eds. Pp. 38–48. New York: Foundation Center.

Sánchez-Korrol, Virginia. 1994. *From Colonia to Community: The History of Puerto Ricans in New York City, 1917–1948*. Berkeley: University of California Press.

Sánchez, José Ramón. 1990. "Housing Puerto Ricans in New York City, 1945–1984: A Study in Class Power." Ph.D. dissertation, New York University.

Stevens-Arroyo, Antonio and Ana María Díaz Stevens. 1982. "Puerto Ricans in the States: A Struggle for Identity," in *The Minority Report: An Introduction to Racial, Ethnic and Gender Relations*. 2nd ed. Anthony G. Dworkin and Rosalind J. Dworkin, eds. Pp. 196–232. New York: Holt, Rinehart and Winston.

Torres, Andrés, and Rodríguez, Clara E. 1991. "Latino Research and Policy: The Puerto Rican Case," *Hispanics in the Labor Force: Issues and Policies*, Meléndez, Edwin, Rodríguez, Clara E. and Janis Barry Figueroa, eds. Pp. 247–263. New York: Plenum Press.

U. S. Bureau of the Census. 2000. "The Hispanic Population: 2000 Brief" (May) <www.census.gov>.

_____. 2001. "The Hispanic Population: Census 2000," Betsy Guzmán, Economics and Statistics Administration. Washington, D.C: (May). <http://www.census.gov/population/www/socdemi/race/Ombdir15.html>.

_____. 2002. "Hispanic Heritage Month (2002)." CBOS-FF:15 9/3/2002 Hispanic Heritage Month 2002: 9/15–10/15/2002. Washington, DC: Press release from <www://factfinder.census.gove/servlet/Basic FactsServlet>.

_____. 2002a. "Census Analysis Tracks 100 Years of Change." Press release on this report (December 17).

_____. 2002b. "Coming to America: A Profile of the Nation's Foreign Born (2000 Update)." Economics and Statistics Administration. Washington, DC: (February) <http://www.census.gov/population/www/socdemo/foreign.html>.

_____. 2002c. "Coming From the Americas: A Profile of the Nation's Foreign-Born Population From Latin America (2000 Update)." Economics and Statistics Administration Washington, DC: (January) <http:/www.census.gov/population/www/socdemo/foreign.html>.

Whalen, Carmen Teresa. 2001. *From Puerto Rico to Philadelphia: Puerto Rican Workers and Postwar Economies*. Philadelphia: Temple University Press.

CHAPTER FOUR
Commentary

Former Bronx Borough President Fernando Ferrer (left) with United States congressional representatives Nydia Velázquez and Jóse Serrano. (*Records of the Office of the Commonwealth of Puerto Rico. Courtesy: Center for Puerto Rican Studies, Hunter College. Photo: Doel Valzquez*)

Commentary

A Stronger Puerto Rican New York

Hon. Fernando Ferrer,
former borough president of Bronx County, New York

In 1993, I, Fernando Ferrer, son of immigrants raised on Fox Street in the Bronx, served as the Grand Marshal of the Puerto Rican Day parade. That in and of itself was a tremendous honor—a symbol of the distance traveled by me, my family, and the Puerto Rican community. But the most moving part of the experience for me came before I even started marching.

I decided to hold the pre-parade breakfast at the Starlight Roof in the Waldorf-Astoria—the same hotel where my grandmother worked in the kitchen until she retired. She watched her grandson grow up on Fox Street and become the president of Bronx County, the borough she had hoped would provide the opportunities that America had to offer. On that day, she watched as the Puerto Rican community of New York City honored her grandson.

As I led the parade down Fifth Avenue, I thought about how far we had come. It's the same thought I have when I go to Paterson, New Jersey. The Dominicans there know me and want to shake my hand. Or when I'm visiting my daughter's home in Bergenfield, and go to the little Cuban place on the

---

Speech Presented at the Symposium *"Contra Viento y Marea*: Puerto Ricans in New York City, 1945–2000." September 22, 2000

corner, where the people come over and say hello. It's a sign of how far we have come that not only does this city recognize the contributions of its Puerto Rican community, it also recognizes the contributions of Dominicans, Cubans, Central Americans, and South Americans. And not only do they recognize what Puerto Ricans have done to make this city a better place for all Spanish-speakers and for all immigrants, they are also proud. They are proud of me. They are proud of our accomplishments.

This is our moment as Puerto Ricans. So much so that despite the fact that our population as Puerto Ricans is diminishing in the city, our economic and political power only increases. This is our moment as Latinos. So much so that while it used to be okay for a politician campaigning in our communities to speak a few words of Spanish, now, anyone running for office trying to court our population must answer the question: what are you doing to improve our lives?

While Puerto Ricans in New York City have progressed, we have also become less monolithic. Our numbers are decreasing. More of us are moving to the suburbs, staying where we went to college, adopting diverse ideologies. You saw us at the Republican National Convention in Philadelphia. You saw us at the Democratic National Convention in Los Angeles. Now it's more about what we stand for than the opportunity to stand at all. For some, this signals a downturn. But I believe that instead, this makes our entire population stronger.

The explosive growth in the Dominican American presence, the Central American presence, and the South American presence, will enable us as Latinos to contribute even more to the economic and political landscape of our city. We cannot perceive the changing demographics as a death sentence because it isn't. It's an opportunity to build the coalitions that will ensure that the concerns of Hispanic New Yorkers are never forgotten.

These new immigrants will have opportunities to assimilate that Puerto Ricans did not have when they came to this country in the 1950s. There were no welcome mats for us, and there aren't any welcome mats for them. But we've made this a better city for Spanish-speaking immigrants and all Americans through our battles for justice and opportunity. The issues are the same as they were when we arrived. It's about jobs, health care, access to education, overcoming language barriers. Back then it was the Puerto Rican *bodegueros* getting shot, now it's the Dominican livery cab drivers. But the story is the same. The parades might be different, the flags different, but in New York City, the issues that confront our families are the same. Only together will we able to work toward ensuring that we live in strong communities and not ghettos isolated from the great economic opportunities that this country and city can offer us right now.

In 1988, Bronx-based Dominicans approached me, interested in organizing a Bronx Dominican Day parade. We pitched in. At the start of the parade, they played *La Borinqueña* in recognition of the help they received from the Puerto Rican community. That is the vision that I have for Puerto Ricans in the twenty-first century.

We will lend our experience from our battles and victories to the growing populations of Spanish-speakers. We are the same family. My vision is one of ethnic succession. Puerto Ricans must offer it, and the others must play their own role. We needn't worry that we will lose our political power, something that we have fought hard to achieve, something that people like Dr. Antonia Pantoja have been fighting for since I was a teenager fortunate enough to become an *Aspirante*. I firmly believe that Puerto Ricans will only be stronger for it. And as there was a lag in gaining political access and power, there will be a lag in losing it.

We don't stand to lose power the moment we embrace diversity. That isn't the consequence. It is a conundrum for us to be achieving our moment in the sun while the world of a solidified, monolithic Puerto Rican population is setting. But instead of seeing this as a loss, we need to refocus ourselves, accept the diversity, share our knowledge, and not waste any time with regret.

Indeed, we should want our people to move out to the suburbs, or to wherever else they dream to live the comfortable lives they have worked very hard for. It is our responsibility to help Dominicans make that move, to help Colombians make that move, to help all of our successors.

Regardless of their native country, Spanish-speakers are proud of my career—wherever they or their parents came from. In fact, in polls, I have slightly higher numbers from Dominicans than from Puerto Ricans. And if I ever serve as the first Hispanic mayor of New York City, I believe that such an accomplishment will be shared by all of us whose parents and grandparents worked so hard to bring us the American Dream, even if they themselves couldn't enjoy it. My grandmother worked in the kitchen of the Waldorf-Astoria so that I could hold the pre-Puerto Rican Day parade breakfast there.

The younger generation of Hispanic leaders is materializing. They are being elected as we speak. But we won't be able to get more Hispanics elected if we can't get them graduated. They must succeed in school; they must be prepared to use the technology that is required in the workplace; they must be articulate and fluent in both their native language and English in order to participate in the economy. The native language is an asset, but English is a necessity. At the end of the day, Hispanics will not be leaders if they don't speak, read, and write English. And they won't be leaders—in any of the sectors of New York society—if they can't pass their Regents exams, take Advanced Placement classes, and go on to college.

I believe that we are well positioned at this moment to assume leadership in New York City. We can have a Puerto Rican mayor, a Puerto Rican speaker of the city council, a Puerto Rican congressman, a Puerto Rican chair of New York's Democratic Party, and a Puerto Rican Bronx borough president. We have matured into assuming the leadership of our city as Jews, the Irish, the Italians, African Americans, and others have done before us. But while we mature, we cannot lose the sense of urgency that propelled all of us to seek public office.

In 1984, there were 3,128 Latino elected officials. As of June 1999, there were 4,966. We are poised to elect even more, especially in New York. But our future in power is in jeopardy. We must foster the desire for leadership early—in the young. And in order to prepare them to become senators and presidents, first they have to learn how to be readers and writers. Dr. Pantoja understood how important it is to invest in the young. Aspira is still around. But I don't believe that we have the same emphasis on leadership development that we had then. Are we grooming the future borough presidents, chancellors, congressmen, deputy chancellors, judges, physicians, and corporate executives?

Our young people require great services because they have great needs. But we must do more than serve them. We must invest in them. If we teach them what *Aspirantes* were taught—that giving back is an obligation—we provide for their prosperity and that of the Puerto Rican community as well.

It is only in doing so that future Puerto Ricans will experience that walk down Fifth Avenue, with the South Americans and Dominicans, and even the rest of New York City, looking on with pride. That experience was one that made the years of fighting—for housing, jobs, stronger public education—for my people worthwhile. That fight isn't over. If we invest in our young, if we seize the opportunity that a diversified Hispanic community presents us, our parades will be even more of a celebration of not only the Puerto Rican culture, but of all that Puerto Ricans have done to make New York City a better place to live, and to dream.

APPENDIX

Dr. Antonia Pantoja (bottom row, right) with Alice Cardona (bottom row, center), Manny Díaz (back row, left), Jóse Morales (back row 2nd left), Louis Nuñez (back row, 3rd left), Judge John Carro (back row, right) and other community leaders commemorating the twentieth anniversary of the founding of the Hispanic Young Adult Association (HYAA), early 1970s. (*Antonia Pantoja Papers. Courtesy: Center for Puerto Rican Studies, Hunter College, CUNY*)

Appendix

Puerto Ricans In New York: A Historical And Community Development Perspective (1989)

Antonia Pantoja

The political life of an oppressed people depends directly on their full understanding of the nature of power and of their true situation in the power arrangements. If the Puerto Rican community of New York City builds an illusory idea of its power, it will not act in recognition of its present powerlessness.

Our community must develop the political awareness of its reality as part of a city that is the center of power in this nation. A look at ourselves in historical perspective may offer us an opportunity not only to face our persistent and chronic poverty but also to more effectively direct our strength and our creativity as a community. Throughout the difficult years of our existence as a people and a nation, we have evidence of our strong sense of identity and our capacity to survive. Looking at ourselves in the mirror of our history can bring surprises we never suspected. For example, many Puerto Ricans would doubt that we still endure persistent poverty, and even fewer would think that we have had a creative history of organizational development in New York City. Unfortunately, it is a quality of oppressed people to have a distorted picture of their situation in the world in which they live.

This article originally appeared in *Centro de Estudios Puertorriqueños: Bulletin* 2: 5 (spring 1989): 20–31.

I hope in this paper to help initiate a dialogue to assist us in understanding the resources of skills and information available to us to analyze and understand our history as a people of strength. This critical awareness will be instrumental in our decision to establish joint efforts with other oppressed groups to attempt to change collectively the power arrangements that perpetuate our poverty and oppression.

In advancing our political consciousness, we should generate anger. However, raising political consciousness should give us the rational tools to channel the anger into informed and effective action. With that action we should continue to build upon our history and culture in such a fashion that we contribute to the struggle for a just and humane society.

Our current work must be done in a period in history when this country creates and uses technology that makes possible what was once impossible, from computers to artificial hearts. Technology and science, however, can only be of help to poor people when there exists a philosophical foundation and a set of values that bind science to the tasks of practical problem solving and human well being. In other words, there must also exist a political determination that technology serve the welfare of all people. In the U.S., science and technology are subordinated to an economic system whose central objective is profit-making. Problem solving is taught with the philosophy and value base required by this kind of society. Therefore, many educated citizens are aggressive, competitive, self-centered, and profit-motivated.

This is also a historical time in the life of the Puerto Rican community of New York City when it has a significant number of educated people that are knowledgeable in the uses of management, science, and technology. However, these factors have little meaning for the life of the community as a whole. The most obvious reasons for this discrepancy are two. First, too many of these Puerto Ricans with access to knowledge and technological skills place their abilities in the service of the majority society where we Puerto Ricans can only benefit from it if we can pay for it. Second, the type of education these Puerto Ricans have obtained does not teach them problem solving skills with the objective of social change and equality for their community.

The present society permits the success of a few individual members of poor minorities, and exacts a price for that success. The price paid by those Puerto Ricans who "succeed" either by acquiring the highest education, prestige, and wealth, or by being elected to political office, is to separate themselves from the community as their base of accountability. Most of these few successful Puerto Ricans internalize those values and characteristics of the "educated American citizen." When this happens the community loses these "successful" members because they do not bind themselves to their community in a consciously and voluntarily political act aimed at bringing the resources of their education to the life of the community. Although this is a difficult challenge, some of the younger New York born Puerto Ricans are doing this.

Today, many Puerto Ricans feel powerless and, indeed, are powerless. Many consider themselves ineffective in their personal life and in the struggles of their community and of the society at large. Puerto Ricans have become silent and invisible in the city. There is a poverty that is worse than the lack of financial resources and that is the deterioration of a fighting spirit, the loss of self-pride, and the destruction of self-assurance. The problems can be overwhelming. Indeed they are enormous, but we cannot run away from them. They must be resolved; the future of all of us depends on it.

A Historical Legacy of Political Effectiveness

Our history in this city is an extremely important history, and one in which we can feel pride and strength. Long before a War on Poverty ever existed, we started to develop our own institutions. We had developed cooperative economic institutions and methods of teaching English long before manpower training or bilingual education programs ever existed. In sum, we developed an impressive array of service agencies in our short lifetime here in a new home city.

Institution building has been a strength in the Puerto Rican community in New York since the earliest immigrations. The Puerto Rican immigrants of the 1800s and first half of the 1900s helped establish political voting clubs, were an integral part of advocacy organizations that defended Spanish-speaking workers, and published literary and political commentary, magazines and newspapers in Spanish in New York City. They were also a very important force in the building of defense organizations and liberation movements in New York for the Latin American nations.

The following brief overview of the history of institution building by and for Puerto Ricans from the mid-1940s to the present is based on my personal experience and readings as an immigrant.

First Era: 1945 to 1960

At this time two distinct groups lived in New York City. One group consisted of Puerto Ricans who had come during earlier immigrations and had already produced a generation of children born in New York. The other group was comprised of recent arrivals.

At the beginning of this period, Puerto Ricans were immersed in Hispanic organizations, and they accepted the designation Hispanic. The leaders of the Hispanic groups were Anglo-Americans, Spaniards, Colombians, and

Cubans. By the end of this era, we had developed a strong energetic leadership. We called ourselves Puerto Ricans, and effectively challenged and replaced the non–Puerto Rican leadership who had elected themselves spokespeople for Puerto Ricans in the larger society.[1] We developed special interest organizations and social groups formed on the basis of private or public sector employment, small business ownership, or town of origin in Puerto Rico. The membership of these groups included women in the garment industry, postal workers, restaurant, bar and beauty shop owners; and those born in particular towns like Ponce, Guayama, or Cabo Rojo.

All of these organizations provided mutual support and information about social and recreational matters. Largely because of the services it offered to the recently arrived, the Office of Migration of the Department of Labor of Puerto Rico played an important role in this process. Among other things, it organized a council of Puerto Rican organizations that brought the groups together and began the effort to move them from individual social, cultural, and mutual aid groups to an organized body that could offer programs and mediate between our community and the larger society. The organizing leadership of this period was traditional and older, ranging approximately between the ages of thirty-five to sixty.

The main needs and issues in these years centered on learning to survive in an increasingly hostile, alien, fast moving environment and difficult climate. Puerto Ricans continued to encounter racism. We found the schools, police, social centers and government agencies to be indifferent and even hostile institutions. We tried to secure a decent place to live and found it necessary to protect ourselves and our children from the different and sometimes dangerous neighborhoods. It was a struggle to hold the family together. We had to learn English and new skills, and we had to secure jobs.

Although we lived in scattered pockets throughout the city, we began to form community consciousness when a series of articles that abused and misrepresented Puerto Ricans appeared in magazines and newspapers. Various cases of police brutality reached the Spanish-language press, and the community out of its anger developed further cohesiveness. Even with the resulting organizing, our responses and reactions were shy, courteous, and primarily directed and implemented by the leadership of the Office of Migration and with the quiet background support of the citywide council of organizations that the government office had organized.

Second Era: 1960 to 1974

The second era was marked by a sharp drop in the number of immigrants arriving in the city. Events in the overall society that distinguished this time span are the civil rights movement, the student revolts in universities, the rise of the Black Power movement, the youth revolt against the country's internal policies and aggressive involvement in foreign lands, and the assassination of three top national leaders—John F. Kennedy, Robert Kennedy, and Martin Luther King. This ferment had its inevitable impact on the Puerto Rican community.

The early part of this period was a time of growth and stabilization for the Puerto Rican community in New York City. A significant number of the young Puerto Ricans immigrating in the 1940s had reached adulthood in the city and had entered educational programs. These people developed relationships with earlier immigrants, with those born in the city, and with non-Puerto Ricans. One of the results of these contacts with other community members and with the overall society was that the Puerto Rican community, in a very short time, became aware of its poverty, powerlessness and oppression. Puerto Ricans had been robbed of their innocence, having realized that the sacrifice of immigrating had placed them in a worse situation than the one they had left in Puerto Rico. Some members of the group of earlier immigrants emerged from their quiet retreat within the Hispanic groups and the suburbs and joined the recent immigrants in their organizations.

This era marks the emergence of professionally staffed service institutions and institutionalized movements for advocacy. In 1961, for the first time in the life of the community in New York, five foundations awarded funds to the Puerto Rican Forum for the creation of an institution to organize and service Puerto Rican youth. ASPIRA, an idea that a group of young Puerto Ricans professionals had dreamed about for several years, became a reality. Other membership associations became staffed service institutions, like the Puerto Rican Association for Community Affairs and the Puerto Rican Family Institute. A system of social services emerged that offered children and family services, parent education, housing services, training services, basic language instruction, and small business technical assistance. There was even an association of grocers that developed a cooperative buying service, and established a refrigerated warehouse and a large credit union.

Significant changes in the leadership took place during this period. The traditional leadership was confronted in a challenge to the Office of Migration and the Council of Spanish American Organizations. The challenging "young Turks" tended to be college educated, bilingual, and mostly New York–born. Their main issue was the need for the modernization of organizational life. This new group brought administrative, management, and research skills. They began to seek funds to establish ongoing professional services to develop these skills. But most importantly, the young leadership advocated a philosophy of institutional development as opposed to reactive "fire fighting" in social programs. Another major issue between the old and new leadership was the new group's belief that the fate of Puerto Rican New Yorkers belonged in the hands of Puerto Rican New Yorkers. This position was in opposition to the Migration Office's practice of bringing Puerto Ricans from the Island to negotiate the problems of Puerto Rican New Yorkers with the city leadership.

Underlying this smoldering conflict was the unspoken grievance that Puerto Rican New Yorkers held against the island Puerto Rican elite. The attitude of the island leadership and its professionals toward Puerto Rican New Yorkers was considered racist, class-snobbish, and elitist. New York Puerto Ricans also considered the Islanders to be obsequious when dealing with white Americans. During this epoch the young leadership managed to take over the direction of major efforts for development in the community.

Two associations of hometown groups, one in Manhattan and another in the Bronx, became the main advocacy forces. Executives of emergent agencies and a new local political leadership took over the representation of New York Puerto Ricans before governmental and private sector entities. This supersession of the old leadership was completed by the establishment of a citywide program with funds from the War on Poverty, organized and directed by the new leadership.

Also of major significance was the role played by a group of New York Puerto Rican Youth towards the end of this period. The youth became fully immersed in the civil rights movement and in the movement for the independence of Puerto Rico as part of the third world revolutionary struggles. This group directly questioned and confronted the behavior of private and public institutions as unethical and racist in their failure to fulfill their responsibilities to serve Puerto Ricans. One of these groups, the Young Lords, used confrontation politics to force the institutions to correct their practices. Some of their very effective programs included forcing a church located in a Puerto Rican barrio to allow its space to be used to provide services for children, and taking over a hospital when overcrowding and indifference caused people to die while waiting long hours to be seen by a doctor. They burned garbage in the middle of the streets where Puerto Ricans lived when the Department of Sanitation would not collect garbage. These acts were so eloquent and so correct that parents and neighbors joined the group in their confrontations. Organized action of Puerto Rican students in institutions of higher education had the same contagious effect. Confrontations and takeovers of university administrations resulted in the establishment of departments of Puerto Rican Studies throughout the universities and colleges of New York and other neighboring cities.

This period ends with various significant changes. Political shifts in the island placed conservatives and pro-statehood forces in power, this created a new immigration wave of radical university professors and ex-government officials of the losing political party in the Island. This group came to New York and occupied positions as faculty in the Puerto Rican Studies departments and in other institutions that serviced Puerto Ricans. Many New York Puerto Ricans considered such developments as negative to the momentum that the community had enjoyed as a result of their ability to act and take on leadership roles in the life of the group. But the overall momentum of the community continued in various ways. A university and research center were created in Washington, DC, by Puerto Rican New Yorkers. The New York community elected a Puerto Rican congressman, a few New York State assemblymen, and a city councilman. Also, a limited number of top-level positions in federal agencies were filled by Puerto Rican New Yorkers, and leadership from New York City moved into other cities, occupying positions in existing programs and helping create Puerto Rican institutions.

Third Era: 1975 to the Present

During this era, great advancement was made in stabilizing several basic Puerto Rican institutions. Their longevity now spans twenty-five years or more. This period also marks the full development of Puerto Rican professional and labor associations. The community achieves basic successes, such as the case of *Aspira v. the New York City Board of Education,* in which the Supreme Court ordered the board to institute bilingual education.

There are many more accomplishments that could be cited, but the political base is fragmented and deteriorates in a void of an effective leadership. A leadership crisis develops. Agency directors, political leaders, and persons in important positions have been convicted in court or found by their institution's boards to have taken or misused funds. Other heads of institutions have proven to be incapable of performing their responsibilities and have been removed only after causing serious problems within the institution. Others used the institutions for financial gain or personal prestige and influence. Of course, this kind of behavior occurs in the majority community. But when it occurs in the Puerto Rican community the effect is deadly, since we have a limited number of institutions.

The existence of an unethical leadership threatens to destroy the institutions we have and to create a climate of distrust, in our own people. The question can be raised: "Why is this happening at this time in our history? Why has our leadership lost the political consciousness and accountability that was developing during the late 1960s and early 1970s?" I would like to share my initial thoughts as to why this is happening.

- The new political consciousness that began to emerge during the 1960s and 1970s was isolated into the thinking and activities of a few people, especially those in colleges and universities, and never permeated the entire community.
- The breaking of a shared group consciousness allows individuals to fill the void with personal philosophies and ideologies that value self-aggrandizement and individual goals.
- The mechanisms for insuring the accountability of a leadership to its community did not expand beyond the social and personal networks to integrate new leaders that were emerging. In fact these mechanisms, where they existed, have been systematically destroyed.
- Some of the current and recently emerged professional leadership perceive themselves beyond the accountability of the Puerto Rican community. The rejection of our cultural and social context frees them to adopt the values of the overall society, placing them beyond the reach of any social controls that the Puerto Rican community could exercise.

In the presence of these sad and hard realities, what can we do? I do not have the answer. However, I have some thoughts regarding what the approaches must be.

I know that we cannot continue to allow a limited number of self-appointed leaders or political appointees to become the spokespersons and decision makers regarding resources allocated to our community. We also cannot allow the nature of the resources and programs we receive to continue to block true access to rights, privileges, and resources. Millions of dollars secured from public and private sources cannot be spent on training, educating, and counseling people, and still leave them unemployed, poor, and powerless. Programs and strategies built on therapeutic and remedial approaches will never catch up with the powerful and efficient forces of destruction that sap the strength of a community and rob it of self-reliance. Piecemeal, one shot, inadequate assistance creates dependency and addresses the manifestations of the problems, not the root causes. The essential prerequisites for our community development have been destroyed. In my judgment, what is necessary is a comprehensive program of community development. People can develop, and they can be taught to take the steps that will create institutions and relationships to fulfill their needs. People can, and they will, if they are allowed the opportunities and the resources to meet the tasks.

A Plan for Action

I am advocating the establishment of a strategy for community development and community restoration. This strategy must begin with the creation of a Puerto Rican community–owned corporation. As part of the economic plan, this corporation must engage our community in work that produces resources and builds wealth for the group, raising its own internal resources as a base. If we are to have a significant effect on our chronic and deteriorating poverty, we need a comprehensive plan of action developed and implemented by us.

Puerto Rican institutions in New York City need to move beyond objectives of service delivery to developing those strengths needed to break the cycle of deterioration and poverty in which our community is caught. This requires the use of a model for analysis and for action that will help us identify those functions of our community that have been destroyed and those that are still operative for the processes of Puerto Rican community restoration. In order to produce a comprehensive action plan, it is necessary to develop programs that will systematically restore the basic functions of our community, which are:

> **Production, Distribution and Consumption**: Developing institutions, owned by the community, that perform the functions of production, distribution, and consumption of the basic resources needed by Puerto Ricans in New York City. These institutions must create ownership, opportunity, employment, financial, and investment basis, worker-owner ventures for and among our people.
>
> **Socialization of our youth**: Developing or restoring institutions that will assist in socializing young Puerto Ricans with those values that we, as a community, want them to acquire; the behavior that would help in living in the outer community; the search for the accumulated knowledge that the established educational system offers; and the overall values of cooperation, group life, and dedication to social justice.
>
> **Establishing mechanisms for internal controls**: Development of an array of strategies and relationships that will establish a network for social control so that we can exercise some influence on the behavior of our community members when they violate our community norms.
>
> **Developing and Restoring Institutions for Social Integration**: Restoration of those institutions that strengthen our solidarity, and

provide us with enjoyment, recreation, celebration of our culture and our important moments, as well as associations to validate our personal, job, and professional achievements.

Mutual Support: Restoration and strengthening our most effective mutual support institutions. These must be institutions that function with our cultural patterns and that are capable of delivering services and resources to members of our community, especially in times of crisis.

Communication: Restoration and full development of our communications systems. In this category, I include schools, theaters, literary congresses, and artistic endeavors that validate the use of both languages and that create standards through the awarding of prizes for excellence. We must take advantage of our location in the communication center of the world. We must also develop effective means of communicating our history, which I insist is a powerful weapon in our struggles to secure change and social justice.

Defense: Establishing access to and developing mechanisms for monitoring the larger societal institutions. We must make sure that we have community institutions that play a "watch-dog" role to see that those in the total societal defense function (the police, the courts, the legislative body, and so on) do not violate our civil, political, and economic rights.

These seven functions are part of the components of a model of community development-community restoration that cannot be presented here in full. My desire to share at least this outline of the model is born out of a preoccupation to offer some assistance to produce a comprehensive action plan for elevating the social, cultural, and economic level of the New York Puerto Rican community and its institutions through the development of broad-based strategies and approaches of mutual benefit to the private, public, and community sectors. The timing is right for the production of such a plan. The knowledge base exists and is accessible to the builders of the plan; the technology and the human resources exist. We, as a community, have the financial basis. Other assistance can be obtained from those friends and supporters within the foundation and industrial communities. The need is acute and pressing!

Further research is also necessary. A survey of existing Puerto Rican institutions in New York will reveal which functions need to be restored or developed. Also as part of this plan of action, we must build strategies to include layers and levels of participation by groups, associations, institutions, and individuals in the community. This participation is essential, because it will insure the learning process and the *concientización* of the total community.

This approach of working with people is not only different in the obvious ways that I have already mentioned, but it also has the following differences from programs that are created by the yearly funding fads of the government, or the priorities that foundations and industry set for their giving, or the latest answers of social scientists to societal problem. In this approach, we do not start by labeling the people who suffer problems as the problem—for example, "the Puerto Rican problem of New York City." Rather we identify the problem at its roots and not at the level they are manifested. The community, through its working units, selects the problems and the strategies of action to be undertaken. In this approach, the people who are members of the community are participants in the resolution of their own problems and they grow in acquiring knowledge, skills, and value positions. But they also become owners and controlling elements of as many of their own institutions as possible.

The usual responses to these ideas is that it is difficult to do, that it will cost a lot of money that we, a poor community, do not have, and that it would be a lot of work. The answer is: "Yes, it would cost a lot of money." But we spend a lot of money on meaningless and ineffective programs. Yes, it will be a lot of work. But then we, Puerto Rican New Yorkers, have been forged with strong backbones that include not only courage but constancy and determination.

Notes

[1] In actuality, there were quite a number of Puerto Rican and Hispanic organizations led by Puerto Ricans from the 1920s to the 1940s. These included the Porto Rican Brotherhood of America, Federation of Puerto Rican Clubs in New York City, La Liga Puertorriqueñ e Hispana, and others See Virginia Sanchez Korrol, *From Colonia to Community: The History of Puerto Ricans in New York City* (Berkeley: University of California Press, 1994).

CONTRIBUTING ESSAYISTS

JOSÉ E. CRUZ is an associate professor of political science and Latin American and Caribbean studies at the Albany campus of the State University of New York. He is the author of *Identity and Power: Puerto Rican Politics and the Challenge of Ethnicity* (1998) and contributor to *Adios Borinquen Querida: The Puerto Rican Diaspora, its History, and Contributions* (2000).

ANGELO FALCÓN is the Senior Policy Executive for the Puerto Rican Legal Defense and Education Fund and author of numerous articles and reports on Puerto Rican/Latino politics and policy issues affecting these communities.

GABRIEL HASLIP-VIERA, is currently the director of the Program in Latin American and Latino Studies at City College, CUNY, and most recently, the author of *Crime and Punishment in Late Colonial Mexico City, 1692-1810* (1999), and editor of *Taino Revival: Critical Perspectives on Puerto Rican Identity and Cultural Politics* (2001).

FÉLIX. V. MATOS-RODRÍGUEZ is director of the Center for Puerto Rican Studies at Hunter College, the City University of New York. He is the author of *Women in San Juan: 1820-1868* (2001), and co-editor of *Puerto Rican Women's History: New Perspectives* (1998).

FRANCISCO RIVERA-BATÍZ is an associate professor of economics and education in the Department of International and Transcultural Studies at Teachers College, Columbia University. He is co-author of *Island Paradox: Puerto Ricans in the 1990s* (1996) and co-editor of *U.S. Immigration Policy Reform in the 1980's: A Preliminary Assessment* (1991), among other works.

CLARA E. RODRÍGUEZ is professor sociology at Fordham University, and is most recently the author of *Changing Race: Latinos, the Census, and the History of Ethnicity in the United States* (2000) and *Heroes, Lovers and Others: The Story of Latinos in Hollywood* (2004).

VIRGINIA E. SÁNCHEZ KORROL is a professor of Puerto Rican and Latino Studies at Brooklyn College, City University of New York. She is the author of *From Colonia to Community: The History of Puerto Ricans in New York City* (1994), co-editor of *The Way it Was and Other Writings* by Jesús Colón, and co-editor of the forthcoming encyclopedia, *Latinas in the United States*.

ANA CELIA ZENTELLA is professor of ethnic studies at the University of California, San Diego. She is the author of *Growing-up Bilingual: Puerto Rican Children in New York* (1997) and "Latino@ Languages and Identities" in *Latinos: Remaking America* (2002), among other publications.

www.ingramcontent.com/pod-product-compliance
Lightning Source LLC
Chambersburg PA
CBHW022110150426
43195CB00008B/344

Brain Obesity

How Our Brain Can Control Overeating and Obesity?

Hamed Ekhtiari, Meghedi Vartanian

metacognium
www.metacognium.com

Brain Obesity

Authors
Hamed Ekhtiari, MD, PhD
Meghedi Vartanian, MSc

This edition is published in 2022
Copyright © 2022 by Metacognium LLC. All rights reserved.

ISBN-13: 978-1-7347408-3-7
Illustrator: Laleh Ziyaee
Art Director: Mohsen Farhadi
Page Layout: Arash Sarikhani
Editors: Victoria Vultee, Behnaz Sadr, Jordan James, Khashayar Niki Maleki, Emily B Roze

The material of this book is not intended to replace the services of your physician, therapist, or caregiver. Since the recovery process for each person is unique, you should consult with your own physician or therapist to evaluate the symptoms you may have, or to receive suggestions for appropriate interventions.

This book is written based on the findings in cognitive neuroscience and authors have tried their best to make it as accurate and up to date as possible. However, it may contain errors, oversights, or materials that is out of date at the time you read it. The authors and publisher disclaim any legal responsibility or liability for errors, oversights, and out-of-date materials, or the reader's application of the information or advice contained in this book.

Copyright © 2022 by Metacognium LLC. All rights reserved.

This book may not be reproduced, in whole or in part, including illustrations, in any form (beyond that copyright permitted by Sections 107 and 108 of the U.S. Copyright Law and except by reviewers for the public press), without written permission from the publishers.

Printed in the United States of America